FRESH FROM THE
COUNTRY

The Natural Foods Cookbook

FRESH FROM THE
COUNTRY

The Natural Foods Cookbook

Susan Restino

KEY PORTER BOOKS

Copyright © 1987 by Susan Restino

Canadian Cataloguing in Publication Data

Restino, Susan
    Fresh from the country

Includes index.
ISBN 1–55013–015–3

1. Cookery. 2. Cookery (Natural foods). I. Title.

TX715.R48 1986   641.5   C86-095001-8

Key Porter Books Limited
70 The Esplanade
Toronto, Ontario
Canada M5E 1R2

87 88 89   6 5 4 3 2 1

Design: Marie Bartholomew
Illustrations: Susan Restino
Cover Photo: Whitmer/Miller Services
Typesetting: Computer Composition of Canada
Printed and bound in Canada

Contents

Preface

This is a book about cooking with foods fresh from the country. At the same time, I have to admit to somewhat urban tastes: we like to eat well. I'm liable to whip up a fast Hollandaise Sauce to serve on the freshly-cut asparagus, simmer my chicken in wine, and scoop out the baked potatoes to mash their fillings with milk, butter and chopped chives.

This book is about the cooking I do at home on our farm in the Cape Breton highlands, where I live with my husband and one of our two daughters (the other lives in Vermont and has gotten into making her own *Coq au Vin*). We eat meat, but not a lot. I do all my own baking at home, using mostly whole grains and fruits. We like snack foods that aren't laden with sugar and heavy fats. We freeze and store food for the winter; there are sections in this book on how to do that. There's also a pantry chapter at the end about herbs, and what's in foods, and how to convert measurements.

A lot of people ask me what this book is about: "What's your angle? Where are you coming from? Is it for women with jobs, microwaves, wood stoves? Is it for vegetarians, fat people, computer operators, campers or kids?" I'd have to say, all of the above, and more. It's for people who have never cooked before, and for people who are always looking for a new recipe. It's for international cuisine — I like to cook with a real variety of flavors — and for those who prefer to cook with what they grow. Here in New England and the Maritimes our diet is governed less by international boundaries than by the number of growing days there are in the summer.

This is also a cookbook for active people. If you're going to get anything done in the day, besides cooking the meals, you need recipes which work well and don't take up a lot of extra time. These are the ones I cook with, plus a few special ones we only use once in a while. I'm sure you'll recognize them.

This is my second cookbook. The first was about cooking on a wood stove, with whole foods. I wrote it when we moved from suburban New England to a Maritime farm, built a small cabin, cleared land, gardened, made cheese and soups and bread and pickles and beer. This second cookbook reflects developments in our lifestyle. We have built a much larger and warmer house, wired it, taken jobs, and learned the essential culinary truth that if you want to compete with fast foods, you have to produce something which tastes better.

But we still cook on a wood stove.

Susan Restino

Breakfast & Brunch Dishes

To many people, breakfast is a very personal meal. Most of us are a little sleepy and hurried in the morning, so we need to make breakfast simple. On the other hand, we all want it to be something that we really enjoy eating. The important thing is to find a meal that fills all our needs — and it really doesn't matter whether it's eggs on toast, leftover lasagne or a blender special. If it keeps our insides happy until lunchtime it probably has the right ingredients. In general, they are a serving of protein, a little roughage, a little fat and some vitamin C.

If you're fed up with the high prices and low food values of commercial breakfast cereals, try making your own. They're delicious because the ingredients are fresh. The recipes that follow are in quantity —

store them in an airtight container in a cool place.

Eggs are another good choice for breakfast and brunch because they cook so rapidly. There are many ways to prepare eggs, if they are fresh, free-range ones. Commercially produced eggs are difficult to fry and almost impossible to poach, because the whites are so runny. If you can't get home-grown eggs, better stick to boiling or scrambling them.

Everybody loves pancakes; they're moist, hot and easy to eat. Pancakes are often served with maple syrup, but there are alternatives such as molasses, applesauce, sour cream and fruit sauce, which have more food value and less sugar. They can also be made with fruit in them.

A CUP OF SOMETHING HOT

Almost everybody likes a cup of something hot in the morning. Coffee and tea are favorites, but not everybody can drink them early in the day. Fortunately, there are now a wide variety of herbal teas. And there are other things as well. How about hot lemonade? Great for a stuffy head. Hot grape or apple juice is also delicious. And the ultimate simplicity: Chinese peasants start their day with a cup of hot water, taken slowly, before the morning chores.

Hot Lemon Tea

This is a great favorite around our house, especially in the winter. Use either fresh or bottled lemon juice.

1 Tbsp.	lemon juice	15 mL
1 Tbsp.	honey	15 mL
1 cup	boiling water	250 mL

Combine in a large mug; serve hot.

1 serving

VARIATION

HOT PURPLE TEA Add to Hot Lemon Tea, above: 2 Tbsp., (30mL) blackberry, currant juice or grape concentrate

Raw Tiger's Milk

There are many different versions of this mixture, many of which are carefully balanced to give you maximum nutrition during times of severe stress. My problem is that under stress I don't have the time to mix a complicated drink.

1 cup	milk	250 mL
1	egg	1
2 Tbsp.	Engivita brewer's yeast	30 mL
1 Tbsp.	molasses	15 mL

Combine ingredients and mix thoroughly.

1 serving

Finnish Berry Shake

This is easy to make with a blender, but possible without. If using frozen berries, thaw for two hours, until slushy but still partly frozen. Use strawberries, raspberries, dewberries or baked apples.

1½ cups	cold milk	375 mL
2 Tbsp.	liquid honey	30 mL
3 Tbsp.	fresh or frozen berries	45 mL

Blend until berries are pulverized. Or mash berries with a fork, then add milk and honey and beat with a rotary beater for one minute.

1–2 servings

Blender Combo

If you don't have a blender handy, mash the banana, then shake everything together in a bottle.

1½ cups	whole *or* skim milk	375 mL
5 Tbsp.	instant skim milk powder	75 mL
½	banana	½
½ cup	orange juice	125 mL
1	egg *or* egg yolk	1
2 Tbsp.	liquid honey	30 mL

1–2 servings

HOW TO CHOP ROLLED OATS

Coarse rolled oats can be finely chopped in a blender or a grain grinder for finer texture. To use the blender, half fill it with rolled oats, cover, and give it a short buzz. Stir and buzz, covered, again. Continue until the oats are mostly chopped but not pulverized. To use the grinder, set it to a very coarse setting and run the oats through once.

Light Granola

This is a very light, dry version of granola.

1/3 cup	vegetable oil	80 mL
1/3 cup	honey	80 mL
1/3 cup	water	80 mL
pinch	salt	pinch
6 cups	rolled oats	1.5 L
1 cup	coconut	250 mL
1 cup	sunflower seeds	250 mL
1/2 cup	hazelnuts, ground	125 mL

In a small saucepan mix oil, honey, water and salt. Heat gently (so that the honey and oil will mix). Meanwhile, mix remaining ingredients together in a large bowl, using your hands. Give the liquid mixture a last stir before pouring it over the dry ingredients. Mix everything together with your hands and strew the uncooked granola over cookie sheets or baking pans, thinly, so that there are no lumps.

Bake for 30 minutes at 200°F (100°C). Cool and store in an airtight container.

9 cups (2.5 L)

Scotch Oatmeal

Always have something else with oatmeal for breakfast. Milk is easy, but it could be eggs, or cheese, or meat, or even tamari soy sauce and roasted sunflower seeds. Any of these will greatly increase the level of protein in a cup of oatmeal.

2 cups	water	475 mL
1/2 tsp.	salt	2 mL
1 cup	Scotch oatmeal, ground	250 mL

Add salt to water and bring to the boil. Add oatmeal. Cover, lower heat and simmer for 1 hour. If it gets very thick, stir in a little water so that it won't scorch on the bottom.

2 servings

Familia

A favorite of the Swiss, who eat it with yogurt and fresh fruit for breakfast or snacks.

3 cups	rolled oats, chopped	725 mL
1 cup	wheat germ, roasted	250 mL
1 cup	dried currants	250 mL
1 cup	unroasted almonds, chopped	250 mL
1 cup	dried apples or apricots, chopped	250 mL

Mix by hand; store in an airtight container in a cool place.

6 cups (1.5 L)

Roasted Oatmeal

2 cups	rolled oats	475 mL
3½ cups	water	850 mL

Put rolled oats in a heavy iron skillet over steady heat and roast, stirring constantly, for about 5 minutes, until they begin to smell nutty. Add water, cover and steam for 10 minutes.

Serve with tamari soy sauce, gomasio, roasted sunflower seeds, and/or butter.

4 servings

Roasted Oat Cereal

4 cups	rolled oats	1 L
1 cup	wheat germ	250 mL
1 cup	walnuts, chopped	250 mL
1 cup	unsweetened coconut	250 mL
1 cup	dried apples, chopped	250 mL
1 cup	raisins or chopped dates	250 mL
2 Tbsp.	Engivita brewer's yeast	30 mL

Mix all ingredients together. Spread on cookie sheets and roast for 30 minutes at 200°F (100°C).

Store in an airtight container. Serve with milk and fruit.

9 cups (2.5 L)

Steamed Cracked Wheat

You may buy cracked wheat or grind your own in a grain mill. In either case it makes a very nice thick cereal.

2 cups	water	475 mL
½ tsp.	salt	2 mL
1 cup	cracked wheat	250 mL

Bring water and salt to the boil in a heavy pot. Add wheat slowly, stirring. Cover closely, lower heat and simmer for 20 minutes. Serve with milk and sugar, or tamari soy sauce and butter, or maple syrup and cream.

4 servings

Scrambled Eggs With Variety

Obviously, this is a recipe with all sorts of possibilities. You might add bits of smoked fish or ham, sautéed tofu cubes, or a splash of Tabasco sauce. It's a great thing to make for brunch.

2 Tbsp.	butter or safflower oil	30 mL
1	small onion, chopped	1

½	green pepper, chopped	½	
6	mushrooms, sliced	6	
4–5	eggs	4–5	
¼ cup	cream *or* evaporated milk	60 mL	
	paprika		

Heat butter or oil in a heavy skillet. Sauté onion, pepper and mushrooms. Break eggs into a bowl and add cream or evaporated milk. Beat well and pour over vegetables. Tilt the pan and lower heat. Stir after 1 minute. Tilt the pan, let it cook another minute, then stir again, making sure all uncooked egg gets to the bottom. Remove from heat the instant they are done. Sprinkle with paprika.

3–4 servings

Eggs Benedict

This is the sort of thing you get served in bed at the Ritz. It can actually be made more successfully at home – and served hot off the stove, which is the best way to eat it.

3 Tbsp.	butter	45 mL
	juice of 1 lemon	
3	large eggs	3
2	English muffins, halved	2
2	slices ham	2

First, set the table and get out all your ingredients. Melt the butter and lemon in the top of a double boiler. Sizzle ham lightly in a slightly buttered pan, over mod-

erate or low heat. Add one egg to sauce and beat until thick. Remove from heat and cover to keep warm, leaving the bottom half on the stove to poach eggs in. Toast muffins and poach the remaining two eggs. Lay muffin half on plate, top with ham, poached egg, a scoop of sauce and another muffin half. Serve at once.

2 servings

Whole Wheat French Toast

Whole wheat bread is perfect for French toast; slightly stale whole wheat is even better.

4–5	eggs	4–5
¼ cup	milk	60 mL
6	slices bread	6
5 Tbsp.	vegetable oil	75 mL

Break eggs into a shallow dish and add milk. Beat well. Dip slices of bread into egg mixture. Heat oil in a heavy skillet. Lay French toast pieces in hot oil so they do not overlap. Fry about 2 minutes per side (don't let oil smoke). Drain on absorbent paper and serve hot.

Serve with butter, maple syrup, molasses, or applesauce and sour cream. If necessary, French toast can be kept in the oven for up to 15 minutes at 200°F (100°C).

4 servings

ABOUT PANCAKES

To add extra nutrition to pancakes you may add up to 2 Tbsp. (30 mL) Engivita brewer's yeast, wheat germ or defatted soy flour to a batch. To cook pancakes successfully nothing can replace the cast-iron skillet. Heat it up first, adding a few drops of cooking oil, then reduce heat to medium. Pour in batter to make three 4 in. (10 cm) pancakes at a time in an ordinary-sized skillet. Larger pancakes are hard to turn, and if you leave part of the skillet empty, it will start to smoke. If you have small children, you can make each one a "turtle" by dripping batter around the central pancake to make head, feet and tail.

let, and heat them up, before pouring on 3 Tbsp. (45 mL) batter for each pancake. Cook pancakes over moderate heat, flipping once, until browned on each side. Serve hot, with butter and maple syrup or molasses.

15 pancakes

VARIATIONS

BLUEBERRY PANCAKES Add 1 cup (250 mL) fresh or frozen blueberries to the batter just before you cook the pancakes.

BANANA OR APPLE PANCAKES Slice the fruit thinly and lay it, in small circles, on a hot, greased skillet. Pour batter over fruit and cook, at high heat, until browned on underside. Turn over carefully. Add a few drops of oil to skillet each time more fruit is added.

Whole Wheat Pancakes

In order to make more, faster, I use two skillets and cook three pancakes at a time in each.

4	eggs	4
1 cup	water	250 mL
1/2 cup	skim milk powder	125 mL
1 cup	whole wheat flour	250 mL
1/2 cup	unbleached white flour	125 mL
2 tsp.	baking powder	10 mL
pinch	baking soda	pinch
1/2 tsp.	salt	2 mL

Beat together the eggs, water and skim milk powder. Sift in remaining ingredients. Put a few drops of oil on each skil-

Oatmeal Pancakes

A good recipe for hearty appetites.

2 cups	milk	475 mL
2 cups	rolled oats	475 mL
1/4 cup	vegetable oil	60 mL
4	eggs, beaten	4
2 Tbsp.	brown sugar	30 mL
1 cup	whole wheat flour	250 mL
1/2 tsp.	salt	2 mL

Combine milk and rolled oats and let sit for 5 minutes. Add oil, eggs, sugar, flour and salt, and beat thoroughly. Cook on a hot, lightly oiled griddle, making pancakes about 4 in. (10 cm) across.

20–25 pancakes

Potato Pancakes

Not at all like ordinary pancakes, these morsels are crunchy on the outside, soft inside, and delicious with applesauce and sour cream for breakfast or brunch.

4	small potatoes	4
2	eggs	2
$^1/_2$ cup	flour	125 mL
$^1/_2$ tsp.	salt	2 mL
1	onion	1
4 Tbsp.	vegetable oil	60 mL

Peel and grate potatoes; twist them in a towel over the sink to remove excess moisture. Beat eggs in a bowl. Add flour, salt, and potatoes. Grate in peeled onion. Heat oil in skillet. Spoon about 3 Tbsp. (45 mL) of the mixture on the skillet and spread it out to around 4 in. (10 cm). Fry cakes on both sides until golden brown.

14–16 pancakes

Cornmeal Pancakes

Tender, crisp and light, these are my family's favorites.

2 cups	cornmeal	475 mL
4 Tbsp.	molasses	60 mL
1 tsp.	salt	5 mL
3 Tbsp.	corn oil	45 mL
2 cups	boiling water	475 mL
$^1/_2$ cup	white flour	125 mL
1 cup	milk powder (not instant)	250 mL
2 tsp.	baking powder	10 mL
2	eggs	2
	cooking oil	

Measure cornmeal, molasses, salt and oil into a heavy ceramic bowl. Stir as you pour boiling water over them, then cover and let sit for a few minutes. Sift in flour, milk powder and baking powder and beat well. Beat the eggs separately, then beat them into the mixture. Preheat skillet, coating lightly with a few drops of cooking oil. Make 3–4 in. (8–10 cm) pancakes, turning when the tops are bubbly and the edges slightly dry.

Serve with butter, maple syrup, or molasses.

14–16 pancakes

Blintzes

Blintzes are culinary feats, to be carried out on a gloriously late Sunday morning or for a midnight feast.

FILLING

$1^1/_2$ cups	cottage cheese	370 mL
2	egg yolks	2
1 Tbsp.	soft butter	15 mL
1	lemon peel, grated	1

CRÊPES

3	eggs	3
2 cups	water	475 mL
1 cup	instant skim milk powder	250 mL
1 cup	white flour	250 mL
$^1/_2$ tsp.	salt	2 mL
$^1/_4$ cup	vegetable oil	60 mL

In a sieve, place cottage cheese and work out as much cream as you can, using a spoon. (If you have dry curds, you can skip this stage.) Turn into a bowl and add egg yolks, butter and lemon peel. Mix together and set aside until needed.

In a shallow bowl, beat eggs. Add water, milk powder, flour and salt. Beat briefly with a fork or whisk. Heat skillet and spread a few drops of oil on it. Pour batter into skillet as thinly as possible, making 6 in. (15 cm) rounds. Cook over medium heat for about 2 minutes, until the top is moist but not sticky. Turn them out on to a cookie sheet or smooth counter, *uncooked-side down*. Don't stack them. Place on each blintz, in a short line, 1 heaping Tbsp. (15 mL) cottage cheese filling. Tuck in the edges at the ends of the line, then roll up the blintzes. Let sit for 5 minutes before frying or baking.

To fry blintzes, heat oil in a deep pan until the oil is hot enough to brown a cube of bread. Lay blintzes in carefully, one at a time, seam-side down, so they aren't touching. Brown about 4 minutes to a side, turning once. Remove with a slotted spoon, draining for a moment over the pot before you roll it in absorbent paper to remove excess oil. Lay cooked blintzes on a platter and keep warm in a 200°F (100°C) oven, until serving.

To bake blintzes, place them in a slightly oiled pan, seam side down, and bake at 400°F (200°C) for 15 minutes.

Serve with applesauce, maple syrup or sour cream.

14 blintzes

Fresh Herb Omelet

For cream you can substitute evaporated milk.

5	large eggs	5
2	egg yolks	2
¼ cup	light cream	60 mL
¼ tsp.	freshly ground pepper	1 mL
3 Tbsp.	unsalted butter	45 mL
2 Tbsp.	chives, chopped	30 mL
2 Tbsp.	parsley, chopped	30 mL

In a large mixing bowl, beat together eggs, egg yolks, cream and pepper with a whisk. Heat butter in a cast-iron or heavy cast-aluminum skillet until it sizzles. Hold the pan by the handle as the omelet cooks, tilting it from side to side to loosen the eggs. Lower heat if the eggs bubble and bulge. After about 2 minutes, sprinkle chives and parsley over eggs. Tilt the pan and fold one half of the omelet over the other with a spatula. Continue to cook another minute. Remove from heat and serve at once.

4 servings

ABOUT OMELETS

For 1 person allow 2 eggs;
For 2 people allow 3 eggs;
For 4 people allow 5 to 6 eggs;
For 5 to 6 people allow 8 eggs and use a very large pan.

For larger groups, make more than one omelet, since more than 8 eggs will not set, and more than 6 is difficult. No omelet should take more than 5 minutes to cook.

VARIATIONS

CHEESE OMELET Cheese may be added along with or instead of herbs. Use ½ cup (125 mL) Monterey Jack or Cheddar cheese, grated.

MUSHROOM OMELET Mushrooms should first be sautéed in butter. Use ½ cup (125 mL) sliced fresh mushrooms and 3 Tbsp. (45 mL) unsalted butter.

Soups & Stocks

Home-made soups and stocks are an important part of a well-rounded kitchen. Soup and sandwich lunches are infinitely more satisfying than cold meals, especially in the winter.

Soups are not expensive or difficult to make. Most are based on vegetable or bone stocks, which do require long cooking. However, if you don't have time for it, use a Crockpot, or speed up the job with a pressure cooker. Store stock in the fridge for use within five days, or freeze.

There are many things you can do with stocks and soups; they increase the power of the kitchen. Stocks are the bases of many sauces as well as soups. When unexpected guests arrive at dinnertime, you can stretch a meal by starting with a soup-and-cracker course. Soup can be run through a food mill for instant baby food. And a hot bowl of soup is a marvelous pick-me-up when you need extra energy.

There are really two stages to making soup. The first is making stock, a chronic affair in our house. There's always a pot of bones and vegetables on the back burner, or stashed in the fridge, to make a good hearty base for the day's *zuppa*. The second stage starts about half an hour before lunch, when I decide what to make with what we have. These are my basic recipes, but I seldom make a soup without some innovation — a sprinkling of a different herb, a chopped vegetable, a splash of wine. The essence of soup cookery is in the flavor, so don't be afraid to dip in and try it, as you adjust the taste. Soup may be accompanied by crackers, sandwiches or bread and butter or cheese.

Vegetable Stock

2 Tbsp.	vegetable oil	30 mL
2	carrots, chopped	2
1	onion, chopped	1
2	ribs celery, with leaves, chopped	2
2 qt.	water	2 L
6	sprigs parsley	6
1	bay leaf	1
1 tsp.	salt	5 mL
3	peppercorns	3

Heat oil in a large pot and sauté onion, carrots and celery until soft. Add remaining ingredients and bring to the boil. Reduce heat and simmer gently for 1 hour. Strain and use at once or refrigerate for up to 3 days. To keep it longer, freeze it.

2 qt. (2 L)

Fish Stock

1 fish	(head, tail, skin and bones)	1
2 qt.	water	2 L
1	onion	1
1	clove	1
1/2 cup	white wine	125 mL
1	rib celery, with leaves	1
3	white peppercorns	3
1	bay leaf	1
1 tsp.	coriander seeds	5 mL
1 tsp.	salt	5 mL

Combine all ingredients in a large pot and bring to the boil. Reduce heat and simmer gently for 1 hour. Strain and use at once or refrigerate for up to 3 days. To keep it longer, freeze it.

2 qt. (2 L)

Chicken Stock

Chicken makes wonderful stock, a base for superb soups and sauces. You may use chicken backs or the bones left over from any chicken dish. Boiling will sterilize them, even if they've been to the table. Avoid necks of commercial birds, as they may contain drug residues.

	bones from 1 chicken	
2 qt.	water	2 L
2–3	celery tops	2–3
1	carrot, diced	1
1	bay leaf	1
4	peppercorns	4
2 Tbsp.	marjoram	30 mL
1 tsp.	salt	5 mL

Cover bones with water and add all other ingredients. Bring to a rapid boil for 15 minutes, then reduce heat and simmer, covered, for about 2 hours.

Chicken stock can also be made in a pressure cooker. Fill cooker no more than two-thirds full of water, bones and vegetables. Bring to 15 lb. pressure (100 kPa) and lower heat according to pressure cooker instructions. Pressure cook chicken stock 30 minutes. Cool stock completely before removing lid.

Strain and cool finished chicken stock. Refrigerate up to three days. To keep it longer, freeze it.

2 qt. (2 L)

Beef Stock

You can make a similar stock using venison instead of beef.

2	cloves	2
1	onion	1
2 lb.	beef shank or flank	1 kg
2 lb.	beef or venison bones	1 kg
2 qt.	water	2 L
2 tsp.	salt	10 mL

Stick the cloves into the onion. Combine all ingredients in a pressure cooker or large pot and cover with water. Cook at 15 lb. pressure (100 kPa) for 1 hour or simmer for 6 hours over low heat. Strain broth into containers and cover tightly when cool. Refrigerate for up to 1 week or freeze.

2 qt. (2 L)

Broccoli Tamari Soup

After the heads of broccoli have been cut in the garden, miniature heads keep appearing along the sides of the stalks. There never seem to be enough to make a complete vegetable serving, but you can use them in a soup, where they combine nicely with the rich tamari flavor.

2 cups	broccoli stems	475 mL
1	onion, chopped	1
1/2 tsp.	salt	2 mL
2 cups	broccoli florets	475 mL
1 cup	tamari soy sauce	250 mL

Cut broccoli stems into rough chunks, cover with water, add onion and salt and bring to the boil. Cover and simmer for 30 minutes. Strain broth or remove vegetables with slotted spoon and add the broccoli florets. Simmer until florets are barely done, about 5 minutes. Lower heat. Just before serving, add the tamari.

4 servings

Clear Onion Soup

With a loaf of French bread, a good cheese, a salad, and a bottle of wine: the most rewarding meal on earth.

2–3	onions	2–3
3 Tbsp.	unsalted butter	45 mL
3 Tbsp.	whole wheat flour	45 mL
1 qt.	Chicken Stock or Vegetable Stock	1 L
4	slices stale French bread	4
6 Tbsp.	grated cheese	90 mL

Slice the onions very thinly. In a heavy soup pot, heat butter to bubbling hot, and sauté the onions over medium heat until they are golden brown. Reduce heat slightly and sprinkle the flour into the pan. Stir with a whisk as you add the stock. Cover the pot and simmer 20 to 30 minutes. Ladle the soup into individual pots. Heap grated cheese on bread slices and float one in each pot. Place under broiler for 3 to 4 minutes, until cheese is toasted.

4 servings

Gourmet Magic Cream Of Potato Soup

This is a wonderful recipe because it can be made with the most mundane ingredients, is marvelously versatile, and pleases everyone.

2 Tbsp.	butter	30 mL
1	small onion, diced	1
	or	
1/2 cup	green onions, sliced	125 mL
2 Tbsp.	unbleached white flour	30 mL
2 cups	water	475 mL
1 1/2 cups	uncooked potato, cubed	375 mL
1 tsp.	salt	5 mL
	pepper	
2 cups	light cream or milk	475 mL
2 Tbsp.	chives, chopped	30 mL
4 Tbsp.	butter	60 mL

Heat butter in a heavy soup pot, and sauté onion for 3 minutes. Sprinkle flour over them, reduce heat a little and cook, stirring, for 1 minute. Stir in water and add potatoes, salt, and a generous grating of pepper. Bring to the boil, then reduce heat and simmer, covered, for 10 to 15 minutes, or until potatoes become soft. Remove from heat, and mash the potatoes with a fork or potato masher. Add cream or milk, mix, and heat gradually over medium heat. Do not boil.

Serve each bowl of soup garnished with chives, a pat of butter, and a dash of paprika.

4 servings

VARIATIONS

CLAM CHOWDER This creamy delicacy is much loved by Maritimers and New Englanders. You may use fresh or canned clams, or even mussels, provided they are well washed. If using fresh shellfish, clean them thoroughly (see page 82) and separate them into a dish of soft parts and another of tough necks. Reserve juice by opening shellfish over a bowl.

1	rib celery, chopped	1
1 cup	clam necks, chopped	250 mL
1 cup	clam soft parts, chopped	250 mL
1 cup	clam juice	250 mL

Sauté celery along with onion, and add clam necks to soup along with potatoes. Use clam juice as part of the water. Add the soft clam parts when you add the milk or cream. Serve with soda biscuits.

CREAM OF ASPARAGUS SOUP

12	fresh asparagus spears	12
1 cup	water	250 mL
1/2 tsp.	salt	2 mL

Cut the spears in half, reserving the green tops. Peel the lower stems and chop into 1/2 in. (1 cm) pieces. Add to soup along with potatoes. Boil the tops separately in a small pan with salted water for 6 to 10 minutes. Remove and chop the tops into ¼ in. (.5 cm) pieces; they should be very small. Add their water to the soup. When the soup is almost ready to serve, garnish with chopped asparagus tops. Omit chives.

CREAM OF MUSHROOM SOUP

24	fresh mushrooms	24
3 Tbsp.	butter	45 mL

Remove mushroom stems, chop fine, and add them to the soup along with the potatoes. Meanwhile, heat butter in a small skillet, slice mushroom caps vertically, and sauté until golden over medium heat. Add them to the soup along with the milk. Serve hot with toast.

CORN CHOWDER You may use fresh, frozen or canned corn. Add along with the potatoes:

1 cup	corn	250 mL
¼ cup	green peppers, diced	60 mL

CREAM OF CHICKEN SOUP Dark meat has the most flavor, light is more tender. A mixture is good.

1 cup	cooked chicken, chopped	250 mL
2 cups	chicken broth	475 mL
3 Tbsp.	parsley, chopped	45 mL

Add chopped chicken to soup along with potatoes. Use chicken broth instead of water. Garnish with parsley instead of chives.

FISH CHOWDER The most popular fish for this is haddock, but you can use any fresh or cooked fish or leftovers.

1 cup	fish	250 mL
2 cups	Fish Stock (page 10)	475 mL
½ tsp.	celery salt	2 mL
1 tsp.	white wine	5 mL

Add fish to soup along with the potatoes. Use fish stock (or substitute water). Flake the fish when you mash the potatoes, and season with celery salt and wine.

Borscht

Borscht is a good sweet-and-sour fall soup, best served with pickled herring, rye bread, thick yogurt or sour cream garnished with chopped dill, and dill pickles.

3 cups	Beef Stock (page 11) *or* Vegetable Stock (page 10)	725 mL
4 cups	canned tomatoes	1 L
½ cup	green onions, chopped	125 mL
2 cups	raw beets, grated	475 mL
½ tsp.	salt	2 mL
¼ tsp.	freshly ground pepper	1 mL

Combine all ingredients (including juice with canned tomatoes) in a pot or Crockpot. Bring to the boil, then simmer for 45 minutes, or until beets are tender.

4–6 servings

Bean Soup

1 cup	dried navy beans	250 mL
2 cups	cold water	475 mL
6 cups	boiling water	1.5 L
1	ham bone	1
1	large onion	1
3	cloves	3
3	ribs celery	3
1	carrot	1
1	clove garlic	1
1	bay leaf	1
1/2 tsp.	salt	2 mL
	pepper	

Soak beans overnight in cold water. Drain in morning, and put in a large pot with boiling water, ham bone, onion stuck with cloves, celery, carrot, garlic, bay leaf, salt and freshly grated pepper. Boil rapidly, covered, for 30 minutes, then simmer, covered, for about 2 hours until the beans soften. Remove 1/2 cup (125 mL) of the cooked beans and set aside. Using slotted spoon, remove the vegetables, bay leaf and bones, then purée remaining beans, meat and liquid. Return whole beans to pot and adjust seasoning. (Alternatively, you can leave the vegetables in, to be puréed with the beans).

4–6 servings

VARIATIONS

U.S. SENATE BEAN SOUP

1 cup	marrow beans	250 mL
1	potato	1

Use marrow instead of navy beans, and add a potato along with the beans. Mash potato when you mash beans.

TOMATO-BEAN SOUP

1 cup	stewed tomatoes	250 mL
1 tsp.	basil	5 mL

Use tomatoes in place of some of the water in cooking the beans, and flavor with basil.

BLACK BEAN SOUP

1 cup	black beans	250 mL
1	lemon	1
4	eggs, hard-boiled	4

Use black beans in place of navy beans, and omit carrot. Serve with wedges of lemon and sliced hard-boiled eggs.

Home-Made Chicken Soup

There's no substitute for the real thing. Cures colds, broken hearts, and wild beasts.

6 cups	Chicken Stock (page 10)	1.5 L
1 cup	sliced carrot	250 mL
1 cup	small shell pasta	250 mL
1/2 cup	frozen peas	125 mL
1/4 cup	parsley, chopped	60 mL
1 cup	cooked chicken, chopped	250 mL
	salt and pepper	

Bring the stock to the boil in a large pot. Add carrots and pasta and boil for 5 minutes. Add peas and parsley and boil 5 minutes longer. Add chicken and salt and pepper.
Serve with crackers and cheese.

4 servings

Egg Lemon Soup

Thick, warm and lemony, this soup is wonderful for a cold that's getting better, or a tasty meal after a long hike.

6 cups	Chicken Stock (page 10)	1.5 L
½ cup	brown rice	125 mL
4	egg yolks	4
3 Tbsp.	lemon juice peel of 1 lemon, grated	45 mL

Put stock and rice in a large pot, cover, bring to the boil, reduce heat, and simmer for 45 minutes, or until rice is done. Meanwhile, beat egg yolks until frothy in a mixing bowl with a whisk. Wash, dry, and grate the lemon peel; then cut and squeeze out the lemon juice. Add both to the egg yolks. When rice is done, pour a little of the hot soup into the egg yolks, beating as you do, then return the mixture to the pot, stirring constantly. Simmer for 5 minutes, being careful not to boil, until it thickens slightly. Serve at once, with toast.

4–6 servings

Split-Pea Soup

3 Tbsp.	ham or bacon fat	45 mL
1	onion, sliced	1
4 cups	water	1 L
1	ham bone (optional)	1
3	carrots, chopped	3
1 cup	split peas	250 mL
½ tsp.	salt	2 mL
1	bay leaf	1

Heat fat in a deep, heavy soup pot. Sauté onion for 3 to 5 minutes, then add water, ham bone, carrots, split peas, salt and bay leaf. Bring to the boil and cook for 20 minutes, then reduce heat and simmer, covered, for 2 to 3 hours. Remove ham bone and bay leaf.

Serve with croûtons fried in bacon fat, corn bread, and hard-boiled eggs.

4–6 servings

Golden Soup

Use a large squash or pumpkin for this creamy, delicious soup.

1	winter squash	1
2 cups	boiling water	475 mL
2 Tbsp.	safflower oil	30 mL
1	onion, chopped	1
2 cups	instant milk powder	475 mL
1 tsp.	coriander	5 mL
1-2 tsp	salt	5-10 mL
	freshly ground pepper	
	whole milk	

Clean squash and cut into large chunks; place in a heavy pot with boiling water, cover closely, and cook for about 20 minutes, or until squash is tender. Meanwhile, heat the oil in a heavy skillet and sauté onions for 3 to 5 minutes before adding them to the squash. When the squash is soft, put it through a food mill or food processor and return to the pot. Add the powder, milk, coriander, salt, and pepper. Thin with whole milk as needed.

4–6 servings

❖❖

Scotch Broth

This is especially good if you cook it one day and serve it the next.

2 Tbsp.	safflower oil	30 mL
2	carrots, sliced	2
1	onion, chopped	1
1	rib celery, chopped	1
4 cups	water	1 L
1	lamb or beef bone	1
1/4 cup	tomato paste	60 mL
	pepper	
1 tsp.	salt	5 mL
1/4 tsp.	thyme	1 mL
1	bay leaf	1
1 cup	pot barley	250 mL
1/2 cup	navy beans	125 mL
1 cup	cooked lamb or beef, diced	250 mL
1 cup	fresh or frozen peas	250 mL

In a heavy deep soup pot, heat the oil and sauté the carrots, onion, and celery. When they are limp, add the water, bone, tomato paste, pepper, salt, thyme and bay leaf. Bring this to a rapid boil and pour in barley and beans. Boil the soup for 30 minutes, then simmer, covered, for 4 hours. Ten minutes before serving, add the meat and peas. Cook until peas are done.

4–6 servings

Minestrone

Definitely our favorite soup for all time: an exotic meal in itself. You may use fresh or frozen green beans.

3 Tbsp.	safflower oil	45 mL
1	onion, chopped	1
2	ribs celery, chopped	2
1	clove garlic, crushed	1
2 qt.	water	2 L
1 tsp.	salt	5 mL
1 cup	pot barley	250 mL
1 cup	navy beans	250 mL
2 cups	stewed tomatoes	475 mL
1/2 cup	egg noodles	125 mL
1/2 cup	cooked meat	125 mL
1/2 cup	green beans	125 mL
1/4 tsp.	thyme	1 mL
1/4 tsp.	oregano	1 mL
2	basil leaves, chopped	2

In a heavy, deep soup pot, heat oil and sauté onion, celery, and garlic. After 5 minutes add the water (or substitute beef stock), salt, barley, beans and tomatoes. Bring to the boil and cook for 30 minutes, then lower heat and simmer, covered, for 3 hours. Ten minutes before serving, add noodles, diced meat, beans, and herbs.

5–7 servings

❖❖

Vegetables & Salads

Growing your own vegetables is one of the great joys in life. There is always something magical about planting and growing things to eat; it's a way of participating in the seasonal changes. Early spring begins with plans and preparations, choosing seeds and starting some indoors. Before you know it, the first radishes and lettuces are ready for the table. The season proceeds through various kinds of greens and peas, and suddenly explodes into a cornucopia of plenty: beans, corn, zucchini and yellow squash, early broccoli, cauliflower and carrots. There are all sorts of lovely things to put in salads: tomatoes, cucumbers, green peppers, green onions, different kinds of lettuce and tender greens, and fresh chopped herbs. Through the fall, vegetables continue to ripen. Some, like broccoli, cabbage, cauliflower and brussels sprouts actually grow better when the weather gets colder. And it's the early frost that turns the pumpkins orange, hardens the onions, and sweetens the apples that taste so good with carrots and beets. Last of all, we dig the potatoes, as winter sets in.

Vegetables can be frozen, canned, dried and processed, but fresh is best. Children seem to know this instinctively; after turning down platefuls of tender cooked peas, beans, broccoli or brussels sprouts, they'll happily munch up all of the raw carrots, turnips and cucumbers in the house. Even if you don't have a garden of your own, it makes sense to eat some vegetables in season, throughout the year.

They're available at farmers' markets where you can buy potatoes, onions and apples by the bagful, or choose from lovely mounds of cabbages and pumpkins. Some may be stored fresh; others frozen. See Food Storage, page 155.

Fresh Asparagus

The great secret lies in the freshness of the asparagus. The thicker, earlier stalks are the most tender.

24	fat asparagus spears	24
2 cups	water	475 mL
3/4 cup	Hollandaise Alvino (page 42)	180 mL

Cut asparagus spears in half. Put the water in the bottom of a vegetable steamer and bring to the boil. Steam the bottom halves for 7 to 10 minutes, then add top halves and steam for 7 to 10 minutes. Meanwhile, make Hollandaise. Serve hot or cold.

4 servings

Beets With Sour Cream

2 cups	water	475 mL
4	large beets	4
1 cup	sour cream	250 mL
1/2 tsp.	dill, basil, chervil	2 mL
1/2 cup	fresh parsley, chopped	125 mL

Bring water to the boil in a heavy pot. Dice, slice or cut the beets in chunks about 2 in. (5 cm) square. Put them in the pot, in a steamer or on a rack. Cover tightly and steam for 1 hour, or until tender. Meanwhile, combine the sour cream and the herbs. Serve beets with sour cream poured over them.

4 servings

Mediterranean Bean Dish

Use either fresh or frozen green beans.

2 Tbsp.	olive oil	30 mL
1	onion, chopped	1
1/2	green pepper, chopped	1/2
1	clove garlic, crushed	1
4 cups	green beans, chopped	1 L
2 cups	canned tomatoes	475 mL
1 tsp.	basil	5 mL
1/2 tsp.	salt	2 mL
1/4 tsp.	pepper	1 mL

Heat oil in a heavy skillet and sauté onion and pepper for 5 minutes over rapid heat. Add garlic, sauté for 1 minute, then add beans, tomatoes (with juice), basil, salt and pepper. Cover and cook gently for about 10 minutes, or until beans are tender.

4–6 servings

Sautéed Beets And Carrots

1 1/2 cups	beets	375 mL
2 Tbsp.	light oil	30 mL
1 1/2 cups	carrots,	375 mL
1/2 cup	water	125 mL
2 Tbsp.	tamari soy sauce (optional)	30 mL

Slice and steam beets for 15 minutes. Cut carrots in finger-sized pieces. Heat oil in a heavy skillet and sauté carrots for 5 to 10 minutes, then add the beets and the water, and soy sauce if desired. Cover the skillet and steam for 15 minutes.

4 servings

Broccoli Romani

1½ lb.	fresh broccoli *or* frozen broccoli	675g
3 Tbsp.	olive *or* safflower oil	45 mL
1	clove garlic, crushed	1
½ tsp.	anchovy paste	2 mL
2 Tbsp.	sherry	30 mL
1 tsp.	tamari soy sauce	5 mL

If the broccoli is uncooked, chop it into florets, and peel and chop the stem into manageable pieces. Peel stem pieces. Steam over boiling water for 10 to 12 minutes, or until barely done. Remove from heat and drain.

Heat oil in a serving casserole over moderate heat and gently sauté crushed garlic. Add anchovy paste, sherry and tamari and mix with a fork. Remove from heat. Toss broccoli in the flavored oil and serve, or keep warm up to 10 minutes by covering.

4 servings

CABBAGE FACTS

Cabbages have an extraordinary amount of vitamin C, most of it concentrated in the outer and greener leaves. This vitamin is water-soluble, so it is better to steam rather than to boil cabbages. There is also a fair amount of iron and calcium in cabbage; the calcium, however, is only available to your body if you eat or drink dairy products or eggs at the same time.

We grow three types of cabbage. *Summer*, or *Savoy*, which grows to be quite large, develops a pale green, crinkly head. It's great for coleslaw and stir-fry, but doesn't keep past December. *Purple cabbage* resembles the ordinary Ballhead, but it's sweeter and more tender – excellent for cooking. *Ballhead*, the kind you see in most stores, will keep in a good root cellar until spring.

Sweet Cabbage

3 Tbsp.	safflower oil	45 mL
3 cups	cabbage, shredded	725 mL
2	apples, chopped	2
1	onion, chopped	1
2 Tbsp.	brown sugar	30 mL
1 Tbsp.	cider vinegar	15 mL
1 Tbsp.	catsup	15 mL
2 tsp.	tamari soy sauce	10 mL

Heat oil in a heavy skillet. Toss in cabbage, apples and onions, cooking over high heat for 5 to 10 minutes; or until they begin to brown. Mix sugar, vinegar, catsup and soy sauce in a small bowl. Add to cabbage, and stir-fry for 1 or 2 minutes before serving.

4 servings

Tart Red Cabbage

A good accompaniment to a big pot of stewed meat, root vegetables and corn-bread – a meal as colorful as fall.

1/2	red cabbage	1/2
2 cups	water	475 mL
3 Tbsp.	safflower oil	45 mL
1	onion, sliced	1
2 Tbsp.	red wine vinegar	30 mL
3 Tbsp.	brown sugar	45 mL
2 Tbsp.	cornstarch	30 mL
1/2 tsp.	salt	2 mL

Slice cabbage into four wedges with a bit of core in each to hold them together. Steam on a rack over the water for 15 minutes. Meanwhile, heat oil in a large, heavy skillet and sauté onion. When cabbage is done, add it carefully to the onions and sauté for about 1 minute on each side. Stir vinegar, sugar, cornstarch and salt into liquid remaining in pot when it has had a minute to cool. Then heat this again, stirring until clear and thick. Pour the sauce over the cabbage, cover, and simmer for 5 minutes.

4 servings

Stuffed Whole Cabbage

Stuffed cabbage is well worth the preparation. A medium-sized to large cabbage, scooped out in the center, stuffed with your favorite filling and topped with Cream Sauce is an elegant and wonderfully filling dinner dish.

1	compact winter cabbage	1
1 cup	Béchamel Sauce (page 42)	250 mL
1 1/2 cups	filling (below)	375 mL

Remove any loose leaves from cabbage. Slice 2 in. (5 cm) off the top, and scoop out the middle, leaving a shell about 1 1/2 in. (4 cm) thick. Put the cabbage upside-down on a rack in a heavy pan with an inch or two (3–5cm) of boiling water and steam it for 10 minutes. Take it out. You should be able to scoop out more, if needed.

Stuff cabbage loosely with fillings. Return to pan, right side up, and steam for 15 to 20 minutes. To serve, place on a platter, and top with sauce.

Slice as you would a pie.

6–8 servings

CABBAGE FILLINGS To assemble fillings, first beat egg and herbs together, then mix in other ingredients, stirring to moisten.

TOFU FILLING

1	egg, beaten	1
1 tsp.	curry powder	5 mL
1/2 cup	cooked cabbage, chopped	125 mL
1 cup	sautéed tofu, crumbled	250 mL
2 Tbsp.	sautéed onion, chopped	30 mL
2 tsp.	tamari soy sauce	10 mL

PESTO FILLING

1	egg, beaten	1
1 Tbsp.	Garlic Pesto (page 46)	15 mL
1 cup	cooked rice	250 mL
1/2 cup	cooked soy grits	125 mL
1/4 cup	Tomato Paste (page 44)	50 mL
2 Tbsp.	sautéed onion, chopped	30 mL

MEAT FILLING

1 cup	cooked bulgur	1
1/2 cup	sautéed ground meat	125 mL
2 Tbsp.	sautéed onion, chopped	30 mL
1	clove sautéed garlic, crushed	1
1	egg, beaten	1

Cabbage Rolls

1	large cabbage	1
1 1/2 cups	Stuffed Cabbage filling	375 mL
2 cups	Fresh Tomato Sauce (page 43)	475 mL
1 cup	mozzarella cheese, grated	250 mL

Use inner leaves of cabbage. Choose those that don't have heavy ribs in the center. Steam them, 4 or 5 at a time, for about 5 minutes. Pile the steamed leaves on a plate.

Meanwhile, mix one of the fillings for Stuffed Whole Cabbage (previous recipe), and oil a baking pan. To fill the leaves, lay each one on the counter, and put a couple of spoonfuls of stuffing on it, along the width of the leaf. Fold both sides up over the filling. Now roll the leaf up towards the seam. Place it seam-side down in the pan.

When they are all done, cover them with Fresh Tomato Sauce. Top with cheese. Bake, uncovered, at 350°F (175°C) for about 30 minutes.

4 – 6 servings

Cabbage Tamari

3 cups	cabbage, shredded	750 mL
4 Tbsp.	safflower oil	60 mL
1 Tbsp.	tamari soy sauce	15 mL

Heat oil in a heavy skillet. Sauté the cabbage over high heat, stirring once or twice, for 5 minutes, or until it begins to look translucent. Add soy sauce (you can make a milder version by adding half tamari and half water). Cover tightly; steam over medium heat for 5 minutes. Serve while cabbage is somewhat crisp.

2 servings

Corn On The Cob

In my father's house, one first put a large pot of water on the stove to heat. When the water was boiling, the table set, the meal cooked, we then (and only then) went down to pick the corn. For corn on the cob we only picked the perfect ears, pale yellow, the tops not yet ripened. Within minutes (in the corn patch) they were stripped and cleaned of silk. Then we sprinted back and plunged them into the boiling water. They were cooked for about 5 minutes, then lifted out and served forth, with plenty of butter and salt. After that we had dinner.

The reason for all this bother is that as soon as corn is picked, the sugar in it begins to convert to starch. Corn picked a few hours before cooking will still be sweet, although not quite as sweet as by the above method. In a day or two, however, it is pretty boring.

Corn is one of the few vegetables I cook in a large amount of water; that is because there are few vitamins to be lost. However, if you prefer, there is another way to cook corn, although you should only do a few ears at a time this way.

6–8	ears of corn	6–8
½ cup	water	125 mL
½ cup	milk	125 mL

Heat water and milk in a cast-iron kettle or large pot. Steam fresh ears of corn for 5 to 10 minutes, or until tender. Serve at once.

3–4 servings

Corn Pudding

2 cups	fresh corn	475 mL
¾ cup	cream	180 mL

Grate corn into a bowl. Add cream and mix until the corn mixture is as thick as half-melted ice cream. Pour into a greased shallow baking dish. Bake in a slow oven, about 300°F (150°C) for 1 hour. Serve hot.

4 servings

Corn Fritters

These definitely fall into the category of treats – something to be made for disappointed children (who were going on a picnic) on a rainy afternoon. The children, of course, do most of it!

12	ears of corn	12
3	eggs	3
1 Tbsp.	flour	15 mL
1 tsp.	salt	5 mL
3 Tbsp.	butter or corn oil	45 mL

Grate the ears of corn. Separate the eggs and beat the egg whites until you can turn the bowl upside down. Mix the egg yolks into the corn, along with the flour and salt. Gently, with your hands, mix together the egg whites and corn mixture. Heat butter or oil in a skillet and fry the batter as pancakes, until light brown.

Serve hot with molasses.

12 fritters

Sautéed Carrots

Carrots have a phenomenal amount of vitamin A. They are also tasty, when sautéed, and have a cheerful color.

2 Tbsp.	vegetable oil	30 mL
3 cups	sliced carrots	725 mL
2 Tbsp.	sesame seeds	30 mL
1/4 cup	water	60 mL

Heat oil in a heavy skillet over high heat. Add carrots and sauté rapidly, stirring as needed, for 10 minutes. Add sesame seeds and cook, stirring, for 3 minutes longer. Then add water, cover, and steam (still over high heat) for 5 minutes or until water is taken up.

4 servings

Cauliflower With Buttery Crunch

1	cauliflower	1
3 Tbsp.	butter	45 mL
3 Tbsp.	vegetable oil	45 mL
1/2 cup	very fine bread crumbs	125 mL
2	cloves garlic, crushed	2
2 Tbsp.	fresh parsley, chopped	30 mL
2	hard-boiled eggs	2

Break cauliflower into florets and steam over boiling water for 10 to 15 minutes in a tightly lidded pot. Meanwhile, melt butter and oil together in a small skillet. Add bread crumbs and garlic and sauté for 5 minutes. You may also add parsley and chopped hard-boiled eggs. Combine with steamed cauliflower.

4 servings

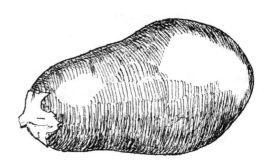

Eggplant Parmigiana

This dish is an all-day affair with the stove and eggplant. Fortunately, you can assemble it one day and bake it the next.

4 cups	Mama Restino's Sauce (page 44)	1 L
2	small eggplants	2
2	eggs	2
1/2 cup	milk	125 mL
1/2 cup	flour	125 mL
1/2 cup	olive *or* safflower oil	125 mL
1 cup	Parmesan cheese	250 mL
2 cups	mozzarella cheese	475 mL

Prepare sauce. Slice the eggplants into 1/4-in. (1 cm) pieces. Set them to dry on a rack or paper towels for about 1 hour. Mix eggs and milk. Dip the slices of eggplant in the egg-milk mixture, then the flour. Let sit for 1 hour in a cool place, to dry a bit. Then fry them in the oil until golden, turning once. Drain on absorbent paper. Grate and combine the cheese.

Place in layers in an oiled baking dish: eggplant, sauce and cheese. Repeat twice more. Set aside until the next day in a cool place, or bake at 350°F (175°C) for 1/2 to 1 hour, until the cheese browns on top.

4 servings

Imam Bayaldi

"The priest fainted," the Turkish name for this recipe proclaims, when his bride served him this exotic stuffed eggplant. For this dish one needs small, whole, unblemished eggplants, one half for each sublime serving.

2	small eggplants	2
¼ cup	olive oil	60 mL
1	large onion, finely chopped	1
1	clove garlic, crushed	1
2	large tomatoes, chopped	2
1 Tbsp.	Tomato Paste (page 44)	15 mL
pinch	sugar	pinch
pinch	pepper	pinch
½ tsp.	salt	2 mL
2 Tbsp.	fresh parsley, chopped	30 mL
½ cup	stale bread crumbs	125 mL
3 Tbsp.	pine nuts, roasted	45 mL

Cut the eggplants in half lengthwise. Scoop out the pulp, leaving ¼ to ½ in. (about 1 cm) of shell. Chop the pulp. Heat olive oil in a heavy iron skillet. Add onion and garlic and sauté until translucent. Add tomatoes, tomato paste, chopped eggplant, sugar, pepper and salt. Simmer for 20 minutes, then allow to cool.

Brush eggplant shells with olive oil. Place in a baking dish. Add parsley, bread crumbs and pine nuts (to roast, allow 10 minutes at 300°F, 150°C) to the cooled mixture in the skillet. Fill the eggplant shells, packing the mixture into a firm mound. Bake in a 350°F (175°C) oven for 20 minutes. Remove from the oven as soon as the eggplant shells are cooked. Keep warm before serving, if necessary.

Serve with bulgur or brown rice, beans, meatballs or sausage, and a lightly dressed salad.

4 servings

COLLECTING FIDDLEHEADS

Fiddleheads, the tightly curled heads of emerging ostrich ferns, are gathered in the early spring. They're a wonderful excuse to go traipsing up and down rivers and streams; all you need is a pair of rubber boots and a couple of plastic bags in your pockets. The tan, papery covering on each new fiddlehead is easy to pick off (not fuzzy) and should be removed as soon as you get home, before cooking or storing, as it's quite bitter. Fiddleheads may be refrigerated for up to four days in a perforated plastic bag or open container. They also freeze quite nicely.

Steamed Fiddleheads

This is only possible with a small quantity of fiddleheads.

1 cup	fiddleheads	250 mL

Clean fiddleheads well. Place in a vegetable steamer over boiling water. Cover pot and steam for 10 to 12 minutes. Serve with butter or Hollandaise Alvino (page 42).

2 servings

Boiled Fiddleheads

Most people cook fiddleheads this way. It's easier, and if there are any husks left on, they'll fall off in the water.

4 cups	fiddleheads	1 L
2 qt.	water	2 L
1 tsp.	salt	5mL

Pick fiddleheads clean. Immerse them in boiling water and salt and cook rapidly for 7 minutes. Drain at once and serve with butter or Hollandaise Alvino (page 42).

4–6 servings

ABOUT GREENS

It's very important to wash greens thoroughly. If they're not very sandy, put them in a wire basket or salad spinner and submerge in cold water. Then spin or whirl the basket outdoors to remove the moisture. If they're definitely gritty, wash each leaf separately — then whirl in the basket. In either case, the only way to be sure they're clean is to taste a few. No amount of fancy cooking later will make anybody want to eat sand.

After you wash them, consider the stems. If you can nip them off with your fingernail, they're tender; if not, they will take much longer than the greens to cook. Fold the leaf lengthwise, underside out, and tear out the stems and any tendrils that come with it. If the leaves are very large, you may want to tear them into smaller pieces.

One pound (450 g) of uncooked greens equals one cup (250 mL) of cooked greens. You should allow ½ cup (125 mL) of cooked greens per serving. Greens should never be cooked in aluminum pans; they pick up a metallic taste, not to mention some questionable qualities.

Italian Greens

Use mild-flavored greens, such as spinach, chard, lettuce or lamb's quarters.

2 Tbsp.	light oil, butter *or* drippings	30 mL
1	onion	1
1	clove garlic, crushed	1
1 lb.	greens	450 g

Heat oil, butter or drippings in a heavy skillet. Slice or chop onion and add with garlic to skillet. Sauté until transparent. Add washed greens. Cover the skillet closely. Simmer for about 5 minutes, or until wilted and tender.

4 servings

VARIATION

PEPPERY GREENS IN MILK Cook as above, but when you put in the greens add 1 cup milk (250 mL). This is especially good for peppery greens such as mustard, dandelion, turnip tops and radish greens. Cover and simmer over low heat so that the milk does not boil.

Aemono

This is an authentic Japanese dish, except that the Japanese serve it cold, and I like it better hot. Use a tender green, such as spinach, young chard, lamb's quarters or lettuce.

2 Tbsp.	dark sesame oil	30 mL
1 lb.	greens	450 g
1/4 cup	sesame seeds	60 mL
1/4 cup	tamari soy sauce	60 mL

In a heavy skillet, heat oil. Add washed greens. Cover and simmer over low heat until the leaves wilt – about 5 minutes. Meanwhile, in another pan, roast sesame seeds until brown. When the greens are cooked, add the seeds and tamari.

4 servings

Sautéed Jerusalem Artichokes

Jerusalem artichokes, available in the early spring, taste a little like parsnips, only they're more tender and crisp. They may be eaten raw or cooked.

12–20	Jerusalem artichokes	12–20
1	onion	1
3 Tbsp.	butter	45 mL
1/2 cup	water	125 mL

Slice artichokes 1/2 in. (1 cm) thick. Chop onion coarsely. Heat butter in a heavy skillet. When the butter is hot, add vegetables and sauté until browned, about 5 minutes, stirring occasionally. Add water. Cover tightly and steam for 7 to 10 minutes. Serve at once.

4 servings

Kohlrabi In Cream Sauce

Non-gardeners may not be familiar with kohlrabi, a member of the cabbage family. The part you eat is the stem, which swells into a round, pale green vegetable, about as big around as an apple. Kohlrabi must be picked and eaten before it reaches its maximum girth, or the center will become tough and woody with little white fibers. Tender kohlrabi has a texture rather like the inner flesh of a broccoli stem, but it is somehow crisper, sweeter and finer.

3	small kohlrabies	3
1 cup	milk	250 mL
3 Tbsp.	butter	45 mL
3 Tbsp.	flour	45 mL
	salt	
	parsley	

Peel and cut kohlrabies in 1/2 in. (1 cm) slices. Simmer them gently in a pan with the milk. They should be tender in about 15 minutes — pierce with a fork to be sure. Meanwhile, in a separate pan, make a roux with the butter and flour. Let the roux foam for about 2 minutes on low heat. Add the milk from the kohlrabies, and beat rapidly until the sauce thickens. Season with salt and parsley. Add the cooked kohlrabi to the sauce.

4 servings

Baked Onions

Leave the onions in their jackets, but cut shallow crosses in both ends to keep the insides from popping out. Bake at 325°F (160°C) for about 1 hour.

Walnut Parsnips

2 cups	parsnips, sliced or quartered	475 mL
1 cup	carrots, sliced or quartered	250 mL
1/2 cup	chopped walnuts	125 mL
1	onion, chopped	1
1/2 cup	stock	125 mL
1 Tbsp.	brown sugar	15 mL

Arrange parsnips and carrots in an oiled casserole and cover with walnuts, onion, either chicken or vegetable stock and sugar. Cover and bake at 350°F (175°C) for 45 minutes.

4 servings

Sweet And Sour Sugar Snaps

1/2 cup	water	125 mL
2 Tbsp.	vinegar	30 mL
3 Tbsp.	brown sugar	45 mL
1 Tbsp.	cornstarch	15 mL
3 Tbsp.	vegetable oil	45 mL
1	onion	1
1	green pepper	1
3 cups	sugar snap peas	725 mL

Mix 1/4 cup (60 mL) water, vinegar, brown sugar and cornstarch in the top of a double boiler. Set over boiling water, covered, and cook for 10 to 15 minutes, stirring occasionally. Meanwhile, heat oil in a heavy skillet or wok. Chop onion and green pepper, and add with peas to skillet. Sauté, and

after about 5 minutes of stirring and frying add remaining 1/4 cup (60 mL) water. Cover and steam for 2 to 3 minutes. Add sauce and serve at once.

4 servings

Sautéed Parsnips and Peas

6	parsnips	6
3 Tbsp.	vegetable oil	45 mL
1/2 cup	stock	125 mL
1 cup	frozen or fresh peas	250 mL
2 Tbsp.	parsley, chopped	30 mL
2 Tbsp.	butter	30 mL

Slice parsnips 1/4 in. (1/2 cm) thick, diagonally. Sauté them in oil in a heavy skillet, stirring to brown as many surfaces as possible in about 10 minutes. Then add stock (chicken or vegetable), and peas. Steam, covered, for 5 minutes over high heat. Add parsley and butter, toss well, and serve at once.

4 servings

FRESH PEAS

We can never plant enough peas. Like sweet corn, they should be picked and shelled just before cooking, but if that's impossible, keep them cool and shell at the last moment. Peas are sweetest when slightly underripe; older peas tend to be starchy. To improve old peas, add to the pot a dash of sugar and a few leaves of mint or marjoram.

POTATO STORAGE

Potatoes should be stored in a dark, damp place. Exposure to light will cause concentrations of toxic *solanine* to appear as greenish patches on the potato skin.

New potatoes are sweet and waxy, the skins thin and tender. Over the winter, however, the quality of potatoes changes. They become starchier, the skins thicker. New potatoes are preferred for boiling; old potatoes are the best for frying and baking.

Always wash store-bought potatoes thoroughly. Commercial potato crops are routinely sprayed with a wide range of pesticides, fungicides and herbicides. For this reason you may prefer to peel them, although this makes them much less nutritious, since all of the vitamin C and iron in potatoes is concentrated in a thin layer just under the skin.

Baked Stuffed Potatoes

Before I moved to the Maritimes, I never used to give much thought to potatoes. Since then, I've heard discussions about their comparative qualities that rival those you hear about beef in Chicago, cheese in Denmark, or wine in Paris. Potatoes can be white, brown, pink or a glossy blue-black purple. They can be sweet, bitter, round, oval, long or lumpy; their skins can be thin or thick, smooth or crusty. The quality that Maritimers prize most, though, is the light, fluffy dryness of a potato "so mealy it flies apart in the pot." Such a potato need never be mashed, saving a lot of time and energy in kitchens where potato is daily fare.

Start these well before dinner, or make them up to 24 hours ahead and refrigerate until the final baking. Choose evenly shaped potatoes, about 2½ in. (6 cm) in diameter and 3–4 ins. (8–10 cm) long.

6	potatoes	6
1 cup	milk	250 mL
½ cup	instant milk powder	125 mL
3 Tbsp.	butter	45 mL
1 tsp.	salt	5 mL
2 Tbsp.	chopped chives	30 mL
1 tsp.	onion juice paprika	5 mL

Bake potatoes at 425°F (220°C) for 45 minutes. When they can be easily pierced with a fork, take them out and cut each one carefully in half. Scoop out the middles, turning each shell upside down on the counter as you do so.

Beat milk, dried milk, butter, salt, chives and onion juice into potato filling. (To extract onion juice squeeze pieces of fresh onion in a garlic press.)

Refill potato skins, heaping the filling up on top somewhat, and put stuffed potatoes in the wells of a cupcake tin. Sprinkle tops with paprika. Bake at 350°F (175°C) for 20 minutes.

3–6 servings

Scalloped Potatoes

6	medium potatoes	6
1	onion	1
6 Tbsp.	unbleached white flour	90 mL

1 tsp.	salt	5 mL
3 Tbsp.	butter	45 mL
	paprika	
2 cups	whole milk	475 mL
½ cup	instant dried milk	125 mL

Slice potatoes and onion as thinly as possible. In a well-buttered casserole, make layers consisting of potato slices, onion slices, a sprinkling of flour and a dash of salt. Chop butter in pieces and sprinkle on top, and finish with a sprinkling of paprika. Mix milk and dried milk and cook over medium heat until hot but not boiling. Pour milk over potatoes. Cover casserole and place over low heat for 20 minutes. Preheat oven to 350°F (175°C). When potatoes can be pierced with a fork, remove lid and put casserole in the oven. Bake 15 to 20 minutes.

4–6 servings

Country Potato Chips

A nice snack on a snowy day, these potato chips are eaten while still warm.

2	potatoes	2
2 Tbsp.	vegetable oil	30 mL
	salt	

Scrub and slice potatoes as thinly as possible. Heat oil in cast-iron skillet over high heat. Put a few slices of potato in the pan, not overlapping. Fry until golden; turn them with a spatula and cook until golden. Drain, and salt lightly. Eat as soon as you can. Make more.

2–3 servings

Country Home Fries

We often make these for breakfast, using about half the amount of potatoes you'd want for dinner.

5	medium potatoes	5
1	onion	1
5 Tbsp.	vegetable oil	75 mL

Chop potatoes into ½ in. (1 cm) cubes. Put them into a saucepan in about 1 in. (2 cm) water, cover tightly, bring to the boil and cook until soft, about 10 minutes. Remove from heat and drain off any remaining water. Dice onion, and heat oil in a cast-iron skillet. Add potatoes and onions, and cook over rapid heat until browned on all sides, turning as necessary.

4 servings

﹀﹀

Sautéed Squash

The best size for summer squashes is about 8 in. (20 cm) long. For these dishes, the squashes are parboiled before frying, which helps to firm them up. To parboil, simply bring a pot of water to the boil, immerse squash, and cook for 10 minutes. Remove and drain, after which you may dice or slice it.

ZUCCHINI FRY

3 Tbsp.	vegetable oil	45 mL
2	zucchini squashes	2
1	large onion, diced	1
2 Tbsp.	tamari soy sauce	30 mL

Parboil and dice or slice squash. Heat oil in a heavy skillet over high heat. Add vegetables and cook until lightly browned on one side, about 5 minutes. Turn, add tamari, and cook over moderate heat for 5 minutes.

4 servings

YELLOW SQUASH WITH CHERVIL

3 Tbsp.	vegetable oil	45 mL
2	yellow squashes, parboiled	2
1	small onion, diced	1
2 Tbsp.	lemon juice	30 mL
1/4 cup	fresh chervil, chopped	60 mL

Heat oil in a heavy skillet over high heat. Add vegetables and cook until lightly browned on both sides, about 10 minutes. Add lemon juice, cover and steam for 5 minutes. Add chervil, toss and serve.

4 servings

Tzimmes

1	medium winter squash	1
1 cup	sliced carrot	250 mL
1/4 cup	corn oil	60 mL
1/2 cup	liquid honey	125 mL
1 Tbsp.	lemon juice	15 mL
1/4 tsp.	salt	1 mL
1/4 tsp.	nutmeg, grated	1 mL
1	lemon peel, grated	1
4	tart apples	4

Slice squash into flat slabs, about 1/4 in. (.5–1 cm) thick. Place pieces on a rack over hot water and steam for 10 minutes. Add carrots to the squash and steam for 5 more minutes. Mix together oil, honey, lemon juice, salt, nutmeg, and lemon peel. Oil a casserole. Slice apples. Layer squash, apples and carrots, ending with carrots on top. Pour oil and honey mixture over and cover tightly. Bake at 350°F (175°C) for about 30 minutes. Remove the lid for the last 10 minutes of cooking.

5–7 servings

Fried Green Tomatoes

Choose firm, light green tomatoes.

4	green tomatoes	4
1/2 tsp.	salt	2 mL
1	egg	1
2	cloves garlic, crushed	2
1/2 cup	wheat germ	125 mL
1/2 cup	fine bread crumbs	125 mL
1/4 cup	olive oil	60 mL

﹀﹀

Slice tomatoes, not too thin, and sprinkle with salt. Beat the egg in a small bowl and add garlic. In another bowl mix the wheat germ and bread crumbs. Dip tomato slices in egg, then in crumbs. Heat olive oil. Fry slices four or five at a time, not touching or overlapping, turning them as they brown. Dry on absorbent paper.

4 servings

Stuffed Winter Squash

2	medium acorn squashes	2
3 Tbsp.	safflower oil	45 mL
1	onion, finely chopped	1
1 cup	whole wheat bread crumbs	250 mL
2 Tbsp.	wheat germ	30 mL
2 Tbsp.	fresh parsley	30 mL
1/2 tsp.	summer savory	2 mL
1/4 tsp.	thyme	1 mL
1/4 cup	pecans, chopped (optional)	60 mL
	ground pepper	

Halve and clean squashes before placing on a rack over 2 in. (5 cm) boiling water. Cover tightly and steam 20 minutes or until almost tender. Meanwhile, heat safflower oil in a heavy skillet and sauté onion until tender; then add bread crumbs, wheat germ, parsley, savory, thyme, pecans and pepper. Oil an ovenproof serving dish and place squashes on it, carefully, right-side up, and fill cavities with stuffing. Cover lightly with foil and bake at 350°F (175°C) for 15 to 20 minutes.

4 servings

Himmel Und Erde

"Heaven and Earth", as the old German title proclaims, is this marriage of applesauce and turnips. Fresh turnips need not be peeled, but by spring the skins will be woody and should be removed.

1	medium turnip	1
1 1/2 cups	applesauce	375 mL
2 Tbsp.	butter	30 mL
2 Tbsp.	brown sugar	30 mL
1/2 tsp.	cinnamon	2 mL
1/4 tsp.	ginger	1 mL

Wash turnip and chop into chunks the size of walnuts. Place in a pot with 1 in. (2 cm) water and bring to the boil. Cover and cook for 15 minutes, or until turnip is soft. Using a fork or potato masher, roughly mash turnips in remaining cooking water. Don't get all the lumps out. Add applesauce, butter, sugar, cinnamon and ginger. Stir well. Serve hot.

4 servings

Stir-Fried Vegetables

This dish is the backbone of summer garden meals around our house. It starts with freshly gathered vegetables, goes through a lot of chopping and slicing, and ends with very brief cooking.

Suggested Combinations:

Spring: carrots, onions, Jerusalem artichokes and/or parsnips;

Summer: beans, zucchini, corn and/or mushrooms;

Fall: cauliflower, broccoli, green pepper, kohlrabi and celery;

Winter: cabbage, carrots, onions, celery and mung bean sprouts.

The only vegetables I never add are potatoes or tomatoes.

3 Tbsp.	vegetable oil	45 mL
2–3 cups	vegetables, chopped	475-725 mL
2 Tbsp.	tamari soy sauce	30 mL
1/4 cup	water	60 mL

Heat oil in a wok or cast-iron skillet. First add carrots or other root vegetables. Stir to coat with oil and cook over high heat for 5 minutes. Add any firm vegetables, such as onions, beans, zucchini, cabbage, and celery, and cook for 5 minutes more. Add any leafy vegetables or sprouts, plus tamari sauce and water. Cover pan tightly and steam for a final 5 minutes. Serve with rice.

CHOPPING ONIONS QUICKLY

To slice onions quickly and efficiently, use a long sharp knife. First slice off the top and bottom, then peel off skin with your fingers. Next slice a small piece off one side so you can lay the onion on its side without slipping. Slice as thinly as possible. To chop the onion, first cut it in half through the "equator". This makes it easy to lay the flat halves on the cutting board and chop them into pieces as large or small as you like.

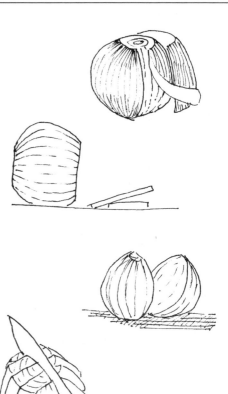

Picnic Potato Salad

and dressing, and toss thoroughly. Add alfalfa or cress sprouts in little bunches, just before serving.

6–8 servings

Every cook from Texas to Newfoundland must have his or her own method of making potato salad; it's the favorite summer food of potluck suppers, barbecues and gatherings of all kinds. Waxy new potatoes make a better salad than flakey old ones, but you can get better results in either case by dicing the potatoes before you cook them, and by steaming, rather than boiling. Old potatoes should be peeled; younger ones need not be.

Coleslaw

Coleslaw is a versatile dish. Kohlrabi, radishes, Jerusalem artichokes and turnips may be grated into it, for color and flavor, and leafy sprouts add special nutritional value.

4 cups	diced potatoes	1 L
1 cup	Vinaigrette (page 36)	250 mL
2	hard-boiled eggs	2
2 or 3	ribs celery	2 or 3
1	green pepper	1
2 cups	sugar snap or snow peas	475 mL
2 cups	lettuce, shredded	475 mL
1/2 cup	green olives	125 mL
1/2 cup	Home-made Mayonnaise (page 37)	125 mL
1 cup	alfalfa or cress sprouts	250 mL

2	ribs celery	2
3 cups	cabbage, shredded	725 mL
1/4 cup	chopped shallots or chives	60 mL
2	carrots, grated	2
1/2 cup	raisins	125 mL
1 cup	lettuce, roughly chopped	250 mL
1/3 cup	red wine vinegar	80 mL
1/4 cup	safflower oil	60 mL
1/4 cup	white sugar	60 mL
1/2 tsp.	dried mustard	2 mL
1/2 tsp.	curry	2 mL
1/2 tsp.	salt	2 mL
2 Tbsp.	mayonnaise	30 mL
2 Tbsp.	yogurt	30 mL

Steam potatoes in a tightly lidded pan in 1 cup (250 mL) water for 10 minutes, or until barely tender. Remove from heat, drain, and mix in half the vinaigrette. Refrigerate. Dice eggs, celery, green pepper. Cut peas in diagonal slices. Add lettuce and olives. Beat together the remaining vinaigrette and mayonnaise. Combine potatoes, salad,

Dice celery and add to cabbage. Add chopped shallots, carrots, raisins and lettuce. Combine vinegar, oil, sugar, mustard and salt in saucepan and bring to the boil. Cool this mixture before beating in the mayonnaise and yogurt. Add to salad and toss well. Refrigerate for 2 hours or more before serving.

4 servings

SPROUTS FOR SALADS

From a few tablespoons of tiny seeds comes a veritable jungle of sprouts. It's easy to grow your own. Use ordinary canning jars with two-piece lids. Remove the flat part of the lid and replace it with a 6 in. (15 cm) square of plastic window screening. For a pint (475 mL) jar use: 2 Tbsp. (30 mL) alfalfa seeds;

For a quart (1 L) jar use: 4 Tbsp. (60 mL) alfalfa seeds.

Put the seeds in the jar and fill with cold water. Screw on screen top. Soak seeds for 5 to 12 hours. Drain off water. Rinse seeds with cool water and drain again. Place the jar at a slight angle, so it drains continually. It should be at room temperature, but not in full light, for best results. However, the only thing that can really go wrong with sprouts is that you can forget to water them for more than 24 hours. Try to rinse them more often: every 6 hours is best. Depending on how well you remember, they will be fully sprouted in four or five days. They will grow little green leaves if placed in full sunshine. They keep up to a week if refrigerated, but should be rinsed daily.

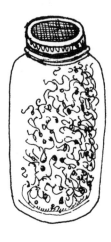

Endless Summer Salad

For the dog days of summer, here's an endlessly changing salad, full of everything fresh from the garden.

For something to contrast with fresh leafy and crunchy vegetables, keep a few stashes of cooked things in the refrigerator:

potatoes
green or yellow beans
cauliflower
grain, such as rice or bulgur
cooked dried beans
Better yet, you can keep these marinated in:
3 parts light oil
1 part vinegar or 2 parts lemon juice
Add to the marinade (but be careful to keep out of the salad):
1 clove raw garlic
1 sliced onion

When you're ready to eat, wander through the garden and woods for the rest of it. Depending on your plantings, findings and the month you may use:

ANY HANDY GREENS: lettuce, small leaves of cabbage, broccoli, or cauliflower; small greens from spinach, chard, beets, or lamb's quarters;

FOR SPICE AND TANG: mustard greens, sorrel, nasturtium leaves, watercress, cowslips, chopped or sliced radishes, green onions, peppers, raw peeled broccoli stems and the florets;

FOR SWEET, TENDER MUNCHING: raw peas, snow peas, tiny green beans, sprouts, chopped cucumbers, raw summer squash, celery, corn sliced off the cob;

FOR COLOR: day lily blossoms, nasturtium blossoms, and the lovely blue flowers of borage;

FOR UNEXPECTED FLAVORS: fennel, thyme, savory, basil, parsley;

FOR ADDED RICHNESS: things fresh and marinated, such as tomatoes, cucumbers, mushrooms, and summer squash chunks.

YOU MAY ALSO ADD: sunflower seeds, sesame seeds, buckwheat groats that have been soaked in water for 24 hours.

Toss all of this in just enough oil to lightly coat all the tender green leaves; then add vinegar to taste. The usual proportions are:

**3 parts oil
1 part vinegar or 2 parts lemon juice**

but I find it safer to taste as I go. You may also add, by the same system:

**salt, pepper, herbs
gomasio (roasted ground sesame seeds)
tamari soy sauce
grated Cheddar or Parmesan cheese
yogurt
bits of chopped ham, hard-boiled eggs**

Tomato-Cucumber Salad

3	ripe tomatoes	3
1	cucumber	1
3 Tbsp.	olive oil	45 mL
1 Tbsp.	wine vinegar	15 mL
1 tsp.	fresh chervil	5 mL
1 Tbsp.	fresh chives, chopped	15 mL
1 tsp.	salt	5 mL
1/2 tsp.	pepper	2 mL
2 Tbsp.	fresh parsley, chopped	30 mL

Chop, slice or cut in wedges tomatoes and cucumbers. Soak them overnight in a mixture of the oil, vinegar, chervil, chives, salt and pepper. Just before serving add the parsley.

4–6 servings

VARIATION

TOMATOES IN SOUR CREAM Follow the above recipe, but instead of oil and vinegar, use:

1 cup	sour cream	250 mL
1/4 cup	milk or plain yogurt	60 mL

Caesar Salad

1	romaine lettuce	1
1/4 lb.	fresh whole mushrooms	125 g
1 cup	alfalfa sprouts	250 mL
1	anchovy fillet	1
2 Tbsp.	blue cheese	30 mL
1	hard-boiled egg yolk	1
1	clove garlic, crushed	1
1 Tbsp.	lemon juice	15 mL
1/2 tsp.	dry mustard	2 mL
1/4 cup	olive oil	60 mL

Chop lettuce coarsely. Slice mushrooms and add to lettuce. Add alfalfa sprouts.

In a small bowl mash together the anchovy fillet, blue cheese and egg yolk. Add to this mixture the garlic, lemon juice, mustard and olive oil. Mix all together well. Add to the salad and toss well just before serving.

4 servings

Croûton Garnish

3 Tbsp.	safflower oil	45 mL
1	clove garlic, crushed	1
1/2 cup	whole wheat bread cubes	125 mL

Heat oil until very hot. Add crushed garlic and stir into oil. Then add brown bread cubes. Cool croûtons before sprinkling on top of salad.

Vinaigrette

Olive oil is traditional for this French salad dressing, but I use part safflower oil.

1/3 cup	white wine vinegar	80 mL
1/3 cup	olive oil	80 mL
1/3 cup	safflower oil	80 mL
1 tsp.	salt	5 mL
1	clove garlic, crushed	1
2 tsp.	Dijon mustard	10 mL
1 tsp.	tamari soy sauce	5 mL
	grating of pepper	

Combine ingredients and store in a jar. Shake well before using.

1 cup (250 mL)

Astoria Mayonnaise

1/2 cup	Vinaigrette	125 mL
1/4 cup	Home-made Mayonnaise	60 mL
2 Tbsp.	tomato catsup	30 mL
1 Tbsp.	green onion, finely chopped	15 mL
1 Tbsp.	green pepper, finely chopped	15 mL
3 drops	Tabasco sauce	3 drops

Shake vinaigrette and measure it into a mixing bowl. Add mayonnaise, beating constantly. Add catsup, onions, green pepper and Tabasco; beat well.

1 cup (250 mL)

Home-made Mayonnaise

Mayonnaise-making is a vigorous art, requiring a blender or a whisk and wide bowl. The bowl and ingredients should be chilled before starting. Keep home-made mayonnaise in a closed container in the refrigerator for no more than four days. If you make it regularly, label your jars, with the expiry date clearly marked. Never allow mayonnaise to stand, warm, for a few hours. Keep mixtures containing mayonnaise chilled as well.

3	egg yolks, chilled	3
1 cup	safflower oil	250 mL
1 cup	olive oil	250 mL
2 Tbsp.	white wine vinegar	30 mL
1 Tbsp.	fresh lemon juice	15 mL
1 tsp.	salt	5 mL
1/4 tsp.	Dijon mustard	1 mL

Put yolks in bowl, and beat briskly 2 to 3 minutes, until lighter in color. Add the first spoonful of oil drop by drop, beating constantly. Add the next half a cup or so of it in a very thin stream, beating constantly as the yolks expand and take up the oil. The more you add, the easier it gets, up to a point. After all the oil is in, you may beat in the vinegar, lemon juice, salt and mustard.

If the mixture separates, you can rescue it by starting all over with fresh egg yolks and oil, and add the separated mixture when it's about half made.

2–3 cups (475–725 mL)

Roquefort Cheese Dressing

1/4 cup	Vinaigrette	60 mL
1/2 cup	Home-made Mayonnaise	125 mL
2 Tbsp.	Roquefort cheese, crumbled	30 mL
1/2 tsp.	Worcestershire sauce	2 mL
3 Tbsp.	fresh parsley, chopped	45 mL

Shake vinaigrette and measure it into a mixing bowl. Add mayonnaise, beating constantly. Add cheese, Worcestershire sauce and parsley; beat well.

1 cup (250 mL)

ONION JUICE

To extract the juice from an onion, cut through its equator. Holding half in your palm, make shallow slits in the cut side, 1/2 in. (1 cm) deep, in a grid pattern. By squeezing the edges and scraping the surface with a serrated knife, you will get about 1 tsp. (5 mL) onion juice.

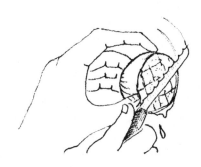

Vegetable Dips

ROQUEFORT DIP

1/2 cup	sour cream	125 mL
1/4 cup	blue cheese	60 mL
	pepper	

Add sour cream to blue cheese gradually, mashing with a fork or spoon in a small wooden bowl. Grate in pepper. Serve with slices of apple and turnip, crackers.

3/4 cup (180 mL)

CREAM CHEESE ONION DIP

1/2 cup	sour cream	125 mL
1/4 cup	cream cheese	60 mL
1 tsp.	onion juice	5 mL
1/4 cup	chives, chopped	60 mL

Add sour cream and onion juice to cream cheese gradually, mashing with a fork or spoon in a small wooden bowl. Add chives and mix well. Serve with crackers, potato chips, or sticks of cucumber, celery, and cherry tomatoes.

3/4 cup (180 mL)

CHEDDAR DIP

2	hard-boiled egg yolks	2
1/4 cup	butter	60 mL
2 tsp.	Dijon mustard	10 mL
	cayenne pepper	
1/2 cup	Cheddar cheese, grated	125 mL

Mash egg yolks with butter in a small wooden bowl. Add mustard and a few grains of cayenne, and mix well before adding the grated cheese. Serve with crackers, bread sticks, radishes.

3/4 cup (180 mL)

SPRING DIP

1/2 cup	sour cream	125 mL
1/2 cup	plain yogurt	125 mL
1 Tbsp.	lemon juice	15 mL
1	clove garlic, crushed	1
1 tsp.	dried mint or	5 mL
1 Tbsp.	fresh mint, chopped	15 mL
pinch	salt	pinch
2 Tbsp.	fresh parsley, chopped	15 mL

Mix sour cream, yogurt, lemon juice, garlic, mint and salt several hours before serving and allow to sit, covered, in refrigerator. Garnish with chopped parsley and serve with crackers or vegetables.

1 cup (250 mL)

Vegetable Marinade À La Greque

1 cup	Chicken or Vegetable Stock (page 10)	250 mL
1 cup	dry white wine	250 mL
1/2 cup	safflower oil	125 mL
2 Tbsp.	lemon juice	30 mL
6	sprigs parsley	6
1	clove garlic, crushed	1
1 tsp.	tamari soy sauce	5 mL
1/2 tsp.	summer savory	2 mL
5	peppercorns	5
1/2 tsp.	salt	2 mL
1/2 tsp.	celery seeds	2 mL

VEGETABLE SUGGESTIONS Choose those you like, in season.

1 cup	sliced Jerusalem artichokes	250 mL
1 cup	carrot sticks	250 mL
1 cup	turnip strips	250 mL
1 cup	celery strips	250 mL
1 cup	fennel hearts	250 mL
1 cup	small radishes	250 mL
2 cups	strips of pickling cucumbers	475 mL
1 cup	sliced small summer squash	250 mL
1 cup	small fresh beans	250 mL
2 cups	broccoli florets	475 mL
2 cups	cauliflower florets	475 mL

Cook marinade ingredients together in an enameled or stainless steel pot for 15 to 20 minutes. Strain and cool until use, or heat at once and cook vegetables, one variety at a time in boiling marinade until just tender (about 5 minutes for most vegetables). Remove and cool vegetables as each is done, then cool marinade and pour it over the vegetables. Refrigerate, covered, for 4 to 12 hours. To serve, drain the vegetables and arrange them on a platter with a variety of dips and mayonnaise in small containers.

12–20 servings

Hummus

This pungent, eye-watering Middle Eastern spread is adored by garlic lovers everywhere. Serve with pita bread, chopped lettuce, tomatoes and cucumbers.

3/4 cup	chick-peas	180 mL
3 cups	water	725 mL
1	onion	1
1/2 tsp.	salt	2 mL
2–4	cloves garlic, crushed	2–4
1/4 cup	olive oil	60 mL
1/2 cup	tahini	125 mL
	juice of one lemon	
2 Tbsp.	parsley, chopped	30 mL

Soak chick-peas overnight in water. In the morning, drain and rinse them, then replenish water. Add onion and salt and bring to the boil for 10 minutes, then lower heat and simmer for 5 hours, or until soft. Discard onion and put chick-peas through a food mill or mix in a blender until smooth. Add garlic, olive oil, tahini, parsley, and lemon juice.

1 1/2–2 cups (375–475 mL)

Antipasto Grill

These broiled vegetables are a good first course for a long dinner party. Serve with Vegetable Dips.

1	small eggplant	1
1	small zucchini	1
1	large yellow pepper	1
1	large red pepper	1
1/4 cup	olive oil	60 mL
3 Tbsp.	red wine vinegar	45 mL
1/2 tsp.	salt	2 mL
1	clove garlic, crushed	1
1 Tbsp.	Parmesan cheese, grated	15 mL
1 tsp.	Dijon mustard	5 mL

Parboil eggplant and zucchini for about 10 minutes. Slice and parboil peppers for 2 minutes. Drain vegetables and slice eggplant and zucchini 1/4 in. (1 cm) thick. Shake oil, vinegar, salt, garlic, cheese and mustard together in a bottle. Preheat grill and oil grill pan. Either dip vegetables in mixture or paint it on. Broil pepper pieces for 10 minutes, eggplant and zucchini for 3 to 5 minutes, turning all vegetables once during broiling and re-coating as necessary. Arrange on platter and serve.

6–8 servings

Sauces & Preserves

A good sauce is a worthy thing, and often the touch that turns an ordinary meal into something special. Let's face it — some foods are kind of boring. Others are on the dry side. A good sauce can save the day, if you know how to make it.

Pickles and relishes, jellies and jams can also add that special touch to a sandwich or holiday feast. They, of course, have the added advantage of being prepared in advance. Just open and serve, but it's still your own.

To make a good sauce, you don't need a lot of equipment: a heavy iron skillet in which to sauté a few chopped vegetables, and a small heavy deep pan in which to cook a small amount of liquid. I like a cast-iron enameled pan with a wooden handle. The tools I use most are a spring-type stirring device, and a small whisk or rotary beater to beat egg sauces.

To make preserves, you'll need a larger pot, made out of stainless steel or enameled. Canning jars with their heavy glass and perfect-seal lids are nice, but any country cook worth his or her salt knows that you can re-use commercial preserve jars and their lids, and so add interesting shapes and dimensions to your canning.

You'll also need tongs for lifting hot jars and a cup funnel to get hot liquid into the jars without spilling.

It's important in all cooking to use the freshest ingredients, but essential when you plan to bottle fruit or vegetables for long storage. For the best quality in texture and flavor, pick produce when it's barely ripe, on a clear, cool morning. Bottle, brine, or cook it that very day. You'll be amply rewarded in another season, when you dip into preserves which still retain their essence, fresh from the country.

Velouté and Béchamel Sauces

This simple method of thickening a sauce or soup is basic to much of Canadian and American cookery.

3 Tbsp.	butter or safflower oil	45 mL
3 Tbsp.	white or whole wheat flour	45 mL
1 cup	milk (for Béchamel) or stock (for Velouté)	250 mL
½ tsp.	salt grating of pepper	2 mL

Heat butter or oil in a small heavy pan over medium heat. When this is hot and bubbly, add flour and stir in as it cooks over gentle heat for 3 to 5 minutes. Don't let it brown. Measure the liquid and add it gradually in three parts, stirring until the mixture thickens after each addition. Add salt and freshly ground pepper. Simmer over very low heat for 5 minutes. This sauce may be cooled and reheated without illeffect if it's reheated slowly, with occasional stirring. It will be a thick sauce. If you want it thinner, add ½ cup (125 mL) milk or stock.

1 cup (250 mL)

Cheese Curry Sauce

1 cup	Béchamel Sauce	250 mL
¼ tsp.	curry powder	1 mL
½ cup	Cheddar cheese	125 mL
1 tsp	tamari soy sauce	5 mL

Combine ingredients and stir over low heat until cheese melts.

1½ cups (375 mL)

Horseradish Sauce

Very nice with boiled beef, corned beef, or meat fondue.

1 cup	Velouté Sauce	250 mL
½ cup	green onions, chopped	125 mL
1 Tbsp.	horseradish (or radishes), grated or prepared	15 mL
1 tsp.	dried mustard	5 mL
1 tsp.	sugar	5 mL
1 Tbsp.	vinegar	15 mL

Heat Velouté in a heavy saucepan. Add remaining ingredients. Simmer over low heat for 5 to 10 minutes.

1¼ cups (310 mL)

Hollandaise Alvino

This is a very simple, uncomplicated version of hollandaise, making just a dab of sauce for each serving. It is best made in a dipper slightly larger than your eggbeater, balanced on top of the broccoli or asparagus. In a pinch, use a double boiler.

4 Tbsp.	butter	60 mL
1 Tbsp.	lemon	15 mL
1	large egg	1

Melt butter and lemon together over boiling water until just before you are ready to serve. Break egg into a small bowl and beat briefly with a rotary beater. Add the egg to the lemon butter and beat until the sauce is thick — about 1 to 2 minutes. Remove from heat at once and serve.

½ cup (125 mL)

Sweet-Sour Sauce

Something to mix with cooked beets, carrots, onions, parsnips, turnips, or fried apples.

¹/₂ cup	brown sugar	125 mL
1 Tbsp.	cornstarch	15 mL
¹/₂ tsp.	salt	2 mL
pinch	dried cloves	pinch
¹/₂ cup	cider *or* white wine vinegar	125 mL

Mix all ingredients thoroughly in top of a double boiler before placing over boiling water. Cook, stirring occasionally, for about 10 minutes, or until thickened.

1 cup (250 mL)

Stir-Fried Vegetable Sauce

A soy sauce flavored condiment for stir-fried meat and vegetables, this is also a very nice sauce for meat balls.

2 Tbsp.	vegetable oil	30 mL
3	green onions, chopped	3
1 cup	vegetable *or* chicken stock	250 mL
	fresh ginger root	
1 Tbsp.	cornstarch	15 mL
2 Tbsp.	tamari soy sauce	30 mL

Heat oil in a small saucepan. Add onions and sauté for 3 to 5 minutes over high heat. Add ³/₄ cup (180 mL) stock and a grating of ginger. Cook gently over medium heat. Meanwhile, mix remaining ingredients (in-cluding stock) in a small bowl. Pour this into the simmering stock in the saucepan and stir gently with a whisk or spring stirrer as it thickens. Simmer for at least 5 minutes before serving. You may serve this separately or mix with cooked vegetables.

1 cup (250 mL)

Fresh Tomato Sauce

Tomato sauce made with fresh tomatoes tastes quite different from sauce made of canned or stewed tomatoes. Light and sweet, it's good on pasta, rice, mashed potatoes, meat, fish, poultry, or by itself.

1	onion, chopped	1
1	clove garlic, crushed	1
2 Tbsp.	olive oil	30 mL
¹/₂ lb.	ground beef	225 kg
3	large tomatoes *or*	3
6	small tomatoes	6
1 Tbsp.	dried *or* fresh basil	15 mL
2 Tbsp.	fresh parsley, chopped	30 mL
	salt and pepper	

Sauté onion and garlic briefly in oil before adding ground beef. Cook over medium heat until meat turns gray. Chop and add tomatoes, basil, and parsley. Cover and cook over medium heat for 10 minutes. Season to taste with salt and pepper.

2 cups (475 mL)

VARIATION

STEWED TOMATO SAUCE Follow recipe above but instead of fresh tomatoes use 1 qt. (1 L) canned tomatoes.

Tomato Paste

The best tomatoes for this are paste, or pear-shaped tomatoes, because they're denser to begin with; but any tomato will do.

1/4 cup	olive oil	60 mL
5	large onions, chopped	5
1	celery head, chopped	1
30–40	ripe tomatoes	30–40
1 Tbsp.	dried or fresh oregano	15 mL
1 Tbsp.	dried or fresh basil	15 mL
1 tsp.	dried or fresh marjoram	5 mL
10	peppercorns	10
10	cloves	10
2	sticks cinnamon	2

Heat oil in a deep, heavy stainless steel or enameled pan. Sauté onions and celery for 5 to 10 minutes. Chop tomatoes in quarters and add them, along with spices. Simmer very slowly for about 4 hours, stirring from time to time, to make sure nothing sticks to the bottom. If the bottom burns, don't scrape it; instead, transfer the paste to another pan and discard the burned part. After 4 hours, put it through a sieve or foodmill, first discarding the whole spices. Simmer until the pulp becomes too thick to cook safely on top of the stove. Spread it about 1/2 in. (1 cm) thick on an oiled pyrex, enameled, or china plate or tray, and cut grooves through it with a knife to help it dry through. Cook for 2 to 3 hours in a very slow, 200°F (100°C) oven. When the paste is thick enough, rub your hands in olive oil. Shape paste into 3 in. (8 cm) patties and submerge them in olive oil. They will keep up to 3 months in a cool place, in a covered container.

10–15 patties

Mama Restino's True Spaghetti Sauce

This is a sauce for pasta, gnocchi, ravioli, or anything that doesn't fall apart. It's good stuff. Don't put any prepackaged bottles of "sauce" in it.

3 Tbsp.	olive oil	45 mL
2	onions, coarsely chopped	2
2	cloves garlic, crushed	2
1	green pepper, chopped	1
1	rib celery, sliced	1
1/4 lb.	ground meat (optional)	125 g
28 oz.	tomatoes	796 mL
5 1/2 oz.	tomato paste	156 mL
pinch	thyme	pinch
1/2 tsp.	marjoram	2 mL
1 Tbsp.	oregano	15 mL
1 Tbsp.	basil	15 mL
1 Tbsp.	dry red wine	15 mL
1/2 tsp.	freshly ground pepper	2 mL
	fresh oregano	
1/2–1 cup	mushrooms (optional)	125–250mL

Heat oil in a heavy skillet. Sauté onions, garlic, pepper and celery for 3 minutes, then add ground meat and stir-fry until meat is gray. Add tomatoes, tomato paste and remaining ingredients except oregano and mushrooms. Refill paste can with water and add that, too. Turn heat down to the barest simmer and cook, covered, for 20 minutes. Turn off heat but leave sauce covered, from 2 to 6 hours before serving. To serve, reheat, adding a little water if necessary, and a pinch of fresh oregano. You may also garnish your dish with fresh fried mushrooms.

4 cups (1 L)

VARIATION

MAMA RESTINO'S TRUE MAN-ICOTTI, LASAGNE, AND PIZZA SAUCE For elaborate dishes such as manicotti, lasagne, eggplant parmigiana, and so forth, sauce must be made thicker than for spaghetti so that it does not disturb the layers of curds tucked in between the pasta. You may make and refrigerate this sauce for one of these dishes up to a week ahead of time.

Follow the recipe for spaghetti sauce, but instead of a 5½ oz. (156 mL) can of tomato paste, use two 11 oz. (312 mL) cans tomato paste. Add water as needed, but you should finish with a thick sauce. Watch it closely in the last stages of cooking, and stir often.

4 cups (1 L)

Barbecue Sauce

Barbecues are lovely, but this sauce is also delicious coated on baked meats such as chicken, pork, spare ribs, and fish.

3 Tbsp.	safflower oil	45 mL
1	onion, finely chopped	1
2	cloves garlic, crushed	2
5½ oz.	tomato paste	156 mL
1 cup	water	250 mL
3 Tbsp.	cider vinegar	45 mL
2 Tbsp.	soy sauce	30 mL
3 Tbsp.	brown sugar	45 mL
½ tsp.	salt	2 mL
1 tsp.	dried mustard	5 mL
¼ cup	lemon juice	60 mL
½ tsp.	freshly ground pepper	2 mL

Heat oil in heavy skillet and sauté onions and garlic for 3 minutes. Add remaining ingredients. Stir while bringing to the boil, then turn down to simmer and cook, covered, for 30 minutes. Stored in a cool place, this sauce will keep for months. To use it, first coat the meat or vegetables with oil and cook until nearly done. Then cover each side with sauce, cook for 5 to 10 minutes, and turn, until all sides are done.

1–1½ cups (250–350 mL)

ABOUT PESTO

Pesto is simply a mixture of fresh herbs pounded together with a mortar and pestle and thickened with oil. The flavor is so strong that you might not want to use it straight, but it's a great addition to sour cream, bland sauce, or gravy. Pestos can also be mixed with a big dish of rice or pasta. Or, spread very lightly on bread, and toasted in the oven, it makes a midnight snack whose aroma will wake the whole house up.

Refrigerated and tightly lidded, pesto will keep for several weeks. It can also be frozen.

Basil or Parsley Pesto

³/₄ cup	fresh basil or parsley	180 mL
¹/₄ cup	pine or pistachio nuts	60 mL
¹/₂ cup	Romano or Parmesan cheese, grated	125 mL
¹/₂ cup	safflower or olive oil	125 mL

Pound basil, pine nuts and cheese together in a mortar or salad bowl, until thick and paste-like. Add oil slowly, in a thin stream, while continuing to pound mixture. Mix well and store, tightly lidded, in the refrigerator.

1¹/₂ cups (375 mL)

Garlic Pesto

1 cup	fresh basil leaves	250 mL
4	cloves garlic	4
¹/₂ cup	fresh parsley	125 mL
2 cups	pine or pistachio nuts	475 mL
2 cups	safflower or olive oil	475 mL

Pound basil, garlic, parsley and pine nuts together in a mortar or salad bowl. When thick and paste-like, add oil slowly, in a thin stream, while continuing to pound mixture. Mix well and store, tightly lidded, in the refrigerator.

4 cups (1 L)

ABOUT MARINADES

Marinades, I suspect, were first invented to help preserve meat, but they also provide variety, by changing the flavor. They're also great tenderizers.

Marinades are used for some vegetables: cooked green beans, potatoes, Jerusalem artichokes, cauliflower, broccoli, brussels sprouts, and beets, as well as cooked or raw mushrooms, raw cucumbers, tomatoes and summer squashes.

Stew meats and cuts 2 in. (5 cm) thick are marinated for 3 to 6 hours. You may use raw vegetables (such as onions, garlic, celery) to flavor the marinade. A small roast of 2–3 lb. (1–1.5 kg) is marinated 1 to 3 days; a larger roast, 3 to 5 days. In longer marinades, the vegetables should be sautéed first.

Because marinades are acidic, use only Pyrex, ceramic, enameled, or porcelain containers.

Lemon Marinade

A good marinade to use on lamb or chicken, for those tasty morsels in shish kebab or vegetable stew. Mix this quantity for every pound, or half kilogram of meat.

1 Tbsp.	lemon juice	15 mL
1/2 cup	safflower oil	125 mL
1/4 cup	apple juice	60 mL
1 Tbsp.	tamari soy sauce	15 mL
1/2 tsp.	salt	2 mL
	ground white pepper	
1	clove garlic, crushed	1
	grating of fresh ginger	
1/2 tsp.	turmeric	2 mL

Combine ingredients. Marinate pieces of meat for 3 hours, turning them every half hour or so.

1/2 cup	sliced onions	125 mL
1/2 cup	sliced carrots	125 mL
2	ribs celery, sliced	2
2	cloves garlic, crushed	2
3 Tbsp.	safflower oil	45 mL
2 cups	red or white wine	475 mL
1/2 cup	wine vinegar	125 mL
1 tsp.	salt	5 mL
2	whole cloves	2
2	sprigs parsley	2
1	bay leaf	1
2 tsp.	dried or fresh rosemary	10 mL
1 tsp.	juniper berries	5 mL

If the meat is to be marinated more than 24 hours, first sauté the onions, carrots, celery and garlic in safflower oil. Mix together all ingredients and immerse meat. Turn the meat every few hours, and keep it refrigerated and covered while in marinade.

Wine Marinade

This recipe is for a small roast, 2–3 lb. (1 kg). For a larger piece of meat, double it; for stewing-sized pieces or chops, halve it. Whether you use red or white wine, or vermouth, depends on the meat you are marinating and the flavor you want. Strong red meats such as venison and beef are usually combined with red wines, chicken and veal with white. In general, the drier wines are best for marinating; vermouth is excellent.

Yogurt Marinade

Good for bits of pork or lamb to be served in a Middle East concoction. Mix together this amount for every pound, or half kilogram of meat.

1 cup	yogurt	250 mL
1 tsp.	dill or rosemary	5 mL
1	clove garlic, crushed	1
2 Tbsp.	lemon juice	30 mL

Combine ingredients. Marinate meat for 3 hours, turning pieces every half hour or so.

ABOUT CANNING

Jars used for canning may be of any size, as long as they have a rubber seal in the cap, where it meets the rim of the jar. Lids are sealed by a simple, ingenious method. First of all, the jars and lids are sterilized by boiling or steaming them for 5 to 10 minutes. The contents, too, are brought to the boil, before they're ladled into the jar. Next, the jars are filled, but not completely; a small air space is left between the contents and the lid. The air in this space, being hot, has few molecules. Consequently when it cools, the air condenses and shrinks, sucking the soft warm rubber of the lid around the rim of the jar.

To sterilize jars and lids, invert them on a rack in a large pot, with 3 in. (8 cm) water in the bottom. Bring to the boil, cover, and steam the bottles for 5 to 10 minutes. Leave bottles in the container until you are ready to use them.

To make sure bottles, lids, and contents remain germ free, use sterilized tongs, spoons, and funnels.

Mixed Pickles

When the garden is at its height with everything coming in at once, I generally make a huge batch of mixed vegetable pickle. You may use any one of these vegetables alone in this pickle, but I find the contrast of a good mixture makes them much more interesting. After a year they will still be crisp and tart, colorful and delicious.

1 cup	pickling salt	250 mL
1 gal.	water	4 L
1 cup	small radishes	250 mL
2 cups	small carrots	475 mL
2 cups	tiny gherkin cucumbers	475 mL
2 cups	celery, sliced	475 mL
2 cups	small beans *or* snow peas	475 mL
2	green peppers, sliced	2
1	medium cauliflower, cut into florets	1
2 cups	pickling onions	475 mL
2 cups	water	475 mL
3 cups	white vinegar	725 mL
1 cup	honey	250 mL
1/4 cup	mustard seed	60 mL
2 Tbsp.	coriander seed	30 mL

Dissolve salt and water in a large crock or plastic bucket. Chop vegetables into it. Set a plate over them and weight with a jar of water. Leave in a cool place overnight. Next day, drain off brine. Heat remaining ingredients together in a large enameled or stainless steel pot. Add the vegetables and bring to the boil as rapidly as possible. Distribute vegetables in jars and pour pickle over them, leaving ½ in. (1 cm) head room. Do not allow vegetables to protrude over the liquid. Adjust lids. Set in a draft-free place until jars have cooled and lids have sealed.

8 pints (4 L)

Zucchini Relish

2½ lb.	small zucchini	1 kg
3–5	green peppers	3–5
5	large onions	5
5 Tbsp.	pickling salt	75 mL
2½ cups	cider vinegar	600 mL
4 cups	sugar	1 L
1 Tbsp.	dried mustard	15 mL
1 Tbsp.	turmeric	15 mL
1 Tbsp.	nutmeg	15 mL
2 tsp.	celery salt	10 mL
1 Tbsp.	cornstarch	15 mL
1 tsp.	dried chili powder	5 mL

Chop zucchini, green peppers and onions, very fine; remove seeds from peppers. Sprinkle with salt in a plastic container, cover, and keep cool overnight. In the morning, drain and rinse three times.

Wash and sterilize 4 pint-sized (475 mL) canning jars and lids. Mix together remaining ingredients and bring to the boil, then cover and simmer for 30 minutes, before adding vegetables. Bring briefly to the boil before ladling into jars. Adjust lids and rings. Cool.

4 pints (2 L)

Bread and Butter Pickles

The cucumbers you ordinarily see in the market aren't suited to pickling. Pickling cucumbers are much smaller, and have thin, lumpy skin; their flesh is firm; they have little of the pulpy center and very small seeds. Pickling cucumbers should be picked the day you make pickles, for best results.

30	fresh pickling cucumbers	30
10	medium onions	10
1 gal.	water	4 L
1 cup	pickling salt	250 mL
10 cups	white vinegar	2.5 L
7 cups	white sugar	1.75 L
2 tsp.	turmeric	10 mL
1 Tbsp.	freshly grated ginger	15 mL
1 Tbsp.	celery seed	15 mL
1 Tbsp.	mixed pickling spices	15 mL

Slice cucumbers and onions as thinly as possible, discarding tops and bottoms. Submerge them in water and pickling salt in a large crock or plastic bucket. Keep cool overnight.

Wash and sterilize 10 pint-sized (475 mL) canning jars and lids. Mix together remaining ingredients and bring to the boil. Add vegetables and bring to the boil again, for 5 minutes; them commence filling jars. Adjust lids and rings as you fill them. Cool in a draft-free place.

10 pints (5 L)

Prime Kosher Dills

These pickles are nice and crisp, each jar packed with a dill flower for elegance and flavor.

4 lb.	fresh 4 in. (10 cm) pickling cucumbers	1.8 kg
3 cups	water	725 mL
2½ cups	white vinegar	600 mL
¼ cup	pickling salt	60 mL
14	cloves garlic, whole	14
7	dill flowers and leaves	7
28	peppercorns	28

Wash cucumbers and slice them lengthwise. Combine water, vinegar, salt and garlic in a stainless steel or enameled pan; bring to the boil. Meanwhile, sterilize 7 pint-sized (475 mL) canning jars and lids. Push one dill flower into each jar so the petals turn back in a star-like pattern, and snip the stem below the neck of the jar. Put 4 peppercorns and 2 cloves of the garlic from pot in each jar. Pack in sliced cucumbers loosely. Add dill leaf on top. Pour hot pickle juice to within ½ in. (1 cm) of rims and adjust lids and rings. Cool in a draft-free place.

6–7 pints (3–3.5 L)

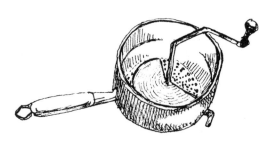

Freezer Fresh Strawberry Jam

It has occurred to more than one modern country cook that there is too much sugar in most jams and jellies. The solution: Freezer Fresh Jams, which use much less sweetener and have real fruit flavors and vitamins because they're cooked much less than ordinary compotes. The secret is that they're stored in the freezer, rather than on pantry shelves. After defrosting, store them in the refrigerator, where they'll last for a week or so.

6 cups	fresh ripe strawberries	1.5 L
2 Tbsp.	plain gelatin	30 mL
1 cup	white sugar	250 mL
1 Tbsp.	lemon juice	15 mL

Wash and hull strawberries. Slice them into a big bowl, then mash them somewhat to make 1 cup (250 mL) juice. Mix the juice with the other ingredients in a large stainless steel or enameled pan. Heat and stir until liquid is clear. Add strawberries and heat, stirring, until mixture just boils. Remove from heat and fill freezer containers to within 1 in. (2 cm) of rim. Cool before freezing.

6 cups (1.5 L)

VARIATIONS

FREEZER FRESH BLACKBERRY OR PEACH JAM Follow recipe for Freezer Fresh Strawberry Jam, substituting blackberries or peaches, but first cook the fruit separately and strain it through a food mill. Cool. Mix gelatin with ¼ cup (60 mL) cold water before adding to fruit.

FREEZER FRESH RASPBERRY JAM
Follow recipe for Freezer Fresh Strawberry Jam, substituting raspberries for strawberries, but increase the gelatin to 3 Tbsp. (45 mL).

Apple Butter

Until the turn of the century, apple butter used to be made in big black iron kettles every fall in households throughout North America. It's a form of applesauce, cooked for a long time with spices until it becomes a flavorful spread. People who have excesses of such fruits tell me that you can make pear butter, plum butter and peach butter the same way.

8 cups	Applesauce (page 112)	2 L
4 cups	apple cider	1 L
	sugar	
6	cloves	6
6	allspice berries	6
¹/₂	nutmeg	¹/₂
1	star anise	1
	(optional)	

Mix applesauce and cider in a stainless steel or enameled pan. Add sugar, if needed, to taste. Cut a piece of disposable cloth in a 6 in. (15 cm) square. Rinse it and put the spices in the middle. Tie up the cloth into a small bag with kite string, leaving a long tail to tie to the handle of the pot, and immerse it in the apple butter. Bring to the boil and simmer, uncovered, over low heat for about 4 hours. Cooking need not be continuous; you can cook it off and on for days. The important thing is to keep the heat low and stir from time to time, so it doesn't burn. It should cook down to about 3 cups (725 mL) of spread with no standing liquid. Ladle into jars, label and refrigerate. It will keep up to 2 months.

3 cups (725 mL)

TO MAKE JELLY

Always use fruit as fresh as possible, for best flavor. Mix almost ripe and ripe fruit. Always remove and discard spoiled fruit. Wash fruit if necessary with cold water.

Work with no more than 4 cups (1 L) fruit juice at one time when you are making jelly. This will boil down to 2 or 3 cups (475–725 mL) of jelly.

When the syrup has boiled for 20 minutes, and is reduced by about a third, it is probably ready to jell when cooled. You will also notice a white foam accumulating on top. Skim this off with a spoon or ladle on to a cool plate and place on the window sill. If, as it cools, it thickens into jelly, it's time to pour the jelly into jars and seal them. (See About Canning, page 48).

Apple Pectin Syrup

Jelly only has three ingredients: fruit syrup, sugar, and the pectin which makes it jell. Pectin is a substance found naturally in the skins of apples, grapes, red currants and some other fruits — but not all. To make jellies from fruits which don't have it, you can mix equal parts fruit syrup and apple pectin syrup. Apple pectin syrup can be made from any fresh, tart apple, but the smaller the better, because smaller apples have proportionately more skin. The quantities given below may be increased, but you will also have to hang more bags.

3 cups	small tart apples	725 mL
1 cup	water	250 mL

Halve apples into a stainless steel or enameled pan. Add water and bring to the boil. Cover and cook over medium heat until apples puff and disintegrate, about 20 minutes. Line a bowl with disposable cloth and empty apples into it. Tie with good string, and hang so bag can drip for 30 minutes.

1 cup (250 mL)

Apple Jelly

Home-made apple jelly has a wonderfully tart and fragrant flavor, quite a bit like currant jelly. The redder the apples, the brighter the color. Crabapples, grown specifically for jelly making, give the final product a dark wine color.

4 cups	Apple Pectin Syrup	1 L
2 cups	sugar	475 mL

Heat syrup and sugar in an enameled or stainless steel pot. Boil for 20 minutes, skimming as necessary. When cooled syrup thickens, bottle and seal.

2–3 cups (475–725 mL)

VARIATION

SPICED APPLE JELLY

2	whole cloves	2
1	stick cinnamon	1
1	piece ginger root	1
3	whole allspice berries	3

Put ingredients in a cloth bag. Tie and cook with Apple Pectin Syrup, when making Apple Jelly, above. Remove before bottling.

Mint Jelly

1 cup	boiling water	250 mL
1 cup	mint leaves, chopped and firmly packed	250 mL
4 cups	Apple Pectin Syrup	1 L
2 cups	sugar	475 mL

Pour water over mint leaves in enameled or stainless steel pot. Let stand for an hour or two. Empty into a disposable cloth and wring to extract all juice. Combine ½ cup (125 mL) mint juice with Apple Pectin Syrup and sugar. Boil for 20 minutes, skimming as necessary. When cooled syrup thickens, bottle and seal.

2–3 cups (475–725 mL)

Red Currant Jelly

Red currants contain natural pectin.

| 4 cups | red currants | 1L |
| 1 cup | sugar | 250 mL |

Bring currants to the boil in a stainless steel or enameled pot. Crush the bottom layer and cook until soft and colorless. Empty into cloth bag and allow to drip for 1 hour. Bring to the boil 2 cups (475 mL) of yielded currant juice, combined with sugar. Boil for 20 minutes, skimming as necessary. When cooled syrup thickens, bottle and seal.

1 cup (250 mL)

Wild Strawberry Jelly

2 cups	wild strawberries	475 mL
3 cups	sugar	725 mL
2–3 cups	Apple Pectin Syrup	475–725 mL

Mash together strawberries and 1 cup (250 mL) sugar in an enameled or stainless steel pot. Allow to sit, covered, for 30 minutes. Hang in a cloth bag to drip for 30 minutes. Measure the strawberry juice yielded and add sufficient Apple Pectin Syrup to make, in all, 4 cups (1 L) strawberry-apple syrup. Add 2 cups (475 mL) sugar. Boil for 20 minutes, skimming as necessary. When cooled syrup thickens, bottle and seal.

2–3 cups (475–725 mL)

Grape Jelly

Grapes, too, contain natural pectin.

| 8 cups | Concord or wild grapes | 2 L |
| 2 cups | sugar | 475 mL |

Bring crushed grapes to the boil in a stainless steel or enameled pot. Cook uncovered until soft, about 30 minutes, then strain through a cloth bag. Bring 4 cups (1L) of yielded juice to the boil with the sugar. Boil for 20 minutes, skimming if necessary. When cooled syrup thickens, bottle and seal.

2–3 cups (475–725 mL)

Raspberry Jelly

4 cups	raspberries, crushed	1 L
2 cups	Apple Pectin Syrup	475 mL
2 cups	sugar	475 mL

Bring crushed raspberries to the boil in an enameled or stainless steel pot. When they are soft, hang them in a cloth bag for 2 hours. Squeeze out the remaining liquid. Then mix 2 cups (475 mL) raspberry juice with the Apple Pectin Syrup and the sugar. Boil for 20 minutes, skimming as necessary. When cooled syrup thickens, bottle and seal.

2–3 cups (475–725 mL)

Blackberry or Elderberry Jelly

4 cups	blackberries *or* elderberries, crushed	1 L
2 cups	water	475 mL
2 cups	Apple Pectin Syrup	475 mL
2 cups	sugar	475 mL

Bring fruit and water to the boil in an enameled or stainless steel pot. When soft, hang them in a cloth bag for 2 hours. Squeeze out the remaining liquid. Mix 2 cups (475 mL) of the juice with the Apple Pectin Syrup and the sugar. Boil for 20 minutes, skimming as necessary. When cooled syrup thickens, bottle and seal.

2–3 cups (475–725 mL)

Rose Hip Jelly

Rose hips have very high amounts of vitamin C. Their pleasant rose flavor and color brighten up many a jar of jelly. Gather them soon after the first frosts.

4 cups	rose hips	1 L
2 cups	water	475 mL
2 cups	Apple Pectin Syrup	475 mL
2 cups	sugar	475 mL

Bring rose hips and water to the boil in an enameled or stainless steel pot. Cover and simmer for 1 hour. Hang in a cloth bag for 1 hour. Squeeze out remaining liquid. Mix 2 cups (475 mL) rose hip juice with Apple Pectin Syrup and sugar. Boil for 20 minutes, skimming as necessary. When cooled syrup thickens, bottle and seal.

2–3 cups (475–725 mL)

Vegetarian Dishes

Eating well without meat is a worthwhile pursuit: good for the mind and body, good for the pocketbook. About half the meals I make are based around a main vegetable course with grains, cheese, eggs, tofu or beans to provide protein.

If you are just learning how to cook without meat, do pay attention to the amount of protein in the meal. Many new vegetarians complain that they or their families eat large amounts of snack foods between meals. Or, denying themselves such pleasures, others feel unaccountably sleepy a few hours after their rice and broccoli. You certainly don't have to go back to hamburgers to get enough protein, but you should remember that the average meat serving — a moderate 3 oz. (75 g) — has more than 20 grams of protein, whereas a cup of brown rice and a serving of vegetables has only a fraction of that. No

wonder the cookie jar is always empty! Even if you add a cup of beans or a square of tofu to the rice and vegetables, you've still got a meal with less than 20 grams of protein. For this reason, it makes sense to add an egg per serving to beans and rice, and serve roasted sesame or sunflower seeds along with the meal. Alternatively, you can include a dessert with extra nutrition in it. And don't skimp on the cheese or tofu, when you're depending on it for energy. If your family eats a lot of sandwiches, make bread with hidden assets such as eggs, milk powder, soy flour or brewer's yeast; or include these ingredients in cakes or cookies.

There is much to be said for the vegetarian diet. More kinds of foods are eaten, making a more balanced daily intake of all the good things we need to be healthy. Meatless meals also tend to be lower in saturated fats, and contain less in the way of unhealthy additives. And, certainly, most of us don't need quite as much protein every day as the average steak-and-potato diet contains. But unless you have arranged to spend the rest of your days meandering slowly through undemanding days and nights, you're going to need what the rest of us need: between 50 and 60 grams of protein a day. Meals are more than an opportunity to rest and enjoy good flavors; they're also the source of our daily energy. Any cook – whether vegetarian or not – develops cooking habits. Shape yours around an understanding of nutritional values, and you'll eat well.

Steamed Brown Rice

2 cups	water	475 mL
1 cup	brown rice (short or long grain)	250 mL
1/2 tsp.	salt	2 mL

Bring water to the boil in a pot with a tight lid. Add rice and salt and bring to the boil again. Cover the pot closely and lower heat. Simmer gently for 40 minutes, or until rice swells. Remove from heat and let stand, covered, for 15 minutes before serving.

4 servings

VARIATION

RESTINO RISOTTO This is a special favorite around our house. Before steaming the rice, heat a heavy skillet over high heat, and roast the dry, uncooked grains, stirring constantly, until a rich nutty aroma and a yellowish-brown color tell you that they are done. Cool rice before adding to hot water. Cook as in Steamed Brown Rice, but simmer for 35 rather than 45 minutes.

TO STEAM BROWN RICE

To steam brown rice, it is necessary to surround each grain of rice in the pot with water or steam for at least half an hour. In order to do this, you must use a pot that holds steam. That means a tight lid, as for example, the lid of a pressure cooker (you don't have to use the pressure). My Dutch oven isn't tight enough; steam leaks out, and the top grains stay dry. Your pot must also be heavy so that the rice doesn't scorch on the bottom.

If you stir the rice while it is cooking, you will loosen the starch and make the rice gummy. Some cooking methods call for washing the rice first: you can do this, but it will cost you some vitamins in the outer layers. In any case, it should not be stirred after water is added. If you want to peek at the bottom and see whether all the water has been absorbed, a quick poke with a small spoon will suffice. Another way to see if the rice is done is to taste a few grains on top.

After the rice is cooked, it is best to let it stand for 15 minutes, in the pot, with the lid on, but the heat off. This will help finish the rice and let each grain "set" before you serve it.

Brown rice takes about 45 minutes to steam. However, if you roast or fry the grains first, they will take slightly less time to cook.

Some people cook rice without salt, but they serve it with soy sauce, which is very salty. Others use as little as possible; about 1/4 teaspoon (1 mL) per cup (250 mL) of dry uncooked rice. I like 1/2 teaspoon (2 mL) per cup (250 mL). You should not take salt for granted — find your own level.

Gomasio

Gomasio, goma shio, or sesame salt, is a garnish of ground sesame seeds and salt, commonly found on the Japanese table; it is served with rice or other bland foods. It tastes a little like peanut butter. Kids love it.

1¹/₂ cups	black, brown or white sesame seeds	375 mL
1 tsp.	salt	5 mL

Roast the sesame seeds in the oven at 275°F (135°C) for 20 to 30 minutes, or in a skillet over low heat, stirring constantly, for 10 or 15 minutes. Add salt. Grind coarsely in a blender, grain mill or with a suribachi (a Japanese mortar with a scored surface) and pestle until the seeds are mostly pulverized – leave about a quarter of them whole so that the gomasio is crunchy rather than pasty.

Gomasio loses much of its flavor within a few days, so you shouldn't try to make too much at one time. Store in an airtight container in a cool place. Sprinkle over rice.

1 cup (250 mL)

Tabbouleh

This is a Middle Eastern salad which is really a meal in itself. Traditionally it is served with pita bread, feta cheese and black olives.

1 cup	fine bulgur	250 mL
1 tsp.	salt	5 mL
1¹/₂ cups	boiling water	375 mL
1 Tbsp.	lemon juice	15 mL
1	clove garlic, crushed (optional)	1
1 tsp.	fresh mint, chopped	5 mL
¹/₄ cup	dark sesame *or* olive oil	60 mL
1	green pepper, chopped	1
1 *or* 2	tomatoes, diced	1 *or* 2
2	green onions, chopped	2
¹/₂ cup	parsley, chopped	125 mL
1¹/₂ cups	fresh spinach, chopped	375 mL
1 cup	cooked *or* canned chick-peas	250 mL
2	hard-boiled eggs, chopped	2

Measure the bulgur into a casserole or tightly lidded pan. Add salt and boiling water, cover, and let stand for 15 minutes. Then mix in the lemon juice, garlic, mint and oil. Cover and chill for 2 to 8 hours. Just before serving, add green pepper, tomato, onion, parsley and spinach. Top with chick-peas and garnish with hard-boiled eggs.

6–8 servings

Spanish Rice

3 Tbsp.	bacon or ham fat	45 mL
1	onion, chopped	1
1	green pepper, chopped	1
3	cloves garlic, chopped	3
2 cups	brown rice	475 mL
3½ cups	water	850 mL
1 cup	Fresh Tomato Sauce (page 43)	250 mL
1 tsp.	fresh basil, minced	5 mL
1 tsp.	salt	5 mL
1 cup	cooked ham or bacon, chopped	250 mL

Heat fat in a heavy saucepan and sauté onion, green pepper and garlic for about 5 minutes, stirring from time to time. Add rice and cook for 2 to 3 minutes, or until golden. Turn off heat for a minute before adding water, tomato sauce, basil and salt. Cover tightly, lower heat, and simmer for 35 to 40 minutes without stirring, until rice swells. Toss in bacon or ham. Let stand for 10 minutes, covered, before serving.

4 servings

Jambalaya

Best fresh, this rice and vegetable dish may also be cooled and reheated the next day. Cooked beans or leftover chopped cooked chicken, or crumbled sautéed tofu may also be added to make it a main course.

4 cups	Restino Risotto (page 56)	1 L
2 cups	vegetables, sliced	475 mL
2 Tbsp.	safflower oil	30 mL
3 Tbsp.	water	45 mL
1 Tbsp.	tamari soy sauce	15 mL

The vegetables should be cut into contrasting shapes and sizes. You may use:
onions: chop fine or slice into thin wedges;
green peppers: seed and cut into slender pieces;
carrots: slice thinly;
zucchini, summer squash: use very small ones, sliced;
mushrooms: cut vertically;
celery: don't use too much, sliced in small chunks;
tomatoes: use only firm flesh; cut in wedges;
fresh parsley: chop, not too fine.
Minutes before the rice is done, stir-fry the vegetables in oil for about 10 minutes. Add water and tamari, cover, and steam for 5 to 7 minutes. Combine with rice and turn into an oiled casserole. Serve hot or keep warm in a low oven (250°F, 125°C) covered, up to 1 hour.

4 servings

Roasted Bulgur

Bulgur, which is a nice light wheat product, resembling rice, is very good mixed with ground or minced meat, such as meatballs, meatloaf, or as a filling for scooped out vegetables. Bulgur used in this way is traditional in Syrian cooking.

3 Tbsp.	vegetable oil	45 mL
1 cup	medium bulgur	250 mL
2 cups	water	475 mL
½ tsp.	salt	2 mL

Heat oil in a heavy saucepan until crackling hot. Add bulgur and cook, stirring, over high heat, for 4 to 5 minutes, adjusting heat to roast bulgur evenly. Remove from heat for 1 minute, then add water and salt. Cover tightly, and cook over very low heat for 15 to 20 minutes. Like rice, bulgur swells slightly when done, and should not be cooked one minute longer.

4 servings

Steamed Buckwheat

Most people prefer buckwheat (also called kasha or groats) roasted before it is steamed. Roasting firms the texture, which is otherwise mushy and dry, and brings out the grain's strong nutty flavor.

3 Tbsp.	vegetable oil	45 mL
1 cup	buckwheat	250 mL
1	onion, diced	1
2 cups	boiling water *or* clear meat broth	475 mL
1/2 tsp.	salt	2 mL
1 cup	plain yogurt rice *or* millet (optional)	250 mL

In a deep, heavy pot heat oil. Add buckwheat and onion. Cook rapidly for 5 to 10 minutes, stirring. Lower heat and add boiling water or broth and salt. Simmer for 15 minutes, until dry. Add yogurt. You may also add cooked rice or millet. Serve at once.

4 servings

VARIATION

TOMATO BUCKWHEAT Sauté green pepper, celery, or ground meat along with the onions. After cooking, substitute tomato juice for yogurt.

Soyburgers

Great for a fast summer supper. Serve with salad and Noodles Alfredo (page 65).

1/2 cup	soy grits	125 mL
1/2 cup	bulgur	125 mL
2 cups	boiling water	475 mL
1 tsp.	salt	5 mL
3 tsp.	tamari soy sauce	15 mL
2	eggs, beaten	2
3/4 cup	bread crumbs	180 mL
1/2 tsp.	sage	2 mL
1 tsp.	summer savory	5 mL
2 Tbsp.	onion, grated	30 mL
2 Tbsp.	parsley, chopped	30 mL
1/2 cup	carrot, grated (optional) vegetable oil	125 mL

Place soy grits and bulgur in a small pan with a tightly fitting lid. Pour boiling water over them and add salt and 2 tsp. (10 mL) tamari soy sauce. Bring to the boil, then lower heat and simmer, covered, for 15 minutes. Remove lid when all the liquid is absorbed and allow the grains to cool. Meanwhile, combine in a bowl eggs, 1 tsp. (5 mL) tamari soy sauce, bread crumbs, sage, summer savory and onion. When the grains are cool, add them to the mixture, along with parsley and carrot. Mix everything well. Thicken with a little flour if necessary and shape into patties. Sauté patties in a lightly oiled pan for about 5 minutes on each side.

4 servings

Southern Grits

This is the basic grits recipe, but there are variations. You may add chopped ham, or serve it topped with fried egg. Cooked fresh corn gives it an interesting texture. You may also allow it to cool, slice it in slabs, and fry it in butter or oil.

2 cups	milk	475 mL
1/2 tsp.	salt	2 mL
1/2 cup	cornmeal	125 mL

Heat milk and salt in a saucepan, being careful not to boil. Add cornmeal slowly, stirring as you add. When it gets thick, cover and turn off the heat. Let stand for 10 minutes.

4 servings

Polenta

2 cups	Southern Grits	475 mL
1	egg, beaten	1
1 cup	cheese, grated	250 mL
	sprinkle of	
	paprika	

Make grits. Allow to cool, uncovered, until warm. Add beaten egg and 3/4 cup (180 mL) grated cheese (any kind—Cheddar is good). Pour into a greased loaf pan and top with 1/4 cup (60 mL) grated cheese and paprika. Bake at 350°F (175°C) for 30 minutes. Serve hot.

4 serving

COOKING TIME	Unsoaked	Soaked	In pressure cooker
soybeans	8 hours	6 hours	45 minutes
chick-peas	6 hours	5 hours	40 minutes
kidney beans	5 hours	3 1/2 hours	30 minutes
black beans	3 hours	2 hours	20 minutes
black-eye peas	3 hours	2 hours	20 minutes
lima beans	3 hours	2 hours	20 minutes
navy beans	3 hours	2 hours	20 minutes
lentils	2 hours	1 hour	10 minutes
split peas	2 hours	1 hour	10 minutes
azuki beans	2 hours	1 hour	10 minutes

French Bean Casserole

1 cup	white *or* navy beans	250 mL
6 cups	cold water	1.5 L
2	whole cloves	2
1	onion	1
1	carrot	1
1	clove garlic	1
1	piece ham fat *or* bacon (optional)	1
1 tsp.	salt	5 mL
1/2 tsp.	pepper	2 mL
2	celery tops	2
2	ribs celery	2
3	potatoes	3
1/2 cup	cooked ham	125 mL
1/2 cup	tomato juice	125 mL
2 tsp.	dried basil	10 mL
1/4 tsp.	thyme	2 mL

DRIED BEANS

Dried beans more than double their size when cooked, and add great richness to casseroles, stews, soups, and salads. Mashed, they can become fillings or fried patties. Combined with grains, dried beans have quite a lot of protein, and are good for you in a great variety of ways.

Always make sure you have cooked dried beans long enough. Soaking them overnight in water to soften them is a good start. In the morning, drain off the water; it may be nutritious, but it causes gas. Add more water and bring them to a full boil for ten minutes before simmering them with your favorite flavorings. Boiling the beans is particularly important with large beans like kidney beans, which can cause digestive problems if they aren't cooked at high enough temperatures.

One way to make sure you aren't caught with half-cooked beans is to cook them one day and serve them the next. I find they taste better the second day, anyway.

Soak beans overnight in half the water. In the morning, drain and replace with fresh water. Stick cloves in onion, quarter carrot, and crush garlic; add to pot with ham fat, salt, pepper, and celery tops. Bring to the boil for 15 minutes, then cover and simmer for about 2 hours, or until beans are tender. Remove ham fat, celery tops, and carrot. Chop carrot and return to pot. Chop and add celery, potatoes, and ham; add tomato juice, basil and thyme. Simmer for 15 minutes, or until potatoes are soft.

4 servings

Pasta Fazule

This is a favorite winter dish which not only fills the empty place in your middle, but also fills the house with a marvelous spicy aroma as it simmers on the stove or in the Crockpot.

1 lb.	dried kidney beans	450 g
2 Tbsp.	safflower oil	30 mL
1	onion, chopped	1
2	ribs celery, chopped	2
2	cloves garlic, crushed	2
2 cups	canned tomatoes and juice	475 mL
1	bay leaf	1
1	ham bone	1
4 cups	cold water	1 L
2 lb.	small macaroni shells	1 kg
1 tsp.	salt	5 mL
1 cup	Italian sausage, sliced	250 mL
1	green pepper, chopped	30 mL
2 Tbsp.	fresh parsley, chopped	30 mL
1 cup	ham, chopped	250 mL

Soak beans overnight in water to cover. In the morning, drain and wash beans. Heat oil in a large pot and sauté onion, celery, and crushed garlic. Add beans, tomatoes, bay leaf, ham bone, and water. Bring to a full boil for 15 minutes, then reduce heat, cover and simmer for 3 hours.

Remove ham bone and bay leaf 30 minutes before serving. Bring a large pot of water to a full boil. Add macaroni and salt, and boil, uncovered, for 15 minutes or until barely tender. Meanwhile add sausage, green pepper, parsley and ham to beans, and simmer for 15 minutes. When macaroni is done, drain it, rinse in cold water, and then add to the beans.

6–8 servings

New England Baked Beans

White pea beans are traditional, but my favorites are the big speckled trout beans.

2¹/₂ cups	beans	600 mL
8 cups	cold water	2 L
1 tsp.	salt	5 mL
1	piece pork *or* ham fat	1
1	onion	1
2	cloves	2
¹/₄ cup	molasses	60 mL
2 tsp.	dried mustard	10 mL
2 Tbsp.	Tomato Paste (page 44)	30 mL
1 Tbsp.	tamari soy sauce	15 mL
1 tsp.	cider vinegar	5 mL

Soak beans overnight in 4 cups (1 L) water. In the morning drain and rinse beans, then replenish with 4 cups (1 L) water. Add salt and pork or ham fat. Stick the cloves into the onion and add that. Bring to a full boil for 15 minutes. Then reduce heat and add molasses, mustard, Tomato Paste, soy sauce and vinegar. Cover and simmer for 2 to 6 hours (see Bean Cooking Chart, page 60). Finish, uncovered, in slow oven, 250°F (120°C) for 30 minutes. Remove pork or ham fat.

Serve with Coleslaw (page 33).

6 servings

Chinese Azuki Beans

Azuki beans are very small, red Oriental beans with a little white stripe. Like lentils, they are quite dry, so are best served with Sweet-Sour Sauce (page 43), and, of course, rice.

3 cups	water	725 mL
1½ cups	dried azuki beans	350 mL
1 tsp.	salt	5 mL
1	onion	1
1	clove garlic	1
6	peppercorns	6
1 in.	fresh ginger root	2 cm
¼	cinnamon stick	¼
10	coriander seeds	10
2	whole cloves	2
1	star anise	1
¼ cup	molasses or plum jelly	60 mL
2 Tbsp.	sweet sherry	30 mL
1 Tbsp.	tamari soy sauce	5 mL

Bring water to the boil. Add azuki beans, salt and onion. Tie garlic, peppercorns, ginger root, cinnamon, coriander, cloves and anise in a small square of cloth, and immerse in beans. Boil for 10 minutes, then cover and simmer for 2 hours. Remove onion and spice bag. Add molasses or jelly, sherry and soy sauce.

4 servings

Brazilian Black Beans

Served with Jambalaya (page 58) and a good green salad, a surprising combination of flavors.

1½ cups	black beans	375 mL
6½ cups	water	1.5 L
1½ cups	dry white wine	375 mL
1	onion, chopped	1
2	cloves garlic, crushed	2
2 Tbsp.	safflower oil	30 mL
3	fresh tomatoes, chopped	3
1	orange, peeled and chopped	1
2	ribs celery, chopped	2
½ tsp.	freshly ground pepper	2 mL
½ tsp.	salt	2 mL
2	bay leaves	2

Soak beans overnight in 4 cups (1 L) cold water. In the morning, drain and rinse beans, then replenish with 1½ cups (375 mL) each of water and wine. Sauté onion and garlic in oil, and add them along with tomatoes, orange and celery. Grate in pepper. Add salt and bay leaves. Bring to the boil and cook for 10 minutes. Then cover, reduce heat, and simmer for 2 hours.

4 servings

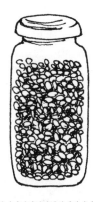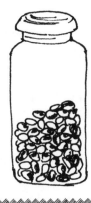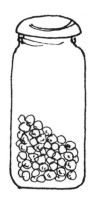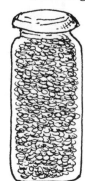

Lentil Stew

In the summer, lentils are a good choice. They take only an hour of cooking to soften, two hours to disintegrate entirely. Cook up a pot of them for use in soups, stews and sauces.

2 Tbsp.	olive oil	30 mL
1	onion, chopped	1
1	green pepper, chopped	1
3	ribs celery, chopped	3
1	zucchini or eggplant, chopped	1
3 cups	water	725 mL
1½ cups	lentils	375 mL
1 cup	tomatoes, chopped	250 mL
1 tsp.	basil	5 mL

Heat oil in a heavy, deep pan. Sauté onion, green pepper, celery and zucchini or eggplant until tender-crisp. Add water, lentils, tomatoes and basil. Bring to the boil and cook for 5 minutes, then cover, lower heat and simmer for 2 hours.

4 servings

Cornmeal-Bean Pie

Beans in a cornmeal piecrust — it looks as good as it tastes.

1 cup	cornmeal	250 mL
2 cups	boiling water	475 mL
2 cups	rolled oats	475 mL
1 Tbsp.	safflower oil	15 mL
1 tsp.	salt	5 mL
1 tsp.	baking powder	5 mL
4 cups	cooked baked beans	1 L

Measure cornmeal into a bowl. Stir as you pour in boiling water. If it becomes lumpy, press through a sieve. Add rolled oats, oil, salt, and baking powder, stirring thoroughly. Press this mixture into the bottom of an oiled pie pan, then push some up around the edges to form a side crust. Fill with baked beans. Bake at 350°F (175°C) for 20 to 30 minutes.

4–6 servings

Chili Con Carne

This is as good without meat as with.

2 cups	pinto or kidney beans	475 mL
8 cups	water	2 L
1	onion, chopped	1
½ lb.	ground meat (optional)	250 mL
3 Tbsp.	bacon or ham fat	45 mL
2 cups	canned tomatoes and juice	475 mL
1 cup	corn	250 mL
1–2 tsp.	chili peppers, flaked	5–10 mL
1	bay leaf	1

Soak beans overnight in 4 cups (1 L) cold water. In the morning, drain and replace with fresh water. Bring to the boil and cook for 15 minutes. Meanwhile sauté onion and ground meat in ham or bacon fat. Add to beans with corn, tomatoes, chili and bay leaf. Cover and simmer for 6 hours, or until beans are tender.

Serve with tortillas and plenty of salad.

4–6 servings

PASTA

Pasta comes in many forms, available at both health food stores and supermarkets. You can even make it yourself, and use a pasta machine to make fancy shapes.

Cooked pasta expands considerably. A one pound (450 g) box will feed four or five people. To cook a pound or so, boil a big pot of water, add salt and a teaspoon (5 mL) of vegetable oil to keep the noodles from sticking together. Add pasta gradually, so the water keeps boiling. If you pack too much in a small pot, the pasta becomes over-starchy.

The thinner the pasta, the faster it cooks. Allow about five minutes for the rice-like bits; twenty, at a full boil, for lasagne noodles. Whole grain noodles take one and a half times longer to cook than white ones.

As soon as the noodles are done, drain them in a colander and rinse with cool water to keep them from cooking any more. Then stir in a little butter or vegetable oil, perhaps a little chopped parsley, and serve.

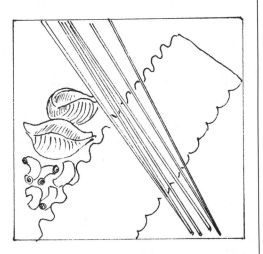

Noodles Alfredo

1 tsp.	salt	5 mL
1 lb.	large egg noodles	450 g
2 Tbsp.	olive oil	30 mL
2 Tbsp.	butter	30 mL
6 Tbsp.	Parmesan cheese	90 mL
3 Tbsp.	parsley, finely chopped	45 mL

Bring to the boil a large pot of salted water. Boil the noodles for 10 minutes, drain and rinse. Turn into a heated dish and toss with oil, butter, cheese and parsley. Serve at once.

4 servings

Spaghetti Carbonara

1 tsp.	salt	5 mL
1 tsp.	vegetable oil	5 mL
1 lb.	spaghetti	450 g
3 Tbsp.	butter	45 mL
4	eggs, beaten	4
1 cup	Cheddar or Monterey Jack cheese, grated	250 mL
3 Tbsp.	parsley, chopped	45 mL
1 cup	cooked ham or bacon, minced	250 mL

Bring to the boil a large pot of salted water with oil for the spaghetti. Boil 10 minutes, drain and rinse. Melt the butter in the pot before returning spaghetti; then add eggs and cheese. Cook, stirring, over moderate heat for 5 minutes, or until eggs are cooked. Add parsley and ham or bacon. Allow to stand, covered, before serving.

4 servings

Clam Spaghetti

1 tsp.	salt	5 mL
1/4 cup	olive oil	60 mL
1 lb.	spaghetti	450 g
3	cloves garlic, minced	3
3 Tbsp.	onion, minced	45 mL
2 tsp.	fresh basil, chopped	10 mL
1 1/2 cups	clam juice	350 mL
1/4 cup	fresh parsley, chopped	60 mL
1/4 cup	fresh fennel, chopped	60 mL
2 cups	clams, fresh or canned	475 mL

Bring to the boil a large pot of salted water for the spaghetti. Add a spoonful of the oil to the top, before adding pasta, to help keep it from sticking together. Boil for 10 minutes, or until barely tender. Meanwhile, heat oil in a heavy skillet and sauté garlic and onion before adding clam juice and herbs. Simmer over low heat until noodles are cooked and you have drained and rinsed them. Then mix noodles, sauce, and clams in a big dish and serve at once with bowls of grated Romano cheese and Italian bread.

4 servings

Lasagne Blanco À La Eleanor

This is a *magnifico* dish which can be prepared early in the day before a splendid party. It is actually better if cooled and reheated.

2 tsp.	salt	10 mL
2 tsp.	safflower oil	10 mL
12	lasagne noodles	12
1 cup	Parmesan or Cheddar cheese, grated	250 mL
1 cup	mozzarella or brick cheese, grated	250 mL

FILLING

1/4 cup	olive oil	60 mL
1	onion, chopped	1
1	green pepper, chopped	1
2	ribs celery, chopped	2
4	cloves garlic, minced	4
2–4 cups	mushrooms, sliced	250–475 mL
1 cup	cooked spinach	250 mL
1 tsp.	fresh basil	5 mL
1 tsp.	dried oregano	5 mL
1/2 tsp.	dried marjoram	2 mL
2	eggs	2
1 cup	ricotta cheese or drained cottage cheese	250 mL
1/2 tsp.	salt	2 mL

SAUCE

1/3 cup	butter	80 mL
1/3 cup	flour	80 mL
3 cups	milk	725 mL
1 tsp.	salt	5 mL
1/4 tsp.	freshly grated nutmeg	1 mL
1/4 tsp.	freshly ground pepper	1 mL

Bring a large pot of water to the boil. Add salt, oil, and, one at a time, 12 lasagne noodles. Boil for 15 minutes. Remove and immerse in cold water.

Grate soft and hard cheeses into separate bowls.

Heat olive oil in a large skillet and sauté the onion, green pepper, celery and garlic. After 3 minutes add mushrooms. Stir and sauté for 5 minutes, then add spinach and herbs, cover, and remove from heat. Beat eggs in a bowl, then beat in ricotta or cottage cheese and salt. Add to cooled vegetable mixture to complete filling.

Heat butter in a small saucepan. Add flour, and cook over low heat 2 or 3 minutes, stirring. Gradually add milk by half cupfuls, stirring after each addition until it thickens. Season with salt, pepper and nutmeg.

Oil a 9 × 13 in. (24 × 32 cm) pan and spread with one-third of the sauce. Sprinkle with one-third of the hard cheese and cover with 4 noodles. Spread half the vegetable filling over the noodles. Cover with another third of the sauce and another third of the hard cheese. Cover with 4 more noodles. Add the other half of the vegetable filling, cover with the last third of the sauce, and add the rest of the hard cheese. Cover with 4 more noodles. Top with a layer of soft cheese. Bake uncovered at 350°F (175°C) for 35 to 40 minutes. Cool at least 20 minutes before serving.

12 servings

Pasta Salad

3 Tbsp.	safflower oil	45 mL
1 Tbsp.	white wine vinegar	15 mL
2 tsp.	lemon juice	10 mL
1/4 tsp.	salt	1 mL
1/4 tsp.	dry mustard	1 mL
1/4 tsp.	paprika	1 mL
1	hard-boiled egg, sliced	1
3/4 cup	cooked green beans, sliced	180 mL
1 cup	cooked cold pasta	250 mL
2/3 cup	kippered herring	160 mL
1/4 cup	black olives	60 mL
3/4 cup	cherry tomatoes, halved	180 mL
1/3	head Boston lettuce, torn into pieces	1/3

Shake oil, vinegar, lemon juice, salt, mustard and paprika together in a bottle. Toss with egg, beans and pasta. Cover and marinate for 2 hours. Just before serving, add herring, olives, tomatoes and lettuce, torn into pieces. Toss thoroughly before serving.

4 servings

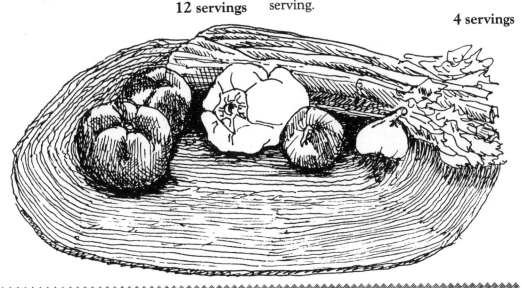

Welsh Rarebit

They've come and they've gone and what's left? A bottle of flat beer, half a loaf of stale bread, and a hunk of cheese as dry as a rock. So—grate, cook, and eat them together.

1 cup	beer	250 mL
1 lb.	Cheddar cheese, cubed	450 g
1	egg, beaten	1
1/2 tsp.	salt	2 mL
1 tsp.	Dijon mustard	5 mL
pinch	curry powder (optional)	pinch
8	slices whole wheat bread	8

Heat beer in a small pan until bubbly but not boiling. Stir in cheese by handfuls. When melted, add egg, stirring constantly over low heat until it thickens. Season with salt, mustard and curry. Pour over toast and serve hot.

4 servings

Swiss Cheese Fondue

A cheese fondue is a hot mixture of cheese and wine, served in a chafing dish at the table. Each person dips crusty cubes of toasted bread into the bubbly cheese with a long fork. French or Italian bread is traditional, but you may also try cubes of whole wheat bread, pieces of apples, and small boiled new potatoes. Fondue requires almost no preparation and very little cleaning up. With salad and a bottle of white wine, it's a perfect intimate dinner.

1	loaf Italian or French bread	1
1 lb.	Emmenthaler (Swiss) cheese	450 g
2 Tbsp.	cornstarch	30 mL
1	clove garlic	1
2 cups	dry white wine	475 mL
3 Tbsp.	Kirsch	45 mL
	salt, pepper	

Cut bread in cubes and toast 15 minutes in a slow oven, 250°F (120°C). Grate cheese and toss with cornstarch. Rub a cut clove of garlic inside the fondue pot. Heat wine in the pot until it bubbles, but don't let it boil. Add cheese by handfuls, stirring as it melts. Add Kirsch. Stir as the fondue thickens, adding salt and freshly grated pepper to taste. Set the dish over heat on the table. Serve with bread cubes.

4 servings

Cheddar Cheese Soufflé

¹/₄ cup	butter	60 mL
¹/₄ cup	unbleached white flour	60 mL
1 cup	milk	250 mL
1¹/₄ cup	Cheddar cheese, grated	310 mL
4	eggs	4
pinch	cayenne pepper	pinch

In a small pan, melt butter over moderate heat. Add flour and stir 2 to 3 minutes. Add milk in thirds, stirring after each addition until the sauce thickens. Then add cheese, and simmer until it melts (about 3 minutes). Cool until sauce is barely warm. Meanwhile, separate eggs. Beat yolks until frothy, then add them to the sauce, stirring well. Beat egg whites until stiff but still moist. Gently fold whites into the sauce and season with cayenne. Turn into a well-greased casserole and bake 30 minutes at 350°F (175°C) or until browned and puffy. Serve at once.

6 servings

Spinach Soufflé

¹/₄ cup	butter	60 mL
¹/₄ cup	unbleached white flour	60 mL
1 cup	milk	250 mL
3	eggs	3
2 cups	cooked spinach	475 mL
3 Tbsp.	onion, minced	45 mL
	fresh nutmeg	

Melt butter over medium heat in a heavy saucepan. Add flour and stir 2 to 3 minutes. Add milk in thirds, stirring after each addition until the sauce thickens. Separate eggs into two bowls. Beat yolks until light, then stir into sauce. Remove sauce from heat. Chop spinach and onion. Add them to the sauce and grate in nutmeg. Preheat oven to 300°F (150°C). Beat egg whites until stiff but not dry; fold them gently into the mixture. Pour into a greased casserole and bake for 30 minutes, or until brown on top. Serve at once.

4 servings

Spinach Pie

1	Flakey Double Piecrust (page 116)	1
2	large eggs	2
¹/₂ tsp.	lemon juice	2 mL
pinch	dried or fresh rosemary	pinch
1 cup	well-drained cottage cheese or ricotta cheese	250 mL
1 cup	cooked spinach, chopped	250 mL

Preheat oven to 400°F (200°C). Roll out two thirds of the pie dough. Line a pie dish, prick with a fork and weight down with a dozen dried beans. Bake 10 minutes. Lower oven temperature to 350°F (175°C). In a mixing bowl, beat eggs, add lemon juice and rosemary, then beat in cheese and spinach. Fill piecrust and cover with remaining third of dough. Bake 30 minutes, or until crust browns evenly.

6 servings

Croûton Quiche

In a good quiche, the crust is half the dish. It should be thick and crisp, accomplished by half-baking before filling. Light cream or evaporated milk is preferable to milk in the filling, because it's less likely to make the crust soggy.

1/4 cup	butter	60 mL
1/4 cup	lard	60 mL
1 1/2 cups	unbleached white flour	375 mL
1/2 cup	wheat germ	125 mL
1/2 tsp.	salt	2 mL
1	egg	1
1/3 cup	cold water	80 mL

FILLING

3 Tbsp.	butter	45 mL
1/2	green pepper, chopped	1/2
1	green onion, chopped	1
1/2 cup	whole wheat bread cubes	125 mL
3	large eggs	3
1 1/2 cups	light cream or evaporated milk	375 mL
1/2 tsp.	salt	2 mL
1/2 cup	sharp Cheddar cheese	45 mL

To make crust, cut cold butter and lard into flour, wheat germ and salt. When the mixture resembles coarse cornmeal, beat together egg and cold water and add liquid gradually, mixing well after each addition. Use as little liquid as possible. Chill,

covered, for 2 hours or longer. Preheat oven to 400°F (200°C) as you roll out crust quite thick, 1/8 in. (3 mm). Line pie pan, prick 5 or 6 times with a fork, and weight crust with a dozen dried beans to keep it from puffing up in the oven. Bake for 10 minutes, until golden. Cool 10 minutes and reduce oven to 325°F (160°C).

To make filling, heat butter in a skillet and sauté pepper, onion and bread cubes. Beat eggs in a mixing bowl until smooth; add cream, salt, cheese, and sautéed mixture. Pour into pie shell and bake at 325°F (160°C) for 30 minutes, until brown and puffy. Serve hot or cold.

4–6 servings

Onion Tart

This resembles a quiche, but has a thicker bottom crust. It is rather dry and should be served with something damp — say, zucchini in tomato sauce, or sweet-sour cabbage.

1 cup	Béchamel Sauce (page 42)	250 mL
1	egg	1
1 1/3 cup	whole wheat pastry flour	325 mL
1/2 tsp.	salt	2 mL
1 tsp.	baking powder	5 mL
1/2 cup	butter	125 mL
1/2 cup	milk	125 mL
2	onions, thinly sliced	2

Make and cool the cream sauce. When cool, beat in the egg. Mix or sift flour, salt and baking powder together, and cut in the butter. Add milk and mix in thoroughly. Spread in a well-buttered 9 in. (24 cm) square pan. Cover with onions. Bake at 425°F (220°C) for 20 minutes.

4–5 servings

Fresh Cheese Patties

1	large egg	1
1 cup	whole wheat bread crumbs	250 mL
1 cup	well-drained cottage cheese	250 mL
2 Tbsp.	whole wheat flour	30 mL
2 Tbsp.	parsley, finely chopped	30 mL
2 Tbsp.	onion, grated	30 mL
pinch	nutmeg	pinch
3 Tbsp.	vegetable oil	45 mL

Beat egg in a mixing bowl; add bread crumbs and soak until soft. Mix in cottage cheese, flour, parsley, onion, and nutmeg. Shape into patties. Sauté in oil until golden on each side.

4 servings

Pizza

Pizza was invented because it's easy to make — there's no need to buy mixes or frozen packages. You can make up the dough days ahead and refrigerate it. To use it, take it out an hour before serving and punch it down; allow to rise until doubled before making the crust.

2 Tbsp.	baker's yeast	30 mL
2 cups	warm water	475 mL
1½ tsp.	salt	7 mL
2 cups	unbleached white flour	475 mL
1½ cups	whole wheat flour	375 mL
2 cups	pizza toppings (see below)	475 mL
2–3 cups	mozzarella cheese, grated	475–725 mL
6 Tbsp.	Parmesan cheese	90 mL
2 cups	Mama Restino's Pizza Sauce (page 44)	475 mL
2 Tbsp.	oregano	30 mL
2 Tbsp.	olive oil	30 mL

Mix yeast and water in a bowl and let sit 10 minutes or until bubbly. Beat in salt and white flour. Work in whole wheat flour, kneading lightly with floured hands until it is one firm mass. Cover bowl and set in a warm place to rise for about 1 hour.

Meanwhile, select pizza toppings. You may use, alone or in combination: sliced pepperoni, half-cooked bacon, sautéed onions, green pepper, or mushrooms. Grate cheeses.

When it has risen, punch down dough and knead. Cut into two pieces. Leave one, covered, in bowl. Preheat oven to 500°F (250°C). Shape the piece of dough into a bun, then flatten and gradually spread into a thin round with a thicker edge, to fit on a well-oiled pizza or cookie sheet. Coat dough lightly with oil, then spread thinly with half the pizza sauce. Arrange pizza toppings on sauce, then cover with half of each cheese and sprinkle with half the oregano. Bake 10 to 15 minutes or until cheese is browned and bubbly. Meanwhile, make up second pizza, ready to go in the oven when the first comes out.

4–6 servings

Crab-Filled Egg Rolls

You can put all kinds of things in egg rolls, so long as they're fresh and a little crunchy: cabbage, celery, onions, chicken, seafood, sprouts, nuts and seeds.

2	eggs	2
2 cups	water	475 mL
1/2 tsp.	salt	2 mL
1 cup	unbleached white flour	250 mL
3 Tbsp.	vegetable oil	45 mL
1 cup	Chinese cabbage, shredded	250 mL
1 1/2 cup	mung bean sprouts	375 mL
1/4 cup	water chestnuts or celery, chopped	60 mL
1 cup	crab meat	250 mL
2 Tbsp.	sherry	30 mL
2 Tbsp.	water	30 mL
1 Tbsp.	flour	15 mL
1/4 cup	oil	60 mL

Beat eggs in a bowl; add water, salt and flour. Heat a skillet (a 6 in., 15 cm, omelet pan is best). Oil with a few drops of vegetable oil; add more as needed. Pour 2 Tbsp. (30 mL) batter in the pan. Quickly tilt pan so the batter spreads. Cook over medium heat about 2 minutes on one side, 1 minute on the other. Don't let them get hard or crisp. Allow pancakes to cool before stacking. Sauté cabbage, mung beans and water chestnuts or celery in hot oil. Add crab and sherry and cover, steam 2 minutes, and remove from heat. Use 2 Tbsp. (30 mL) filling per pancake. Fold sides over filling, then roll them together. Use a mixture of flour and water to glue egg rolls together. Allow to sit 30 minutes before heating 1/4 cup (60 mL) oil to fry them. Fry 5 minutes on each side, or until golden brown. Serve hot, with Steamed Brown Rice (page 56) and Sweet-Sour Sauce (page 43).

15–20 egg rolls

Golden Cheese Balls

These can be served either as an appetizer or as a rich main course in a vegetarian dinner.

1 cup	tofu	250 mL
3	eggs	3
1 cup	sharp cheese, grated	250 mL
1/2 cup	safflower oil	125 mL
3/4 cup	whole wheat flour	180 mL
2 tsp.	baking powder	10 mL
1/2 tsp.	salt	2 mL
1/2 tsp.	mustard	2 mL

Cut tofu into 1/2 in. (1 cm) slabs, wrap in absorbent paper or cloth, and weight slightly with a dish for 10 minutes. Press tofu through a sieve, into a bowl or process it until smooth in a blender or food processor. Beat eggs in a mixing bowl; add tofu, cheese and half the oil. Sift in flour, baking powder, salt and mustard to make a stiff paste. Heat remaining oil in a heavy skillet. Shape batter into balls the size of small plums and fry in successive batches, until golden, on all sides. Remove with slotted spoon to drain on absorbent paper. Serve with Sweet-Sour Sauce, (page 43).

4 servings

Tofu Ratatouille

1	onion, sliced	1
1	zucchini, sliced	1
1	eggplant, chopped	1
1 tsp.	salt	5 mL
2 cups	tofu	475 mL
1/4 cup	vegetable oil	60 mL
1	green pepper, sliced	1
3	cloves garlic, crushed	3
1	large tomato, chopped	1
2	coriander seeds, pounded	2
1 tsp.	basil	5 mL
1/4 cup	parsley, chopped	60 mL

Place onion, zucchini and eggplant in a colander. Sprinkle with salt, and set a plate and a weight on them for 30 minutes. Wrap tofu (cut into four 1 in., 2 cm slabs) in absorbent cloth or paper and lay a board or light even weight on it for 30 minutes. Heat oil in a large heavy skillet. Add zucchini, eggplant and onion, and sauté for 2 minutes. Stir and add green pepper, tofu and garlic. Simmer gently, stirring now and then, for 15 minutes. Then add tomatoes and coriander, basil, parsley. Simmer 15 minutes, covered.

Serve with rice or pasta, and salad.

4 servings

ABOUT TOFU

Tofu is made from the "milk" or liquid extracted from soybeans. A 2 in. (5 cm) cube has about the same amount of protein as a small egg or an equal amount of cheese or chicken, but tofu has no fat and is low in calories and sodium. Most tofu is sold submerged in water, in small plastic tubs. The water should be changed every day. Tofu is best eaten within a week but will keep (if the water is refreshed daily) up to a month. If kept too long, it will sour but it won't kill you! Slightly soured tofu may be freshened by parboiling. Rinse it, then put the tofu in a pan of boiling water and turn off the heat. Let it sit for 2 or 3 minutes, then remove and drain. Use at once. Some dishes are made with fresh tofu, and others are better if the tofu is prepared for cooking by draining, pressing, or freezing, all of which extract water and make the tofu more firm.

To drain tofu: Remove from water and cut into 1/2 in. (1 cm) slabs. Place on a pan or plate, slightly elevated at one end. Allow to drain for about 15 minutes.

To press tofu: Remove from water and cut into 1/2 in. (1 cm) slabs. Arrange three layers of paper towel on a pan with one end slightly raised. Lay tofu on the towel and fold the towel over the tofu. Top with a breadboard or another pan, and a 2-4 lb. (1-2 kg) weight. Press for 1 hour, or until you're ready to cook. For firmer tofu, change the towels every so often.

To freeze tofu: Freezing expels water from tofu; it becomes firmer, spongier and darker in color. To freeze, wrap tofu tightly in two layers of plastic wrap. To thaw, unwrap and place in a pan of boiling hot water. Tofu cut in slabs or cubes will freeze and defrost more quickly. Frozen tofu does not lose protein; in fact, it becomes more nutritious, because some water is lost.

Fish & Shellfish

Fish is excellent food: high in protein and low in fat. In fishing communities throughout North America, where fresh fish is available nearly all-year round, people often eat it for breakfast, lunch and dinner. You might have a little fried mackerel for breakfast, fish steaks for dinner, which is served at noon when the fishermen get back from their day on the boat, and codfish cakes for supper at the end of the day. It is not a bad way to live, and it has never been known to upset anybody's stomach.

HOW TO TELL IF
A FISH IS FRESH

A fresh fish has bright eyes, is pink under the gills, and has a slick or slimy skin. It flops when you handle it. Press your finger against the side; it should bounce up again. "Fat" fish, such as mackerel, lake trout, herring and salmon, will not keep as well as "lean" fish such as cod, haddock or sole. They should be used at once or frozen.

CLEANING FISH

Fish will keep and taste best if cleaned immediately after being caught. If it hasn't been done, spread five or six layers of newspaper next to the sink, to work on. If the fish has large fins and scales, such as carp, or black bass, they will be easier to remove while the fish is whole. Scrape scales off with a curved blade against the grain. You need only get the large scales.

To remove fins, cut slits on either side of each, at a slight angle, and pull them out. This way you also get the bones underneath the fins.

To clean fish, insert the tip of the knife in the vent with the blade edge towards the head. Hold the knife at an angle so you cut only the belly flesh and skin, and slit up to the gills. Remove entrails, cutting them free at the gills. Scrape and rinse cavity clean.

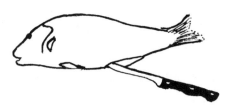

To remove head, cut in a curved line from the top of the head back around the gills on both sides. Bend head back sharply to snap the spine. If the fish is large, you may do this on the edge of the table.

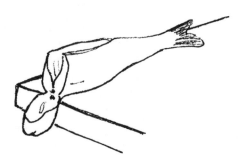

The tail is removed by cutting through it just above the most narrow part. However, to fillet, cut through the flesh on each side but leave the spine intact so the tail is a kind of handle.

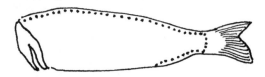

The fine art of filleting is basic to much of fish cookery. The tool for filleting is a slender, flexible, pointed blade about 6 in. (15 cm) long. It should be very sharp. Make a shallow cut down one side of the backbone, across the tail at the narrowest point, and back up the belly to the vent opening. To remove fillet, hold the knife parallel to the ribs, and move it gently back to front in one or more cuts, pulling the fillet away with your other hand.

After you remove the fillets you may wish to skin them. Hold the fillet firmly, skin side down, and slide the knife under the fillet, sawing gently to remove skin.

Another way of deboning fish is to remove the backbone from a good sized fish which you wish to stuff, while leaving the rest of the fish intact. Clean the fish, making the belly cut extra long, right up to the jaw. Then slide the knife on top of the rib cage up to the backbone on each side, from head to tail. The sharper your knife, the less fish will go with the ribcage as you lift it out intact.

A fish is done when the internal temperature reaches 150°F (65°C), and it's amazing how fast that temperature is reached. That's because fish is so lean. The amount of time it takes to cook a fish depends not on the weight but on how thick it is. Fillets and small or flat fish cook in a few minutes. Even large fish take very little time, compared to meat.

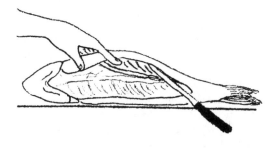

Pan-Fried Small Fish

This method is excellent for brook or lake trout, mackerel, small salmon, smelt and snappers. (Snappers should be scaled soon after you catch them, and the spiny fins and bony bottom section trimmed.)

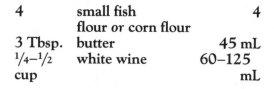

4	small fish	4
	flour or corn flour	
3 Tbsp.	butter	45 mL
1/4–1/2 cup	white wine	60–125 mL

Dust fish lightly with flour or corn flour. You may add seasoning, such as pepper, paprika, tarragon or chervil, but do not add salt, as it dries the fish.

Heat butter in a heavy skillet. When butter bubbles, add the fish and sauté until just golden on each side. If the fish is quite round (as with mackerel) reduce heat and cook very slowly for 5 to 10 minutes, turning three times.

To make an excellent quick sauce, remove fish from pan as soon as it is done and pour in the white wine. Tilt the skillet and let the liquid bubble for a few minutes as it cooks down. Pour sauce over fish. Serve garnished with lemon slices.

2 servings

Cranberry Steaks

4	cod steaks	4
4 Tbsp.	butter	60 mL
1	onion, chopped	1
2	cloves garlic, minced	2
1 Tbsp.	lemon juice	15 mL
1½ cups	whole berry cranberry sauce	375 mL
	parsley	
	lemon wedges	

Preheat oven to 325°F (165°C). Place cod steaks on a buttered dish or in a shallow casserole. In a frying pan, heat the butter and sauté onion for 3 minutes. Add garlic and cook another minute, then add lemon juice. Stir, and pour a little of the mixture over each steak. Bake for 20 minutes, then top each steak with cranberry sauce. Bake for another 5 minutes. Garnish with parsley and lemon wedges.

4 servings

Oven-Fried Fillets

This is an American method of fish cookery, in which fillets (fresh or frozen) are coated with bread crumbs (and only bread crumbs will do!) and baked in a very hot oven. The result is amazingly like deep fat frying – without the fat. This method may also be used for cooking cod tongues and cheeks.

2 lb.	fillets	1 kg
1 cup	milk	250 mL
1 cup	finely sifted bread crumbs	250 mL
3 Tbsp.	vegetable oil	45 mL

Preheat oven to 500°F (260°C). (This is necessary if you want crisp fillets.) Place milk and bread crumbs in separate bowls. Cut the fillets into 8 slender pieces, and roll up each one. Dip in milk, then bread crumbs. Place in a lightly oiled baking dish. Sprinkle or dribble each fillet with about 1 tsp. (5 mL) of oil. Place in the oven and bake for 10 minutes. Do not add liquid to the pan.

4 servings

Sole Fillets In White Wine

To keep fillets from curling as they cook (especially if they are very fresh) score the whitish side that was next to the skin, very lightly, with a sharp knife tip.

Flounder, small halibut, ocean perch, pollock or large trout fillets can be substituted for the sole in this recipe.

4	fillets of sole	4
¾ cup	green onions, chopped	180 mL
⅔ cup	dry white wine	160 mL
2 tsp.	butter	10 mL

Lightly butter a shallow baking dish or heavy skillet. Sprinkle with ½ cup (125 mL) of chopped green onions and place the fillets in the dish. Pour the wine over the fillets. The wine should come up to the middle of the fish, not cover it. Sprinkle with ¼ cup (60 mL) chopped green onions and dot with butter.

To poach in the oven, place dish in a preheated 275°F (135°C) oven, uncovered, for 10 to 12 minutes. To poach on top of the stove, set skillet over medium heat, until it simmers, then reduce heat at once. Cover, and cook gently for about 5 minutes, or until fish is easily flaked with a fork.

4 servings

Bluefish Fillets À La Portugaise

Young bluefish are very tasty; however, their flavor gets stronger as they get older. It is important to clean them at once, store them on ice, and eat or freeze them as soon as possible. They may be filleted or cooked whole, but be careful to remove the dark midline meat, which has a strong "fishy" flavor.

4	bluefish fillets	4
	lemon juice	
1/4 cup	olive oil	60 mL
pinch	thyme	pinch
1/4 tsp.	basil	1 mL
2	cloves garlic, crushed	2
1	Bermuda onion	1
1	large beefsteak tomato	1
1	green pepper	1

Sprinkle fillets with lemon juice and let sit for 15 minutes. Pat dry, then rub with a little olive oil. Arrange fillets for broiling on a foil-covered (outer-side down) cookie sheet. Mix together the olive oil, thyme, basil and garlic, and drizzle this mixture over the fillets. Slice the onion and tomato into thin rounds. Cut the green pepper into thin strips. Arrange overlapping slices of onion and tomato on the fish, with a strip of green pepper between each round. Start broiler when you put the fish in, and cook fillets for 5 minutes under low flame. Then cook for 5 minutes under high heat, or until fish is easily flaked with a fork. Do not turn.

4 servings

Barbecued Bass Fillets

Black bass, a freshwater game fish, is found in rivers throughout North America. There are half a dozen varieties, none of them related to striped bass, which lives around river mouths, in and out of the sea. Black bass can get quite large, but those under 3 lb. (1.5 kg) are considered prime. The skin sometimes has a muddy flavor, so unless it's caught in a clear unpolluted stream, it's best filleted.

4	bass fillets	4
6 Tbsp.	butter	90 mL
2 Tbsp.	lemon juice	30 mL
1 Tbsp.	garlic, crushed	15 mL
2 Tbsp.	tamari soy sauce	30 mL
1 tsp.	celery salt	5 mL
1 Tbsp.	parsley, chopped	15 mL
	green onions, chopped	
4	slices fresh lemon	4

Arrange each fillet on a 6 × 12 in. (15 × 30 cm) rectangle of aluminum foil. Simmer together butter, lemon juice, garlic, soy sauce, celery salt and parsley, for about 3 minutes, then pour a little over each fillet. Top fillets with green onions and a lemon slice. Fold up the foil and seal each along the top, so that steam doesn't escape. Barbecue or bake at 350°F (170°C) for 20 minutes.

4 servings

Stuffed Striped Bass

Striped bass run to vast sizes, but the best for cooking are around 6–8 lb. (2.5–3.5 kg) — perfect for stuffing and baking. These may be deboned before stuffing (see page 75). Line the pan with heavy foil: it's easier to remove the baked fish to a serving platter, where it can be admired at the table.

3 Tbsp.	butter	45 mL
2 cups	fresh mushrooms, sliced	475 mL
1/4 cup	green onions, chopped	60 mL
2 Tbsp.	parsley, chopped	30 mL
1/2 tsp.	rosemary or sage	2 mL
1/2 cup	whole wheat bread crumbs	125 mL
6–8 lb.	striped bass	2.5–3.5 kg
	lemon juice	
3 Tbsp.	sherry	45 mL
	sautéed mushrooms, sliced	

Preheat oven to 400°F (200°C). To prepare stuffing, heat the butter in a heavy skillet. Add mushrooms, half of the green onions, parsley, rosemary or sage. Sauté for 5 minutes. Remove from heat and mix in bread crumbs.

Wipe fish with a cloth. Rub inside and out with lemon juice. Stuff the interior and skewer sides together with toothpicks. Line pan with foil, and rub a little oil on it. Sprinkle with remaining green onions. Place fish in pan. Pour sherry over it. Place fish in oven and reduce heat to 325°F (160°C). Fish vary in size; it is done when the thickest part registers 150°F (65°C) on the meat thermometer, or when the flesh near the backbone is flaky, not translucent. You may baste it a few times during cooking with more sherry. Remove toothpicks before serving, and top with mushrooms.

6–8 servings

Finnan Haddie

1/2 lb.	smoked haddock or hake	225 g
1 1/2 cups	cold milk	375 mL
4 Tbsp.	butter	60 mL
4 Tbsp.	flour	60 mL

Tear fish into bite-sized chunks. Place in a small pan with milk and simmer for 20 minutes. Drain. Make a cream sauce with butter, flour and milk from cooked fish. Serve on mashed potatoes, with a green salad.

4 servings

FRESH SALMON

Fresh salmon does not keep well and should be cooked at once. Whatever you do, don't fry it in butter! Panfrying, which works well for almost any kind of seafood, is a disaster with salmon; it gets mushy and oily. Salmon is best poached. It may then be served hot, plain or with sauce, or cold in salads and sandwiches, or reheated in casseroles. Salmon may also be cut into steaks and grilled. If you have too much of it to eat, it may be frozen.

Poached Salmon

First prepare the liquid in which the salmon is to be poached: you can use either of the two following stocks.

COURT BOUILLON

4 cups	water	1 L
2 cups	white wine *or* vermouth	475 mL
1	large onion, chopped	1
1	bay leaf	1
6	black peppercorns	6
2	celery tops	2
2 Tbsp.	parsley, chopped	30 mL

LEMON STOCK

4 cups	water	1 L
1/2 cup	lemon juice	125 mL
1	large onion, stuck with cloves	1
5	allspice berries	5
2	celery tops	2
1	carrot, sliced	1
5	black peppercorns	5

Simmer ingredients for one or other stock together for one hour, and strain. Let cool. In the best of all possible worlds, you have a fish-poaching pan, which is long and narrow, and contains a removable rack. Butter the rack lightly and place fresh salmon on it. Immerse fish in cooled bouillon or stock, and cover. Place over high heat, bring to the boil, lower heat at once and simmer (do not boil) for 5 to 7 minutes per pound (11 to 15 minutes per kilogram). When the fish is done, remove and skin it.

If you are using a big, round enameled or stainless steel pot, with no rack and a large fish, make sure there is enough liquid to cover the fish when immersed. Put something on the bottom (a couple of spoons will do) and wrap the fish in cheesecloth. Twist the ends, which should be long enough so that you can grasp both ends to lift out the fish when it is done. Proceed as above.

If, however, you have only a medium-sized pot, and the fish is small or you have had to cut it up to fit it in the pot, start it in boiling liquid, then lower heat and simmer. Allow 5 to 6 minutes – if the pieces are around a pound (half a kilogram) – and remove them at once, when done, so they don't become waterlogged. You may strain and save the liquid, cooking it down for fish sauces or soups, or storing it in the freezer if you don't have a use for it right away.

To skin and serve poached fish, remove skin by peeling it back from tail to head; use a knife to free it where necessary. Scrape the flesh carefully, following the grain, to remove the "underskin." You may also make a long, V-shaped cut down the spine to remove the strip of dark meat. Salmon may be served hot with Béchamel Sauce or Hollandaise Alvino (page 42). Or you may cool it and serve with mayonnaise. Cold poached salmon, laid out on a serving dish and surrounded by lettuce, parsley, slices of lemon, tomatoes, cucumber and stuffed hard-boiled eggs, is quite an impressive dish.

6–8 servings

SHUCKING SHELLFISH

Always scrub shells with a stiff brush before opening them, and trim off beards, seaweed, anything that might harbor sand.

Most people steam or bake the shells open. Use a pan with a tight lid. Set shellfish with the most-curved side of the shell down (to hold in liquid when it opens) on a rack, or handful of very well rinsed seaweed, over boiling water. Boil rapidly until the shells open. With thin-shelled varieties, it will take only a few minutes, but we've had some oysters around our house that resisted heat for half an hour. To bake them open, set them on a rack, curved side down, over a baking pan or dish. Bake at 450°F (230°C) or more until open.

As soon as the shells open, even a crack, you may remove them to drain the juice and extract the meat. Don't rinse unless it's absolutely essential, and save the juice.

Many shellfish, such as clams, mussels, cockles and scallops, can be opened raw by running a thin-bladed knife between the shells. Quahogs are stubborn, but as children we learned that if you leave them in cold water, in a quiet place, for an hour or so, and then go to work alone, stealthily slipping them out and quickly inserting the knife, it's a lot easier to work your way through a bucketful. As you open them, use three bowls: one for juice, one for clams, and one for tough neck trimmings or muscles.

Opening raw oysters is an art. It sounds simple: break the "bill" or thin edge with pliers, insert knife, open oyster. But only experience can tell you where the best place to break it is, and how to strike it so that bits of shell don't get inside. Work slowly, and watch your hands: oyster shells are very sharp. Once you get it open, inspect under good light for shards of shell. Rinse (alas) if you suspect. Drain juice into one container, set oysters in another.

After shucking raw shellfish, strain the juice through a sieve lined with muslin. It can be used for making sauce, chowder, or mixed with butter or lemon juice to dip shellfish in as you eat them.

Raw Shellfish and Seafood Sauce

The best shellfish for serving raw are, of course, oysters; but cherrystone clams are a close second, and I've eaten lots of mussels and softshell clams raw and enjoyed them. Large quahogs can be a little tough.

Before serving, strain juice and cut shellfish free; return it to the shell and pour the juice over it. If you like, mix juice with lemon juice or a little white wine. Or serve with the following sauce:

1 cup	stewed tomatoes or tomato catsup, strained	250 mL
2 Tbsp.	wine vinegar	30 mL
1 Tbsp.	horseradish, grated	15 mL
1 Tbsp.	onion, minced	15 mL
1	clove garlic, crushed	1
1/2 tsp.	salt	2 mL
1 tsp.	tamari soy sauce	5 mL
1/4 tsp.	white pepper, ground	1 mL

Combine ingredients and chill for 3 to 4 hours before serving.

1 cup (250 mL)

STEAMED SHELLFISH

When I was about sixteen, I had a friend with a bicycle-built-for-two, and we used to pedal several miles to the nearest harbor and gather mussels. I remember one morning my parents arose to find us steaming a gallon or more of mussels for breakfast. To their absolute horror, we had melted every bit of butter in the house with garlic. They stayed inside muttering into their coffee while we ate mussels on the front porch. All of them.

Clams and mussels should be steamed over water until they just open; any longer and they will be overcooked and tough. Oysters are steamed until the edges just curl.

Shrimp Pesto Pasta

Use fresh or "flash-frozen" shrimp. Fresh shrimp should be shelled and beheaded, and the dark vein along the back should be removed.

3 qt.	water	3 L
2 tsp.	salt	10 mL
2	small potatoes, sliced	2
3/4 lb.	mixed small pasta	338 g
3 Tbsp.	vegetable oil	45 mL
1/2 lb.	shrimp	225 g
1/2 lb.	fresh mushrooms	225 g
4 tsp.	Garlic Pesto (page 46)	60 mL
	fresh parsley, chopped	
	Fruilano or Romano cheese, grated	

Bring water and salt to the boil. Add sliced potatoes and mixed pasta. Cook until just tender, about 10 minutes. Meanwhile, heat oil in a heavy skillet. Sauté mushrooms and shrimp together until mushrooms just brown and shrimp turns pink on both sides (about 3 to 5 minutes). If you are expanding the recipe, cook them separately. Drain pasta and potatoes of all but a few tablespoons of water, and mix in pesto. Serve platefuls of pasta with mushrooms and shrimp on top. Garnish with chopped parsley and pass around a dish of freshly grated cheese.

4 servings

Baked Shellfish

Bake shellfish in a very hot oven until they just open. Take them out and sprinkle with salt, pepper, grated onion, a dot of butter. Cover with a mixture of cooked minced greens and onions. Top with bread crumbs fried in bacon fat.

Bake at 400°F (200°C) for 10 minutes, or until edges curl.

Shellfish Stew

4 Tbsp.	butter	60 mL
1 pint	oysters or other shellfish	475 mL
1 qt.	milk	1 L
1 tsp.	salt	5 mL
pinch	pepper	pinch
	paprika	
	parsley, chopped	

Melt butter in a pot. Add oysters and cook over low heat until edges curl. Add milk, salt and pepper. Simmer for about 5 minutes until the milk is just hot. Serve garnished with paprika and chopped parsley.

4 servings

Poultry

Poultry is my favorite meat, simply because it's so versatile. You can serve it plain or accompanied by almost any kind of sauce — white, lemon, tomato, garlic, wine, or simple gravy. You can roast it, broil it, sauté or boil it, use it in casseroles, salads and sandwiches. And, when you're done, there's a marvelous soup to be made.

Chicken is the most widely used variety of poultry. Today it's mostly from the same stock: a plump white bird with short legs, which grows very rapidly. At five weeks they are sold as "Cornish hens"; at seven weeks they become fryers; and at eight they're broilers. After that they put on fat, reaching anywhere from 5–10 lb. (2.25–4.5 kg) and are sold as roasters. Naturally, the youngest and smallest are the most tender, but have the least amount of flavor.

One problem with chicken is that it doesn't keep very well. Always try to buy it from a source with a rapid turnover, unless you buy it frozen. Fresh chicken should be kept cool and used within two days. Cooked, it will keep up to five days in the refrigerator. Never use poultry with a questionable smell; your nose is an infallible guide.

Turkey is often cheaper than chicken, pound for pound. It has a stronger flavor but you may still cook it in many of the same ways. Duck, goose and wild fowl are also delicious, although more expensive. They generally have more fat and flavor than chicken or turkey, and should be cooked in special ways to allow the fat to drain or be skimmed off.

SUBDIVIDING POULTRY

Many recipes call for uncooked chicken cut into serving pieces. If yours came whole, here's how to cut it up:

TO REMOVE WING: Pull wing tip away from the bird, and make a shallow cut just where the wing joins the body. Then turn the bird over and make a second, deeper cut at a right angle to the first, slipping the knife blade under the bone as you pull the wing outward.

TO SEPARATE LEG AND JOINT: Set the leg on a board, drumstick pointing upward and grasped in one hand. Cut between leg and joint to the bone. Lay down knife, grasp thigh, and bend the joint backward, to separate the cartilage which holds the bones together. Cut through remaining meat.

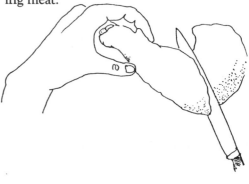

SEPARATING BREAST AND BACK: Set the bird back down, and insert the knife, blade facing backward, through the side of the bird just where the upper and lower ribs meet. Cut through towards the back. Repeat on the other side. Then grasp breast and back firmly and pull them apart as if hinged at the neck. Cut through remaining meat and skin.

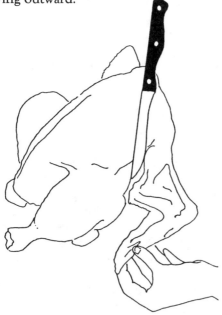

TO REMOVE LEG: Grasp bird firmly by the leg, and starting from the center of the bird, make a gradually deepening cut towards the tail, along the side where the leg connects. Bend the leg outward to disconnect the socket, and then make a second cut, front to back, to remove the entire leg and joint.

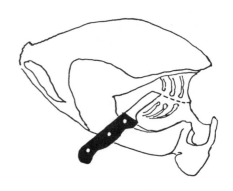

CUTTING THE BREAST IN TWO: This can be done with one well-placed blow of a Japanese cleaver, but it can also be done, less professionally, by simply cutting towards the front and back from the middle, along a line slightly to one side of the central ridge, with the breast turned upside down.

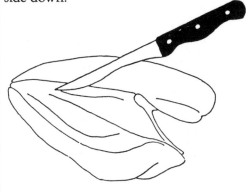

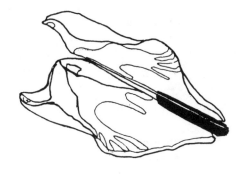

BONING THE BREAST: To remove breast meat entirely from the bone, leave bone whole, but remove skin. Cut a line through the breast meat slightly to one side of the breastbone ridge, as deep as it will go. Peel the flesh back, using the knife to pry and cut free the bottom half of the meat. Breast meat separates easily into two pieces; the inner, smaller one is more tender.

DEFROSTING BIRDS

If the bird is frozen, defrost in the refrigerator, fully wrapped, or the meat will dry out in cooking. Allow:
    24 hours for 6 lb. bird (2.5 kg);
    48 hours for a 12 lb. bird (5.5 kg);
    3 days for anything larger.
You may stuff or not stuff the inner cavity. Birds larger than 9 lb. (4 kg) should be sewed up with cotton string and a sail needle, or secured with metal skewers to hold in the stuffing. Tie the legs together with cotton string; tuck in the wing tips. Set in an oiled pan on a rack. Place in the oven.

Roast Turkey, Chicken or Duck

Any type of bird may be roasted, the best being those under eight months old. The skin should be intact, as it has a thin layer of fat underneath that automatically keeps the bird basted. This fat is thinnest at wing tips and drumsticks, areas that will dry out with long baking, unless basted. In ducks and geese, and older birds of any kind, there is a great deal of fat around the tail. It is customary to poke holes in the skin around the tail area, to release some of the fat as it bakes.

If you have a thermometer, insert it between the thigh and body of the bird; done is 185°F (85°C). If you don't, test by twist-

ROASTING CHART FOR BIRDS			
	Oven Temperature	Minutes per Pound	Minutes per Kilogram	Internal Temperature When Done
Young Chicken	300°F/150°C	35	75	185°F/85°C
Old Chicken	250°F/120°C	60	130	185°F/85°C
Duck, Goose	300°F/150°C	30	65	185°F/85°C
Small Turkey	300°F/150°C	25	55	185°F/85°C
Large Turkey	300°F/150°C	15	35	185°F/85°C

ing the leg, which should feel a little loose when the bird is cooked through. Another test is to slip a knife into the thickest part of the thigh. The juice should run clear, not reddish. A large bird should be basted and covered loosely with foil once it browns, or the meat may dry out under the crisp skin. Smaller birds, on the other hand, should be baked for the last half hour at a slightly higher temperature, 350°F (175°C), to make sure they brown.

A roasted bird will retain heat for quite some time, so you can remove it from the oven up to an hour before serving. Cover with foil and a towel to keep in the warmth.

If you plan to save the bird for future eating, carve one side only, leaving the skin intact on the other side. Cover and refrigerate. Use within 4 to 5 days. Cooked leftover meat may be frozen, but try to use it within a month.

Traditional Bread Stuffing

Economical and delicious, bread stuffing is a favorite with old and young alike. There are many variations, but the important thing (I think) is to use fresh sage and cubed whole wheat bread. You will need about ½ cup (125 mL) stuffing per pound (.5 kg) of bird.

3 Tbsp.	butter or chicken fat	45 mL
1	onion, chopped	1
2	ribs celery, chopped	2
½ cup	mushrooms, sliced (optional)	125 mL
2	cloves garlic, minced (optional)	2
3 Tbsp.	parsley, chopped	45 mL
2 tsp.	fresh sage, chopped or	10 mL
1 tsp.	dried sage	5 mL
1 tsp.	fresh summer savory	5 mL
2 cups	whole wheat bread, cubed	475 mL

Heat butter in a heavy skillet. Sauté vege-tables and seasonings, them combine with bread. Toss and cook over low heat for a few minutes. Stuff bird loosely.

Stuffing for 6 lb. (2.5 kg) bird

VARIATION

CHESTNUT DRESSING

1 cup	whole chestnuts	250 mL
	Traditional Bread Stuffing	

Simmer chestnuts, shells and all, for twenty minutes in water. Remove shells and skins when cool enough to handle. Chop in bits and add to Traditional Bread Stuffing in place of 1 cup of bread crumbs. If using dried chestnuts, soak overnight in water to cover. Then simmer in fresh water until tender.

Stuffing for 6 lb. (2.5 kg) bird

Oysters En Poulet Dressing

5	slices bacon	5
1	small onion, chopped	1
2 cups	whole wheat bread crumbs	475 mL
1–2 cups	cooked oysters	250–475 mL
1/2 cup	oyster juice	125 mL
1/2 tsp.	marjoram	2 mL
1/4 tsp.	thyme	1 mL
1/4 tsp.	nutmeg	1 mL
2 Tbsp.	parsley, chopped	30 mL

Fry bacon over moderate heat until done, but not crisp. Remove from pan, chop and set aside. Sauté onion in the bacon fat. When tender-crisp, turn off heat and re-turn bacon to pan together with remaining ingredients. Toss everything together and then stuff bird loosely. Use any remaining liquid in the gravy.

Stuffing for 6 lb. (2.5 kg) bird

Plum Pudding Dressing

Prunes, nuts and apples make a marvelous contrast to duck, goose or pork.

1 cup	prunes	250 mL
1/2 cup	water	125 mL
3 Tbsp.	butter	45 mL
1/2 cup	onion, chopped	125 mL
3	apples, cored and sliced	3
3 Tbsp.	prune juice	45 mL
1 cup	whole wheat bread crumbs	250 mL
1/4–1/2 cup	walnuts, chopped	60–125 mL

Simmer prunes in water, covered, for half an hour. Meanwhile, heat butter in a skillet and sauté onion until just translucent. Add apples and cook for 3 minutes, stirring constantly. Turn off heat. Add pitted prunes, prune juice, bread crumbs and walnuts. Toss all ingredients together and stuff bird loosely.

Stuffing for 6 lb. (2.5 kg) bird

Gravy Broth & Drippings

Broth for gravy may be started when you put the bird in the oven to roast.

2 cups	water	250 mL
1/2 tsp.	salt	2 mL
1/2 tsp.	pepper	2 mL
	poultry neck, liver, heart and giblets	
3	celery tops	3
1	small onion stuck with 2 cloves	1

Simmer ingredients gently in a small covered pan. When the bird is done, place it on a serving platter and cover lightly with foil to keep it warm. Scrape and pour drippings from the roasting pan into a measuring cup and let them sit a few minutes. When the fat rises to the top, measure out 4 Tbsp. (60 mL) of chicken fat.

1¹/2 cups (375 mL)

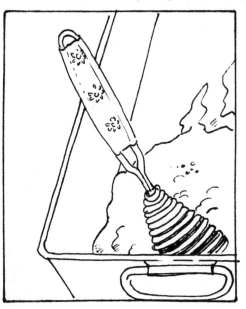

Country Gravy

After you have made gravy a few times, you won't have to measure things any more; you simply heat the drippings, add flour to "take up the fat" and then add liquid, stirring until it looks right. Many cooks do this right in the roasting pan, to save time and dishes. If there isn't enough fat to work with, add some butter or vegetable oil.

4 Tbsp.	rendered chicken fat	60 mL
4 Tbsp.	flour	60 mL
1¹/2 cups	chicken broth	375 mL

Heat the fat in a small, heavy pan, and when it begins to bubble, add the flour, stir, and reduce heat. Cook, stirring occasionally, over low heat for 3 minutes. Then add the broth and drippings, gradually, in three parts, stirring after each addition until the gravy thickens. Cook gravy gently for about 3 minutes. If it gets too thick, add more liquid.

Additions of all kinds can be made to a good gravy. For seasoning, try light herbs such as chopped parsley, chervil or tarragon. You may want to add a dash of salt, a grinding of fresh pepper. To some it isn't gravy unless the liver, heart and giblets are added — all chopped fine, of course. Others prefer a few sliced sautéed mushrooms. You may also substitute a little white wine or sour cream for part of the liquid. Gravy is a terrific leftover. To reheat, add a little liquid (water or milk) and stir until smooth. Then heat gently, stirring from time to time. Add more liquid as needed. Add to chopped, cooked leftover poultry; serve on toast.

1¹/2 cups (375 mL)

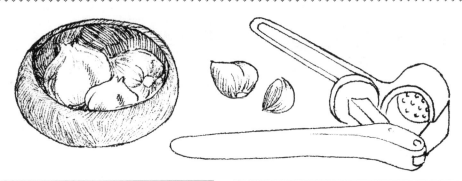

Aioli Chicken

A thick, garlicky sauce for roast chicken, having divine properties. Besides 1 roast chicken you need:

1/2 cup	whole wheat bread crumbs	125 mL
1/4 cup	white wine vinegar	60 mL
6	cloves garlic, crushed	6
6	egg yolks	6
1/3 cup	olive oil	80 mL
2/3 cup	vegetable oil	160 mL
1/4 cup	white wine or water	60 mL

Set bread crumbs to soak in vinegar when the bird goes in the oven. About 15 minutes before serving, crush garlic and beat in egg yolks. Add oil in a fine stream, beating until thick with a whisk or rotary beater. When the chicken is done, remove the bird from the roasting pan and deglaze the pan by adding wine or water. Cook and stir over high heat for about 3 minutes, then add to the sauce. Mash up the vinegar-soaked bread crumbs and add them, too. Pour everything into a small, heavy pan, and whisk gently over low heat until it thickens — and no longer. Pour into a heated serving dish and serve with the chicken.

6 servings

Paté De Maison R.

1 lb.	chicken livers	450 g
3/4 cup	chicken broth	180 mL
1	onion, chopped	1
3	ribs celery, chopped	3
1	egg	1
3 Tbsp.	cognac	45 mL
1/4 cup	cream or evaporated milk	60 mL
1/4 cup	unbleached white flour	60 mL
1 tsp.	salt	5 mL
	ginger, allspice and pepper	
3	strips uncooked bacon	3

Simmer chicken livers in broth with onion and celery for about 10 minutes, or until tender. Put livers and vegetables through a meat grinder or chop very fine. Beat together egg, cognac, cream, flour, salt and a pinch of each of the spices, and mix thoroughly with liver. Shape into a firm loaf in a small, greased casserole, and top with bacon. Bake at 350°F (175°C) for about 1 hour. Cool and chill overnight before serving.

1 1/2 lb. (680 g) loaf

Duck À L'Orange

4½–6 lb. duck	2–2½ kg

DUCK STOCK

2 cups	water	475 mL
	duck neck, giblets	
1	rib celery	1
1	onion	1
3	cloves	3
3	black peppercorns	3

SAUCE

3 Tbsp.	port or sherry	45 mL
2 Tbsp.	arrowroot or cornstarch	30 mL
2 tsp.	unsweetened cocoa	10 mL
2 Tbsp.	red wine vinegar	30 mL
2 Tbsp.	brown sugar	30 mL
1	lemon peel, grated	1
1	orange peel, grated	1
	juice of 3–4 oranges	

Oil pan and roast duck (see page 87).

To make stock, combine water, neck and giblets, celery, the onion stuck with cloves and peppercorns in a saucepan. Allow to simmer while duck cooks.

When the duck is done, place it on a serving platter and cover with foil to keep warm. Pour the considerable drippings into a tall glass and skim off fat as it rises. Set aside. Combine port, arrowroot and cocoa in a small bowl. Mash into a smooth paste, then add 1 cup (250 mL) of the duck stock, the wine vinegar, brown sugar,

lemon and orange peel, and orange juice. In a small, heavy pan, heat ¼ cup (60 mL) of rendered duck fat. Add sauce mixture. Cook over moderate heat, stirring occasionally.

6–8 servings

Country Chicken

This is a simple, delicious way to prepare chicken, much better for you then deep fried. Use a heavy frying pan.

4	pieces chicken	4
¼ cup	vegetable oil	60 mL
½ cup	water	125 mL
¼ cup	white or red wine	60 mL

Dry chicken with paper towel and cook each piece in oil over medium heat until browned on all sides, about 10 minutes per side. Add water, cover, and steam lightly over medium heat for 20 minutes. Alternatively you may bake the chicken 20 minutes at 350°F (175°C). For a special touch, remove chicken from the pan, and deglaze the drippings with wine, swirling and scraping the pan over high heat for a few minutes. Pour this mixture over chicken and serve.

4 servings

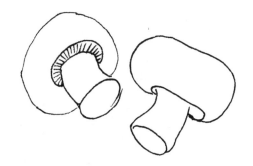

Mediterranean Country Chicken

8–10	pieces chicken	8–10
	flour to dredge	
4 Tbsp.	olive oil	60 mL
1	onion, diced	1
2	carrots, sliced	2
2	ribs celery, sliced	2
1	clove garlic, crushed	1
1	green pepper, sliced	1
1 cup	chicken broth	250 mL
1 cup	tomatoes, chopped	250 mL
1	bay leaf	1
1/2 tsp.	ground pepper	2 mL
2 tsp.	basil	10 mL
2 Tbsp.	parsley, chopped	30 mL
1 cup	broccoli or cauliflower florets	250 mL
1	green pepper, sliced	1
1/2 cup	red or white wine (optional)	125 mL
1/4 tsp.	oregano	1 mL

Dry chicken pieces and dredge in flour. Heat 2 Tbsp. (30 mL) olive oil in a heavy skillet, and sauté lightly the onion, carrots, celery, garlic and green pepper. Remove vegetables from skillet. Heat another 2 Tbsp. (30 mL) olive oil and sauté chicken pieces until golden on all sides. Return vegetables to pan and add chicken broth, tomatoes, bay leaf and seasonings. Cook until liquid just bubbles then cover and cook slowly for 45 minutes. Ten minutes before serving, add broccoli or cauliflower, green pepper, wine and oregano. Serve with pasta or freshly steamed rice.

6 servings

Coq Au Vin

You can make this with just about any kind of wine. I used to make it with amontillado sherry, which was terrific, if a little rich.

6	pieces chicken	6
	flour to dredge	
3 Tbsp.	vegetable oil	45 mL
1	carrot, sliced	1
1	onion, chopped	1
1	clove garlic, chopped	1
1 cup	chicken broth	250 mL
1/2 cup	wine	125 mL
1	bay leaf	1
1/2 cup	mushrooms, sliced	125 mL
1/4 tsp.	thyme	1 mL
	pepper	

Dry chicken pieces and dredge in flour. Heat oil in a heavy skillet and sauté chicken until golden on all sides. Add vegetables together with broth, wine, bay leaf, mushrooms, thyme and a generous grating of pepper. Heat until liquid just bubbles. Cover and simmer slowly for 1 hour.

4 servings

Chinese Peanut Chicken

This is a special dish, involving a lot of preparation but a short cooking time.

3–4 lb.	fryer chicken	1.5–2 kg
6 Tbsp.	sesame or peanut oil	90 mL
2	cloves garlic, chopped	2
1 in.	piece fresh ginger	2 cm.
1 cup	blanched peanuts	250 mL
2	onions or bunch green onions	2
3 Tbsp.	sherry or sweet wine	45 mL
2 Tbsp.	cornstarch	30 mL
2 Tbsp.	tamari soy sauce	30 mL
1/4 cup	water	60 mL
1 tsp.	blackstrap molasses	5 mL

Skin, bone and chop chicken. Toss meat in about 2 Tbsp. (30 mL) sesame or peanut oil, then add garlic and ginger. Grind or pound peanuts into coarse meal. Chop or slice the onions. Heat up a wok or cast-iron skillet over high heat until very hot. Pour in 4 Tbsp. (60 mL) oil, and tilt wok or skillet to coat surface evenly. Add chicken and stir-fry for about 3 minutes, tossing to cook on all sides. Add peanuts, onions and wine. Cook for 1 minute, stirring occasionally, while you mix, then add the cornstarch, soy sauce, water and molasses. Cover and steam until chicken cooks through — about 4 minutes. Serve with brown rice, soy sauce and fresh vegetables.

4 servings

Maccheroni Con Tacchino

3 Tbsp.	olive oil	45 mL
1/2 cup	onion, chopped	125 mL
2	cloves garlic, crushed	2
1/4 cup	celery, chopped	60 mL
1/2 cup	green pepper, chopped	125 mL
1 cup	mushrooms, sliced	250 mL
28 oz	canned tomatoes	800 mL
2 cups	cooked turkey, chopped	475 mL
1 tsp.	basil	5 mL
1 tsp.	salt	5 mL
	freshly grated pepper	
1 lb.	large shell pasta	450 g
2 tsp.	salt	10 mL

Bring to the boil a large pot of water. Meanwhile, heat oil in a large skillet, and add onions, garlic, celery, green pepper, mushrooms. Sauté until tender-crisp. Then add tomatoes, turkey, and seasonings. Cover and simmer. When the large pot of water boils, add pasta and salt.

Cook pasta until tender, rinse under cold water, and mix with sauce. Serve with plenty of Parmesan cheese.

6 servings

Chicken Kiev

To bone chicken and cut fillets from chicken breast, see page 86. Prepare these rolls ahead of time and they will stay together as you cook them.

¼ cup	softened butter	60 mL
¼ cup	parsley, chopped	60 mL
2	cloves garlic, crushed	2 cloves
1½ lb.	chicken breasts	675 g
1	egg	1
1 cup	unbleached white flour	250 mL
½ cup	vegetable oil	125 mL

Place butter in a bowl and mash in parsley and garlic. Lay fillets on a counter, cover with plastic wrap and pound gently with a rolling pin to flatten and enlarge them. Place 1-2 Tbsp. (15-30 mL) butter on each piece of chicken and roll them up tightly. Refrigerate 1 hour. Beat egg in a bowl; put flour in another bowl. Dip each roll in first egg, then flour. Heat oil in a skillet; fry rolls over medium heat about 15 minutes in all, turning as necessary to brown all sides. Serve on beds of hot rice, with lemon wedges.

4 servings

Chicken Risotto

4 Tbsp.	vegetable oil	60 mL
½ cup	onion, chopped	125 mL
2 cups	brown rice	475 mL
2	cloves garlic, crushed	2
1–2 tsp.	curry powder	5–10 mL
4 cups	water or chicken stock	1 L
2 cups	tomatoes, chopped	2
1 tsp.	summer savory	5 mL
1 tsp.	salt	5 mL
1 cup	cooked chicken, chopped	250 mL
1 cup	mushrooms, sautéed	250 mL

Choose a deep, heavy pan with a good tight lid. In this pan, heat the oil, then add the onion, rice, garlic and curry powder. Cook and stir over high heat until the rice turns light brown and the onions are limp. Then add the water or chicken stock, tomatoes (you can use either fresh or canned), savory and salt. Cover and cook for 45 minutes or until all liquid is absorbed. Finally, add the cooked chicken and mushrooms, and serve.

4 servings

Meat Dishes

Today, there is increasing controversy about whether meat is or isn't good for you. On the one hand we hear that saturated fats contribute to heart trouble and high blood pressure. On the other hand, meat has always been a source of strength and vigor. If we can get it, what's wrong with good red meat?

I think the real question, however, is not one of saying "yes" or "no" to meat, but how much? Who's eating it, and when? Supposing you've spent the day puttering around the house, and plan to spend the evening curled up with a good book. A big juicy leg of lamb with gravy and potatoes will probably give you heartburn and add half a pound to your middle. A fillet of sole, or a piece of chicken, with rice and vegetables would be a better choice. On the other hand, if you spent the afternoon digging the car out of a snowbank and are prepar-

ing to set off after dinner on a long trip, maybe a leg of lamb isn't such a bad idea.

In the modern world, with machines to do most of our physical labor, the average individual doesn't have much opportunity to utilize high amounts of fats and proteins. The body, being a frugal organism, stores the excess away for leaner times. If you never do hard physical work, it stays there. Some meats contain more than protein. Pork, ham, lamb and mature beef contain high levels of saturated fats. You'll have need of those fats, and burn them off efficiently, only if you work hard, are out in the cold, or are under stress for long hours. It's important when eating meat (and especially fatty meat) to include a variety of other foods. All of them work together to keep your body healthy, which is what is meant by a "balanced diet."

If you don't do much physical work,

should you eat meat at all? Sure! Just don't overdo it, or exclude other foods. Stick to lean meats, such as veal, venison or lean beef, and vary the menu with chicken, fish and meatless meals. Get plenty of exercise when you do eat meat, and stay away from other saturated fats (gravy, biscuits, pies, heavy desserts) when you serve a meat dinner. The point of all the controversy is that too much meat is just as bad, maybe worse, than too little.

ABOUT PORK

Pork is a fat, juicy meat, and may be cooked at somewhat higher temperatures than other meats. You may put it in an oven preheated to 500°F (260°C), but should immediately reduce the heat in the oven to 350°F (175°C) for roasting. Bake until done to at least 170°F (75°C), or until the juice from the center runs out clear and gray.

Pork should never be rare.

This is because the heat destroys a parasitic larva called trichinae, which is sometimes found in pork muscle. trichinae are actually killed at 131°F (55°C), which is a lot more rare than you would ever want to eat it, but the custom of cooking pork until it is thoroughly gray has served us well, and continues to be popular.

ABOUT VENISON

Venison is a lot like beef, but leaner and a little tougher (depending on the age of the deer). If cooked slowly, however, it makes a good roast. To avoid a gamey taste, remove all venison fat, replacing it with bacon or thin slabs of pork fat, attached to the top with toothpicks.

ROASTING MEAT

The aim in roasting is to produce a piece of tender, flavorful cooked meat. You don't want it to become dry. There are three ways that a roast will become dry and tough: by salting it, searing it, or basting it. Nor should a roast be covered, or cooked in a plastic bag. It will then be steamed, not roasted.

Your roast should be covered with fat. In the case of a leg of lamb or a ham, this is not a problem. Many cuts, however, have a good deal of exposed meat on them, and meats such as rabbit, goat's meat, veal and venison have no fat at all. So you should brush the meat with oil, or rub it with lard, or attach thin slabs of pork or other fat with toothpicks over the top before you put it in the oven.

A roast should be set on a rack in a pan. Otherwise the bottom of it will fry in hot fat.

If you like, you can coat your meat with spices before roasting it. You can use pepper, thyme and marjoram, or rub it with crushed garlic or onions, or use a little of one particular flavor, such as sage with chicken, tarragon with lamb, or mustard with pork.

I like to roast meat at low temperatures. The reason is that the slower meat cooks, the more tender it remains when cooked. This is particularly important if your roast is lean, or if you suspect it of not being very tender to begin with. When roasting very tender or fatty meats, you can get away with higher temperatures and shorter cooking times. However, the trend today is towards lean meats, and many stores now offer grass-fed beef at lower cost than feedlot beef. Grass-fed beef is both leaner and less tender than feed-lot beef. It seems wise to cook your meat more slowly, for longer periods, just to be on the safe side.

ROASTING MEAT CHART

	Oven Temperature	Minutes per Pound	Minutes per Kilogram	Internal Temperature When Done
BEEF				
Standing Ribs				
Rare	325°F/160°C	25	55	140°F/60°C
Medium	325°F/160°C	30	65	160°F/70°C
Well Done	325°F/160°C	40	90	170°F/80°C
Rolled Rump				
Rare	325°F/160°C	25	55	140°F/60°C
Medium	325°F/160°C	35	75	160°F/70°C
Well Done	325°F/160°C	40	90	170°F/80°C
Sirloin				
Rare	325°F/160°C	30	65	140°F/60°C
Medium	325°F/160°C	40	90	160°F/70°C
Well Done	325°F/160°C	45	100	170°F/80°C
VEAL				
Shoulder	325°F/160°C	35	75	170°F/80°C
VENISON, CHUCK OR GOAT'S MEAT				
Rare	250°F/120°C	50	110	135°F/60°C
Medium	250°F/120°C	60	130	150°F/65°C
Well Done	250°F/120°C	70	155	160°F/70°C
LAMB				
Leg	325°F/160°C	35	75	180°F/80°C
Shoulder	325°F/160°C	45	100	180°F/80°C
FRESH PORK				
Loin	350°F/175°C	35	75	170°F/80°C
Picnic				
Shoulder	350°F/175°C	35	75	170°F/80°C
Leg	350°F/175°C	35	75	170°F/80°C
Spareribs	325°F/160°C	30	65	170°F/80°C
CURED PORK				
Picnic	325°F/160°C	35	75	160°F/70°C
Ham	325°F/160°C	30	65	160°F/70°C

⧫⧫

GRAVY MAGIC

Gravy, like cream sauce, is a mixture of fat, flour and liquid. Pork, lamb and well-marbled beef give off enough fat during roasting to make the gravy base. If there isn't enough fat, as is often the case with veal or venison, you may add butter to make up the difference. For the liquid, you can use canned beef or chicken stock or a bouillon cube with water, but the best stock is made by cooking together a little meat, sliced from the roast before cooking, together with an onion, carrot, celery, parsley, salt and water to cover. Bring to a boil, cover, and lower heat to simmer 30 minutes or more. Strain before using in gravy.

To pick up the flavor of a good meat gravy, add any juices released in cooking and carving the roast. If your gravy tastes a little flat, try adding a dash of wine or beer. You can also add a pinch of thyme or summer savory.

If your gravy has no flavor at all and you really want something delicious, add a few dollops of sour cream and a handful of sliced mushrooms, sautéed in butter.

To darken gravy, try adding one of these:

1 tsp. (5 mL) tamari soy sauce;
½ tsp. (2 mL) instant coffee; or
1 tsp. (5 mL) unsweetened cocoa.

The flavor of coffee or cocoa isn't noticeable in a strong meat-flavored gravy such as lamb, pork or beef.

Pan Gravy

3 Tbsp.	fat and meat drippings	45 mL
3 Tbsp.	unbleached white flour	45 mL
1 cup	meat stock	250 mL
	salt and pepper	

When a roast is almost done, pour fat from the roasting pan and measure into a small saucepan. Heat gently; add flour gradually, stirring with a small whisk or spring stirrer. Add stock ⅓ cup (80 mL) at a time, stirring after each addition until gravy thickens. Season to taste with salt and pepper.

1 cup (250 mL)

Steak Secret

This is the sort of thing that makes a cook's reputation.

½ cup	tamari soy sauce	125 mL
2	cloves garlic, crushed	2
2 lb.	well-marbled steak	1 kg
3 Tbsp.	unsalted butter	45 mL
1 cup	mushrooms, sliced	250 mL
½ cup	dry red wine	125 mL

Half an hour before serving, mix tamari and crushed garlic in a shallow dish or platter. Place steak in it, turn once, and let sit at room temperature until ready to

⧫⧫

broil. Pat dry before broiling. While it is cooking, heat the butter in a small pan and sauté mushrooms until golden. Add wine and stir as you cook them over medium heat for 3 or 4 minutes. Pour wine and mushrooms over broiled steak and serve at once.

4–5 servings

Pot Roast

Choose a large piece of meat for pot roasting: beef, venison or goat's meat are all good. Shoulder cuts, chuck and lower leg cuts make great pot roasts. The dish should include some bone in the meat; if not, add a soup bone.

3–4 lb.	piece of beef, venison *or* goat's meat	1.5–2 kg
3 Tbsp.	whole wheat flour	45 mL
3 Tbsp.	vegetable oil	45 mL
1	onion, coarsely chopped	1
1	carrot, chopped	1
3 cups	water *or* broth	725 mL
1/2 tsp.	thyme	2 mL
2 Tbsp.	Italian parsley, chopped	30 mL
2 tsp.	Dijon mustard	10 mL
pinch	freshly ground pepper	pinch
1	bay leaf	1
1	soup bone (optional)	1
1	small turnip, cut in wedges	1
8	small potatoes	8
10	tiny white onions	10
4	carrots, quartered	4
1 cup	green beans, chopped	250 mL
1/2 cup	rolled oats	125 mL
1/2 tsp.	salt	2 mL

Rub the meat with flour and sear it lightly on all sides in oil, a minute or two to a side. Remove it from the pot, add a little more oil if needed, and sauté the onion and carrot. Return meat to the pot and add water or broth, thyme, parsley, mustard, pepper, bay leaf, soup bone. Bring to the boil, then reduce heat and simmer, covered, for 2 hours. Remove bay leaf and soup bone. Add liquid to make about 3 cups (750 mL) if necessary. In the last 30 minutes of cooking, add turnip, potatoes, onions and carrots. In the last 15 minutes of cooking, add green beans, oats and salt. When the sauce thickens and the vegetables are done, remove the meat from the pot and carve.

Serve with biscuits and pickles.

6 servings

Herbed Calf's Liver

Fresh liver from young beef, cooked gently and not too long, is tender and delicious. Because it's rich, you serve less of it than of other meats.

4	strips bacon	4
1	onion, sliced	1
1/2 cup	unbleached white flour	125 mL
	thyme, savory, mint, tarragon	
1 lb.	calf's liver	450 kg

In a heavy skillet, sauté bacon until crisp. Remove and drain bacon on absorbent paper. Sauté onion in bacon fat. Mix flour and herbs and dust liver with mixture. Remove and drain onions. Cook liver 3 minutes on each side. To be sure it's done, cut into the thickest part with a sharp knife. Serve pieces garnished with onion rings and bacon.

4 servings

Boeuf Bourguignon

This is a classic French stew of lean beef, mushrooms and small white onions cooked in a sauce flavored with a light red Burgundy wine. Serve with rice or potatoes and salad.

1½ lb.	stewing beef	675 kg
3 Tbsp.	unbleached white flour	45 mL
2 Tbsp.	vegetable oil	30 mL
1 Tbsp.	butter	15 mL
1	onion, chopped	1
2	cloves garlic, chopped	2
½ cup	red wine	125 mL
1 cup	water	250 mL
2 Tbsp.	Tomato Paste (page 44)	30 mL
2 Tbsp.	Italian parsley, chopped	30 mL
¼ tsp.	thyme	2 mL
¼ tsp.	freshly ground pepper	2 mL
12	small white onions	12
6 Tbsp.	unsalted butter	90 mL
1 tsp.	sugar	5 mL
1 cup	mushrooms, sliced	250 mL

Cut stewing meat in 1½ in. (4 cm) chunks. Rub with flour and sear lightly on all sides in oil in a heavy, deep pot. Remove pieces as done and add 1 Tbsp. (15 mL) butter. Sauté onion and garlic for 2 minutes. Return meat to the pot along with wine, water, Tomato Paste, parsley, thyme and pepper. Bring to the boil, then reduce heat and simmer, covered, for 1½ hours. Meanwhile, cut shallow crosses in the base of each onion to keep them from falling apart. Immerse them in boiling water long enough to loosen their jackets, then peel them. Heat 3 Tbsp. (45 mL) butter in a heavy skillet, and brown the onions. Sprinkle them with sugar and sauté another minute or two, for extra browning. Add them to the meat and cook another 30 minutes. Just before serving, sauté the sliced mushrooms in the remaining butter, and add them to the mixture. If sauce seems thin, simmer uncovered to cook it down.

4 servings

Cocido

Spanish Beef and Vegetable Stew.

1½ lb.	lean stewing beef	675 g
3 Tbsp.	flour	45 mL
3 Tbsp.	vegetable oil	45 mL
½ lb.	sausage	225 g
1	onion, chopped	1
3	cloves garlic, chopped	3
2	celery tops, chopped	2
3 cups	canned tomatoes and juice	725 mL
1 cup	cooked chick-peas	250 mL
3 Tbsp.	parsley, chopped	45 mL
1 Tbsp.	basil, chopped	15 mL
½ tsp.	salt	2 mL
¼ tsp.	freshly ground pepper	1 mL

Cut beef and sausage into cubes about 1½ in. (4 cm) square. Prepare beef by dusting lightly with flour. Heat oil in a heavy deep pot and sear meat lightly. Remove from pan and sauté sausage pieces. Remove from pan and sauté onions, garlic and celery tops for 5 minutes. Then return meats to the pot and add tomatoes, chick-peas, half the parsley, basil, and enough water so that the liquid barely covers the meat. Bring to the boil, then reduce heat and simmer over very low heat, covered, for 1½ hours. Then add salt and potatoes, and cook 30 minutes longer. In the last 10 minutes of cooking, add pepper, remaining parsley and zucchini. Serve as soon as the squash is tender-crisp.

6 servings

covered, for 1½ to 2 hours. About 10 minutes before serving, mix together flour, sugar and water. Stir into stew and cook uncovered, stirring occasionally, until gravy thickens.

Serve with boiled potatoes, or potatoes and turnips mashed together, and green beans.

4 servings

Venison Carbonnade

A rich brown ale or home brew is the secret ingredient in this traditional hunter's stew. It doesn't matter if it is flat.

1½ lb.	venison *or* lean stewing beef	675 g
3 Tbsp.	whole wheat flour	45 mL
2 Tbsp.	vegetable oil	30 mL
1	large onion, sliced	1
2	cloves garlic, crushed	1
1	carrot, chopped	2
1 cup	dark ale *or* beer	250 mL
1 cup	water	250 mL
2 Tbsp.	parsley, chopped	30 mL
½ tsp.	thyme	2 mL
¼ tsp.	freshly ground pepper	1 mL
1	bay leaf	1
1 Tbsp.	red wine vinegar	15 mL
3 Tbsp.	unbleached white flour	45 mL
1½ Tbsp.	brown sugar	25 mL
¼ cup	water	60 mL

Cut meat in cubes 1 in. (3 cm) square. Dust with flour and brown on all sides in oil. Set meat aside and sauté onions, garlic and carrot. Return meat to the pot and add ale or beer, water, parsley, thyme, pepper, bay leaf and vinegar. Bring to the boil, then reduce heat and simmer very slowly,

Hash With Ham

Once you learn to make a fast hash, you'll never be stuck again for something to serve on the spur of the moment.

5	large potatoes	5
1 cup	water	250 mL
1	large onion	1
4	thick slices cooked ham	4
1	green pepper (optional)	1
¼ cup	vegetable oil	60 mL
2 tsp.	summer savory	10 mL
½ tsp.	salt	2 mL
¼ tsp.	freshly grated pepper	1 mL

Wash, peel and chop potatoes into ½–1 in. cubes (1–2 cm). Put them in a pot with water, cover tightly, and bring to the boil. Then lower heat to medium and cook for 10 minutes. Remove from heat and drain. Meanwhile, chop up the onion, ham and green pepper. Heat oil in a heavy skillet. Add onions and green pepper. Sauté 2 minutes, then add ham and potatoes. Season with savory, salt, and pepper. Cook over medium-high heat, uncovered, until bottom browns. Turn with a spatula and cook the other side until browned.

Serve with Coleslaw (page 33) and a poached or fried egg per serving.

4 servings

Country Ham

Unprocessed ham is quite salty, and bene-fits from cooking in liquid before baking.

4–6 lb.	ham	2–2.5 kg
1 cup	cider vinegar	250 mL
1	onion	1
1	carrot, chopped	1
5	peppercorns	5
1	bay leaf	1
1/2 cup	brown sugar	125 mL
15	cloves	15
	cider, water or beer	

Rinse the ham and place it in a large stainless steel or enameled container. Add vinegar and enough water to fill 3/4 of the pot. Add onion, carrot, peppercorns and bay leaf. Bring the pot to the boil, then immediately reduce heat and simmer, covered, for 30 minutes per lb. (65 minutes per kg). If it is a large ham, over 7 lb. (3 kg) decrease cooking time to 20 minutes per lb. (45 minutes per kg).

Preheat oven to 400°F (200°C). Drain the ham and cool it a little; then slice off any outer skin, leaving a layer of fat about 1/2 in. (1 cm) thick. Rub ham with brown sugar. Score fat lightly in a diamond pat-tern. Insert a clove in the middle of each diamond.

Put the ham on a rack in a baking pan. Lower heat to 325°F (160°C), and cook ham, uncovered, for 30 minutes. Moisten brown sugar with a little cider, water, or beer. Bake for another 30 minutes.

Serve with Scalloped Potatoes (page 28) a good green vegetable, mustard pickles, applesauce, and a fruit dessert.

6–8 servings

Crisp-Tender Pork Chops

Chops for this dish should be cut quite thin: 1/3–1/2 in. (8-10 mm). If they are thicker, fry the meat longer on each side, but don't overcook them!

4	thin pork chops	4
1 tsp.	thyme	5 mL
1/4 cup	whole wheat flour	60 mL
1	egg	1
1 Tbsp.	water	15 mL
1 cup	bread crumbs	250 mL
3 Tbsp.	vegetable oil	45 mL
1/2 cup	sherry	125 mL
1 tsp.	tamari soy sauce	5 mL

Rub chops in thyme, then dust with flour. Beat the egg and water in a small bowl, dip each chop in it, then coat each with bread crumbs. Allow to dry 15 minutes.

Heat oil. Fry chops 3 minutes on each side. Remove them from the pan and drain on absorbent paper. Deglaze the pan by adding sherry and tamari over high heat, scraping and boiling until the sauce is re-duced by half. Pour a little sauce over each chop.

4 servings

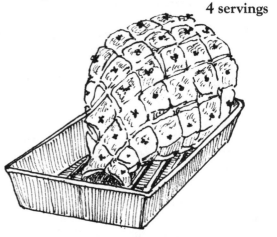

Lamb Stew

For stewing meat, choose flank, shoulder and riblets. I like a combination: bones add flavor, flank has a little fat mixed in, and shoulder comes in solid chunks.

2–3 lb.	stewing lamb	1–1.5 kg
3 Tbsp.	unbleached white flour	45 mL
3 Tbsp.	vegetable oil	45 mL
1	onion, chopped	1
2	stalks celery with leaves, chopped	2
1	carrot, chopped	1
2	cloves garlic, crushed	2
3 cups	water	725 mL
1/2 cup	barley	125 mL
3 Tbsp.	parsley, chopped	45 mL
1/2 tsp.	thyme	2 mL
1	bay leaf	1
4	small onions, peeled	4
2	carrots, quartered	2
4	large potatoes, quartered	4
1 cup	fresh or frozen peas	250 mL
1	leaf fresh mint	1

Cut lamb into pieces about 1 1/2–2 in. (4–5 cm) square. Toss in flour. Heat 1 Tbsp. (15 mL) oil in a heavy skillet until almost smoking, and sear meat on all sides. Remove from pan and add remaining oil. Sauté onion, celery, carrot and garlic until tender. Add the seared meat and water, barley, parsley, thyme and bay leaf. Bring to the boil, reduce heat and simmer, covered, for 1 1/2 hours. Remove bay leaf and add onions, carrots, and potatoes. Simmer for 20 minutes, until vegetables are almost done. Five or ten minutes before serving, add peas and mint leaf. The moment the peas are done, serve.

4 servings

Lamb Chops in Sour Cream

The tenderest chops are from the loin, sirloin and ribs of lamb. If you're using shoulder of lamb, or mutton or goat's meat, cook the meat a little longer.

4	lamb chops	4
2 Tbsp.	vegetable oil	30 mL
1	onion, sliced	1
1	clove garlic, minced	1
1 cup	chicken broth	250 mL
1 cup	sour cream	250 mL
1/2 tsp.	salt	2 mL

Oil a heavy iron skillet lightly and sear lamb chops on both sides until browned. Add a little more oil and sauté onion and garlic until tender. Add broth and simmer very slowly, covered, for 20 minutes. Just before serving, stir in sour cream and salt. Do not allow to boil. Serve with rice and green peas.

4 servings

Shepherd's Pie Topped With Biscuits

When the hot lunch program was started in my old grade school, this was our favorite dinner. Even children who failed to memorize a single verb chart or multiplication table were never absent on Shepherd's Pie Day.

1	egg	1
4 cups	seasoned mashed potatoes	1 L
2 Tbsp.	butter	30 mL
1 Tbsp.	onion, grated	15 mL
1	onion, chopped	1
1 lb.	ground beef	450 g
3 Tbsp.	unbleached white flour	45 mL
1½ cups	beef or chicken broth	375 mL
	Buttermilk Biscuits (page 138)	

Beat egg in a large mixing bowl. Add cooled potatoes and grated onion. Butter a casserole and half fill with mashed potatoes. Heat butter in a heavy skillet, and sauté chopped onion 2 minutes; then add and cook ground beef, stirring, until gray. Sprinkle flour over the ground beef. Stir and cook for 5 minutes. Then add broth, a little at a time, stirring as gravy thickens. When all the broth is added, reduce heat and cook, uncovered, for 15 minutes, until it becomes a thick gravy.

Preheat oven to 400°F (200°C) and make up a batch of Buttermilk Biscuit dough.

Roll out the dough and cut out biscuits. Pour meat and gravy over mashed potatoes and top with biscuits. Bake 15 to 20 minutes, until biscuits are brown. Allow to cool 15 minutes before serving.

4–6 servings

Old-fashioned Meatloaf

1	egg	1
½ cup	dry whole wheat bread crumbs	125 mL
1 lb.	ground beef or beef and pork	450 g
3 Tbsp.	parsley, chopped	45 mL
¼ tsp.	dried thyme	1 mL
2 Tbsp.	catsup or Tomato Paste (page 44)	30 mL
1	clove garlic, crushed	1
½ tsp.	salt	2 mL
¼ tsp.	ground pepper	1 mL

Beat the egg in a shallow mixing bowl and soak bread crumbs in the egg until soft (if necessary, pound them a bit). Add meat, parsley, thyme, catsup, garlic, salt and pepper, and mix thoroughly, using your hands. Shape the mixture into a firm loaf on a greased baking dish. Bake at 300°F (150°C) for 45 minutes. Cool for 10 minutes before slicing.

4–5 servings

Noodles Nonnioff

When I was going to college, I remember my friend Nonny used to cook this up by the gallon, to feed the starving thousands.

1 lb.	broad egg noodles *or* penne	450 g
3 Tbsp.	butter	45 mL
1	large onion, chopped	1
1 lb.	ground beef	450 g
1/4 cup	white wine *or* sherry	60 mL
2 cups	sour cream	475 mL

Bring a large pot of salted water to the boil, and boil noodles or penne for 10 to 15 minutes, until barely done. Drain and rinse. Meanwhile, melt butter in a skillet, and sauté the onion for 3 or 4 minutes; then add ground beef and stir as you cook, until meat becomes gray. Add wine and simmer, uncovered, for 10 minutes over low heat. Add sour cream at the very end, and don't let it boil. Serve with noodles.

4 servings

Meat Cheese Pie

1	Flakey Single Piecrust (page 116)	1
1	onion, finely chopped	1
1/2	green pepper, chopped	1/2
2 Tbsp.	vegetable oil	30 mL
1/2 lb.	ground beef	225 g
2 Tbsp.	whole wheat flour	30 mL
2	eggs, beaten	2
1 cup	ricotta *or* drained cottage cheese	250 mL
1/2 tsp.	salt	2 mL
1/4 tsp.	freshly grated pepper	1 mL
1/2 cup	Cheddar cheese, grated	125 mL
	paprika	

Preheat oven to 400°F (200°C). Roll out piecrust and line a pie dish. Prick the crust 6 times with a fork and weight it with a dozen or so uncooked baking beans. Bake it for 10 minutes. Remove beans. Reduce oven heat to 350°F (175°C). Sauté the onion and pepper in oil for 2 or 3 minutes in a heavy skillet. Add beef and stir as it cooks for another minute or two. Sprinkle with flour and simmer over low heat 5 minutes. Meanwhile, combine eggs, cheese, salt and pepper in a mixing bowl. Spread cooled meat in piecrust. Cover with cheese mixture and top with grated cheese and a sprinkling of paprika. Bake at 350°F (175°C) for 20 minutes, or until browned on top.

4–6 servings

Piroghi

A popular Russian meat pastry, piroghi can be made as one large pastry or many small ones.

	Elsie's Foolproof Piecrust (page 117)	
3 Tbsp.	butter	45 mL
2	onions, chopped	2
1 cup	mushrooms, sliced	250 mL
1/2 lb.	ground beef *or* beef and pork	225 g
2 Tbsp.	unbleached white flour	30 mL
2 Tbsp.	fresh dill, chopped *or*	30 mL
1 tsp.	dried dill	5 mL
1/2 cup	sour cream	125 mL
2	eggs	2
	poppy seeds	

Make up a batch of piecrust, divide in half, and refrigerate. Heat butter in a heavy skillet and sauté onions 4 minutes. Add mushrooms and sauté 5 minutes longer, then add ground meat and cook, stirring, until meat is gray. Sprinkle flour over meat and cook 5 minutes, stirring. Add dill and sour cream and allow to cool before beating in 1 egg.

Preheat oven 400°F (200°C). Roll out one half of pie dough into a long oblong, 10 × 16 in. (15 × 40 cm). Lay filling in a line along the middle, leaving a generous margin, particularly at the ends. Paint edges with water and seal, folding ends up first, then the two long sides. Prick with a fork. Break the second egg into a small bowl and beat it thoroughly; then paint egg on top of the piroghi. Sprinkle over with poppy seeds. Bake at 400°F (200°C) for 30 minutes, or until golden.

VARIATIONS

PIROZHKI Cut dough into 4 in. (10 cm) squares. Heap 1–2 Tbsp. (15–30 mL) in each, paint edges, and fold into a triangle. Prick, paint, and bake only 20 minutes.

CABBAGE-MEAT PIROGHI Make meat filling as above but use:

1/2 lb.	ground meat	225 g
2 cups	shredded cabbage	475 mL

Add cabbage to onions and sauté a minute or two before adding mushrooms. Continue as above.

Moussaka

1	large cauliflower	1
3	strips uncooked bacon	3
1	large onion, chopped	1
1/2 lb.	ground beef	225 g
2 cups	Fresh Tomato Sauce (page 43)	475 mL
2 Tbsp	basil, chopped	30 mL

Break cauliflower into florets and steam them for 15 minutes over boiling water. Meanwhile, chop bacon fine and sauté in a heavy skillet, until crisp. Remove bacon from the pan and add onion; sauté 4 minutes, or until tender, then add ground beef and stir as you cook until gray. Add Tomato Sauce and basil. You may serve at once or put in a casserole and bake up to 45 minutes at 325°F (160°C).

4 servings

Desserts

Desserts are a wonderful invention; we all deserve them. Almost as much fun as the eating is imagining what we want, mixing it up, waiting for the right moment, and finally indulging. But the only way to get exactly what we want, when we want it, is to make it ourselves.

My inclinations range from the tart and crisp to the thick and creamy. On the one hand there are fruit desserts, freshly made with the blueberries, raspberries, rhubarb, cranberries and apples which grow best in New England and the Maritimes. I prefer wild fruit: it has more flavor than domestic varieties. On the other hand there are puddings and custards to tempt the palate. I've included some dessert sauces — almost a lost art, and one which can transform a simple cake into an extravaganza, a pudding into an experience. And, finally, there is ice cream.

It's important to choose the right time of day for a good dessert. They usually have a lot of calories which you have to burn off — else no more desserts! Our preference is mid-afternoon when, on the farm, attention to detail begins to lag, and we need a moment to sit down and think about what we've just done (or haven't done). We stop for tea, and a slice of pie, or a dish of pudding.

Ice cream, of course is for very special occasions. Most often, we make it to celebrate the birthday of a friend. This is partly because it takes a lot of energy to turn the crank of an old-fashioned ice cream maker and, at a birthday party, there are always a lot of willing hands to take over. The choice of flavor is a privilege accorded to the birthday person. Our two-quart (2 L) container is about right for twenty guests — with seconds for the true aficionados of this, the most delicious of desserts.

Rhubarb Crisp

Delicious in the early spring, we mellow the acidity of rhubarb with dried milk powder and a little sugar. Non-instant dried milk (available at health food stores) works best, but you can substitute instant dried milk.

FILLING

3/4 cup	white sugar	180 mL
2 Tbsp.	cornstarch	30 mL
1/2 cup	non-instant milk powder	125 mL
6 cups	fresh rhubarb	1.5 L

TOPPING

6 Tbsp.	unbleached white flour	90 mL
1/2 cup	brown sugar	125 mL
1/4 cup	non-instant milk powder	60 mL
1 tsp.	cinnamon	5 mL
3 Tbsp.	cold butter	45 mL
1/2 cup	rolled oats	125 mL
2 Tbsp.	safflower oil	30 mL
2 Tbsp.	water	30 mL

To make filling, mix sugar, cornstarch and milk powder in a large mixing bowl. Cut rhubarb into 1 in. (2 cm) pieces. Toss in sugar mixture to coat evenly. Empty into an oiled 9 in. (24 cm) square pan. For topping, mix flour, sugar, milk powder and cinnamon. Cut in butter with a fork until finely crumbled. Then mix in rolled oats. Sprinkle oil and water over mixture and toss lightly. Spread over rhubarb filling and press firmly down by hand. Bake at 325°F (160°C) for 1½ hours.

9–12 servings

Strawberry Shortcake

2 cups	fresh strawberries	475 mL
1/2 cup	sugar	125 mL
	Bannock (page 139)	
	whipped cream	

Slice or halve the strawberries, and mix them with sugar. Let them sit an hour, while you bake the bannock and whip the cream. Top slices of bannock with strawberries and cream.

6–8 servings

Fresh Fruit Cocktail

A flexible recipe, fruit cocktail can be varied according to what's available in season. It's great party fare. It's also been known to cure colds single-handed.

2	oranges	2
3	sweet apples	3
1	banana	1
1/2 cup	orange juice	125 mL
1 cup	strawberries, sliced	250 mL
1 cup	fresh blueberries	250 mL
1 cup	peaches, sliced	250 mL
1/2–1 cup	raspberries	125–250 mL

Combine ingredients. To prevent discoloration of apples, bananas and fresh peaches, chop or slice them into the orange juice. Cut all fruit into bite-sized chunks or slices. Serve chilled.

4–6 servings

Fruit Leather

Fruit leather can be made with the pulp of any fruit, but those that are slightly tart are best. You can use 3 cups (725 mL) each:

> **apples;**
> **peaches;**
> **raspberries;**
> **strawberries;**
> **dried apricots** *or*
> > **prunes;**
> **blackberries.**

Cook fruit over low heat with a little water in the bottom of the pan to keep it from scorching. When it's soft, run it through a food mill. Place fruit in a very heavy pot to cook down. Add honey to taste, if you think it is needed.

When it becomes too thick to cook without scorching, spread it ¼ in. (5 mm) thick on oiled cookie sheets. Cover with a light cloth and set it in the sun to dry every day for 1 to 2 weeks. Roll, when dry, into fruit leather sticks, and enclose in plastic wrap.

Blueberry Grunt

You have been picking blueberries all day, under the blazing sun. You step into a kitchen milling with kids, adults, and dogs. In the midst of it all, your mate appears, gives you a loving smile, and says "Well now, how about that blueberry pie?"

Hence the title of this splendid dessert, obviously invented to fill such a need. It takes about five minutes to assemble, and involves no hard work or heating of the oven.

8 cups	fresh *or* frozen blueberries	2 L
½ cup	sugar	125 mL
2 Tbsp.	lemon juice	30 mL

DUMPLINGS

2	eggs	2
⅓ cup	milk	80 mL
1 cup	unbleached white flour	250 mL
1 cup	whole wheat flour	250 mL
½ tsp.	salt	2 mL
1 Tbsp.	baking powder	15 mL
½ tsp.	nutmeg	2 mL

To make the dumplings, beat eggs and milk together. Sift in flour, salt, baking powder and nutmeg, and beat thoroughly. Heat the blueberries, sugar and lemon juice in a large pot. When they bubble, drop the dumpling mixture by large spoonfuls on the top. Cover and cook over medium heat for 15 minutes. Serve in bowls, ladling hot blueberries over the dumplings.

6–9 servings

Applesauce

For years we have made terrific sweet pink applesauce with no added ingredients. The secret is a mixture of tart red apples and bland sweet yellow apples. Wait until after a few hard frosts to pick them — the cold sweetens them.

30	tart red apples	30
30	sweet yellow apples	30
1 cup	water	475 mL

Halve apples and put them in an enameled or stainless steel pot with water, cover tightly, and cook over high heat. The yellow apples will cook first, but continue cooking until all apples are soft. Ladle into a food mill and turn until all the applesauce is through.

Another way to do this is with the pressure cooker. Fill cooker with halved apples and 1 cup (250 mL) of water. Adjust lid on tightly but don't set the valve cover on the valve. When steam begins to blow through the valve, remove the pot from the heat at once. Do not open lid until you cool the pressure cooker completely under running water.

6–10 qt. (6–10 L)

TO FREEZE APPLESAUCE

Line plastic containers with plastic bags. Fill, using cup funnel, seal with gooseneck, and freeze. Once frozen, plastic container may be removed, for reuse.

Applesauce Sundae

1 cup	thick cream	250 mL
1 cup	Applesauce	250 mL
1/2 cup	chopped walnuts or pecans	125 mL
1 tsp.	vanilla or dark rum	5 mL
pinch	cinnamon	pinch

Beat cream until stiff, then mix with remaining ingredients. Spread in a loaf pan and freeze for 1 hour. Remove from freezer and whip with a wire whisk. Refreeze for 15 to 30 minutes.

6 servings

Old-fashioned Apple Crisp

This is a large recipe, triple the size of an apple pie, and a good one to make a lot of. It keeps well and is always popular and nutritious, delicious hot or cold.

12 cups	sliced apples	3 L
1–1½ cups	apple juice	250–375 mL
1 cup	raisins	250 mL
1 cup	brown sugar	250 mL
6 Tbsp.	whole wheat flour	90 mL
1 Tbsp.	cinnamon	15 mL
2 tsp.	allspice	10 mL
1 tsp.	nutmeg	5 mL
1/2 tsp.	cardamom	2 mL

TOPPING

½ cup	butter	125 mL
1 cup	whole wheat flour	250 mL
1 cup	brown sugar	250 mL
1 cup	rolled oats	250 mL
2 cups	sunflower seeds	475 mL
½ cup	walnuts, chopped (optional)	125 mL

Mix apples with apple juice, raisins and sugar. Mix together flour and spices before adding to apples. Butter and fill a large baking pan or three pie pans with the mixture. To make the topping, first cut butter into the flour and brown sugar until well mixed; then add oats, sunflower seeds and walnuts. Bake at 350°F (175°C) for 30 to 40 minutes.

10–12 servings

Baked Stuffed Apples

1 Tbsp.	melted butter	15 mL
1 Tbsp.	whole wheat bread crumbs	15 mL
1 Tbsp.	currants	15 mL
2 Tbsp.	small nut pieces	30 mL
1 Tbsp.	wheat germ	15 mL
pinch	cinnamon grating nutmeg	pinch
4	large perfect apples	4

Mix melted butter with bread crumbs, then mix in the other ingredients. Carve a shallow circle in the top of each apple, and scoop out the core with a small sharp spoon or paring knife. Stuff apples. Place on a greased pan and bake at 350°F (175°C) 30 minutes. Serve hot or cold. You may pour cream over them, or serve with chilled yogurt.

4 servings

ABOUT GELATIN DESSERTS

You may add any fruit to gelatin except fresh pineapple, which has an enzyme that dissolves the gelatin permanently. If you want to use fresh pineapple, cook it first to destroy the enzyme. Canned pineapple is fine — it's cooked in canning.

When gelatin is half chilled and is partially jelled, it can be whipped. This doubles its volume and gives it a light, airy texture.

One last thing I should mention in passing: gelatin is an animal product. If you or your guests are vegetarians, it's off your list — unless you want to bend the rules a little. . .

Lemon Gelatin

This is a basic recipe. It's good with sliced fruit such as bananas, peaches, oranges or berries.

2 Tbsp.	gelatin	30 mL
½ cup	cold water	125 mL
1 cup	boiling water	250 mL
1 cup	sugar	250 mL
2 cups	cold water	475 mL
½ cup	lemon juice	125 mL

Mix gelatin with cold water, then add boiling water and sugar. When all granules have dissolved, add cold water and lemon juice. Chill 1½ to 2 hours, or until set.

4 servings

VARIATIONS

ORANGE GELATIN Substitute for 2 cups (475 mL) cold water:

2 cups	cold orange juice	475 mL

STRAWBERY OR RASPBERY GELATIN Using partially thawed frozen fruit, pour over Lemon Gelatin:

1 cup	strawberries *or* raspberries	250 mL

Fruit Juice Gelatin

Use any fruit juice you like: cranberry, grape, blackberry, pineapple, grapefruit, or a mixture.

2 Tbsp.	plain gelatin	30 mL
1/2 cup	cold water	125 mL
1 cup	boiling fruit juice	250 mL
2 1/2 cups	cold fruit juice	600 mL

Soak gelatin in cold water, then add boiling fruit juice and stir until gelatin dissolves. Add cold fruit juice and chill 1 1/2 hours, or until set. You may also pour the mixture over sliced fruit before chilling.

4 servings

YOGURT MAKING

Yogurt culture, like yeast, is a living organism and is very sensitive to temperature. It "grows" (divides and multiplies) best a little above our body temperature, at 110°F (43°C). Below 70°F (21°C) it becomes dormant. At temperatures over 120°F (50°C) it is killed by heat.

It is not difficult to make and keep making your own yogurt at home. Establish and label one jar "milk culture" and keep it separate from the others. Don't dip in an unsterilized spoon, or leave it around with the lid off. When you make yogurt, date all the jars. Make a new batch weekly, and your culture should remain working for several months.

Even with the best of care, it is necessary to renew yogurt cultures from time to time. You will notice after a while that your yogurt is more sour, less flavorful, and takes longer to make. You may buy a fresh container of yogurt from a store, or buy a packet of freeze-dried culture from a delicatessen or health food store. You may prolong the life of a culture, when you get it, by freezing cubes of fresh culture in a sterile ice cube tray.

To sterilize jars or other equipment, boil or steam them in a covered pan for 15 minutes. Leave in the pan until you are ready to use them; wash your hands before removing them.

Yogurt

If your milk is unpasteurized, fresh from the animal, pasteurize it first by heating over low heat, gradually, to 150°F (65°C), holding it there for 15 minutes, then cooling to 110°F (43°C) before adding yogurt culture.

2 qt.	milk	2 L
1 cup	instant dried milk	250 mL
4 Tbsp.	yogurt	60 mL

Sterilize 4 pint (475 mL) jars and lids, measuring spoons and a whisk or eggbeater, for 15 minutes.

In another pan, mix milk and instant dried milk. Heat milk very gradually, stirring and checking the temperature every two minutes. At 110°F (43°C) remove milk from the heat and whisk or beat in the yogurt. Pour milk mixture into jars and put on the lids. Put the jars in the large pot and pour in water at 110°F (43°C). Keep water temperature constant for 4 to 6 hours, until the yogurt appears firm when a bottle is tilted slightly. Label one jar "milk culture." Label all jars with date before putting them in a refrigerator or in dark, cool storage.

4 2-cup (475 mL) jars

Baked Custard

3	eggs	3
2 cups	whole milk	475 mL
1/3 cup	honey	80 mL
1 tsp.	vanilla	5 mL
pinch	salt	pinch
	grating nutmeg	

Beat together everything except the nutmeg, and pour into a greased casserole or ovenproof custard cups. Set in a pan of hot water (to keep the bottom from toughening). Bake at 300°F (150°C) 1 hour for casserole, 45 minutes for cups, or until knife inserted in the middle comes out clean. Serve with Raspberry Melba Sauce (page 120).

4 servings

Rice Pudding

1	egg	1
1 cup	milk	250 mL
1/2 cup	honey	125 mL
1/4 tsp.	nutmeg	1 mL
pinch	salt	pinch
1/4 cup	dried instant skim milk	60 mL
1 cup	brown rice	250 mL
1/2 cup	currants	125 mL

Mix all ingredients and beat well. Pour into a greased casserole and bake 1 hour at 300°F (150°C) or until knife inserted in the middle comes out clean.

4 servings

Bread Pudding Supreme

3 1/2 cups	stale whole wheat bread	825 mL
2	eggs	2
2 cups	milk	475 mL
1/4 cup	honey	60 mL
1 Tbsp.	molasses	15 mL
1/2 tsp.	cinnamon	2 mL
1/2 tsp.	nutmeg	2 mL
1 tsp.	dark rum	5 mL
1/2 cup	dates, chopped	125 mL
1/2 cup	walnuts, chopped	125 mL

Break bread into pieces the size of hazelnuts. Beat together other ingredients and soak bread in them for 10 minutes. Pour into a greased ovenproof casserole or individual ovenproof custard cups. Bake for about 1 hour at 300°F (150°C) or until a knife inserted in the middle comes out clean. Top with whipped cream or light cream.

6 servings

ABOUT PIECRUST

Piecrust is a mixture of flour and shortening. The idea is to crumble the shortening into the flour in cold, hard little lumps, which will melt rapidly in a very hot oven, spreading out and causing the flour to be cooked in flakey layers. You cannot do this with warm shortening or a slow oven. Chilled ingredients and rapid handling must be used to keep the shortening hard until it goes into the oven.

I have had the best results with pure, home-rendered lard. Hydrogenated, store-bought lard, or vegetable shortening, is smoother, but more care must be taken to keep it cold in mixing. Although butter or margarine has a delicious rich taste, the crust is more expensive and not quite as flakey. A combination of lard and butter gives both the rich taste and the dry texture.

White flour is the only flour that produces flakey piecrust. Whole wheat bread flour is too coarse, and whole wheat pastry flour is difficult to roll and shape. If you want to add nutrition to piecrust, try substituting 1/4–1/2 cup (60–125 mL) wheat germ for part of the flour. The result will be a slightly crunchy, but still reasonably flakey crust.

The liquid used in piecrust is usually water — as cold as you can get it. If your tap water is tepid, chill it with an ice cube.

Sprinkle in liquid gradually, 1 Tbsp. (15 mL) at a time, mixing lightly after each addition. Do not add any more liquid than is necessary to make a single mass or ball, with all the flour adhering, but not sticky. The final working can be done by hand, but with light fingertips (remember, your hands are warm!) Almost any piecrust is easier to work if refrigerated for an hour or two before rolling it out.

Flakey Single Piecrust

1/2 cup	cold shortening	125 mL
1 1/3 cup	unbleached white flour	330 mL
1/2 tsp.	salt	2 mL
3 Tbsp.	cold water	45 mL

Follow instructions for double crust, below.

Flakey Double Piecrust

2/3 cup	cold shortening	150 mL
2 cups	unbleached white flour	475 mL
1 tsp.	salt	5 mL
5 Tbsp.	cold water	75 mL

Using a fork or pastry cutter, cut shortening into flour and salt until it resembles coarse cornmeal. Sprinkle in water a little at a time, mixing after each addition. Work into a single ball. Enclose in plastic wrap and chill for 1 hour or longer before rolling out.

Graham Crumb Crust

1 cup	graham cracker crumbs	250 mL
1/4 cup	melted butter *or* safflower oil	60 mL
1/2 tsp.	cinnamon	2 mL

Mix all ingredients together and press into pie pan firmly. Chill for at least 30 minutes.

Elsie's Foolproof Piecrust

Repeated handling does not drastically change the texture of this crust, which is firm and attractive-looking, although not as flakey as an eggless crust. Excellent for tarts, meat pies, quiche, and custard or pumpkin pies.

1³/₄ cups	cold shortening	400 mL
4 cups	unbleached white flour	1 L
1 tsp.	salt	5 mL
1	medium egg	1
¹/₃ cup	cold water	80 mL
1 Tbsp.	lemon juice	15 mL

Using a fork or pastry cutter, cut shortening into flour and salt until it resembles coarse cornmeal. Beat egg slightly, then add water and lemon juice and beat again. Add liquid to dry ingredients gradually, mixing and shaping dough into two rough balls. Enclose each in plastic wrap and chill for 1 hour or longer before rolling out.

2 double-crust pie shells

Apple Pie

To make a really glorious apple pie with good flavor and texture, you need tart, firm apples. On the commercial market choose Cortlands, Rome Beauty, Gravensteins, or Baldwins. Underripe fruit may be used, but you should increase the sugar and milk, and add 3 Tbsp. (45 mL) butter to the recipe. Skins may be left on in the fall and early winter, but in the spring they become tough and should be peeled.

8–10	tart apples, sliced	8–10
¹/₂ cup	brown sugar	125 mL
3 Tbsp.	whole wheat flour	45 mL
2 Tbsp.	whole milk	30 mL
1 tsp.	cinnamon	5 mL
1 tsp.	nutmeg	5 mL
1	Flakey Double Piecrust	1

Preheat oven to 350°F (175°C). Slice apples into a bowl and sprinkle the other ingredients over them. Mix well. Roll out piecrust, fill, and cover. Prick top of pie. Bake at 350°F (175°C) for 45 minutes.

6–8 servings

Blueberry Apple Pie

¹/₂ cup	sugar (optional)	125 mL
2 Tbsp.	cornstarch or flour	30 mL
¹/₂ tsp.	cinnamon	2 mL
2 cups	cored apples, sliced	475 mL
2 cups	fresh or frozen blueberries	475 mL
1	Flakey Double Piecrust	1

Preheat oven to 400°F (200°C). Mix sugar, cornstarch and cinnamon together in a mixing bowl before tossing with apples and blueberries. Roll out piecrust, fill, and cover. Prick the top of the pie. Bake at 400°F (200°C) for 30 minutes, or until juice bubbles around edges.

6–8 servings

Blueberry Tarts

	Flakey Single Piecrust	
4 cups	fresh or frozen blueberries	1 L
2 Tbsp.	cornstarch	30 mL
1/4 cup	honey	60 mL
2 Tbsp.	lemon juice	30 mL

TOPPING

1	egg	1
2	egg yolks	2
1/2 cup	cream or evaporated milk	125 mL
1/3 cup	honey	80 mL
pinch	salt	pinch

Preheat oven to 400°F (200°C). Roll out piecrust, and line 4 large, individual tart pans. Mix blueberries, cornstarch, honey and lemon juice. Distribute them into the tart shells and bake for 20 minutes.

Meanwhile, mix topping ingredients in the top of a double boiler, cook and stir over boiling water until thick. When thick, in 5 to 10 minutes, remove from heat and cool for 15 minutes. Pour over the cooled blueberry tarts. Chill for 3 hours before serving.

4 large tarts

Custard Pie

	Flakey Single Piecrust	
3	eggs	3
1/3 cup	honey	80 mL
1 cup	whole milk	250 mL
1 cup	light cream or evaporated milk	250 mL
1 tsp.	almond flavoring	5 mL
1/4 tsp.	salt	1 mL

Preheat oven to 325°F (160°C). Roll out piecrust and line pie pan. Beat eggs, then add remaining ingredients and beat well. Pour into pie shell and bake at 325°F (160°C) for 30 minutes. Cool before serving.

6–8 servings

Cranberry Tofu Flan

1 lb.	tofu	450 g
1/4 cup	honey	60 mL
1/2 cup	safflower oil	125 mL
1/2 cup	white sugar	125 mL
1 Tbsp.	vanilla extract	15 mL
2 Tbsp.	lemon juice	30 mL
1/2 tsp.	grated lemon rind	2 mL
1/2 tsp.	salt	2 mL
1	Graham Crumb Crust	1

TOPPING

1 cup	fresh *or* frozen cranberries	250 mL
1/2 cup	sugar	125 mL
2 Tbsp.	honey	30 mL
1 Tbsp.	cornstarch	15 mL
3 Tbsp.	water	45 mL
1 tsp.	almond flavoring	5 mL

Press tofu through a sieve, using a spoon. Add and mix in honey, oil, sugar, vanilla, lemon juice, lemon rind and salt. Pour into graham cracker crust and bake at 350° F (175°C) for 40 minutes. Cool before adding topping.

To make topping, mix cranberries, sugar and honey in a small saucepan and heat gently, covered, until the cranberries pop. Cook over moderate heat about 5 minutes. Meanwhile, mix cornstarch and water. Add to the cranberries and cook 5 minutes or until mixture becomes clear, over low heat, uncovered. Remove from heat and cool before adding almond flavoring. Pour over cooled tofu mixture. Chill 1 hour or longer before serving.

6–8 servings

Reasonable Strudel

This may not be the way they make it in Vienna, but this strudel tastes so good that nobody will mind.

1/2	Elsie's Foolproof Piecrust	1/2
3	tart apples, chopped	3
2 Tbsp.	butter	30 mL
2 Tbsp.	honey	30 mL
1/4 cup	nuts, chopped	60 mL
1/4 cup	currants	60 mL
1 tsp.	cinnamon	5 mL
1/4 tsp.	allspice	1 mL

Preheat oven to 400°F (200°C). On a lightly floured surface, roll out the dough as thin as you can into a long oblong shape. Trim the edges so they are even. Mix together apples, butter, honey, nuts, currants and spices. Distribute evenly, leaving a border around the edges. Brush the edges with a little water, then bring them together and seal. Bake for 20 minutes.

4–6 servings

Butterscotch Pudding

If you've never had an old-fashioned pudding made from scratch, you've no idea how delicious a pudding can be. Start at least 2 hours before serving, so it will have time to set and chill.

3 Tbsp.	butter	45 mL
1/4 cup	unbleached white flour	60 mL
3/4 cup	brown sugar	180 mL
2 cups	whole milk	475 mL
4	large eggs	4

Put the butter, flour and brown sugar in the top of a double boiler, over boiling water. In another pan, heat milk over medium heat until scalding. When the butter melts, stir well, then add hot milk, stirring thoroughly. Separate eggs into two bowls. Beat yolks until foamy, then pour about half a cup of the hot mixture into them, beating steadily as you do. Still beating, pour everything back into the top of the double boiler and continue to stir for about 5 minutes as the mixture thickens slightly. Remove from heat at once. Pour into 4 dessert glasses and chill before serving. You may use egg whites to make Coconut Honey Macaroons (page 151.)

4 servings

Chocolate Pudding

Thick, rich, and uncomplicated. Good with Vanilla Sauce (page 121).

1³/₄ cups	milk	430 mL
¹/₂ cup	sugar	125 mL
¹/₄ tsp.	salt	1 mL
¹/₄ cup	milk	60 mL
3 Tbsp.	cornstarch	45 mL
¹/₄ cup	unsweetened cocoa	60 mL
1	egg	1
1 tsp.	vanilla	5 mL

Heat milk, sugar and salt in the top of a double boiler over medium direct heat until almost boiling. Meanwhile, mix together ¹/₄ cup (60 mL) milk, cornstarch, cocoa and egg, in a bowl, and beat well. Add a little of the hot milk to this, then pour it all back into the pot. Put the top of the double boiler over boiling water, and cook for 5 minutes, stirring every now and then until it begins to thicken. Stir constantly for about 2 minutes as it continues to thicken, then remove from heat and cool. Add vanilla and pour into 4 dessert dishes. Chill 1–2 hours. Serve with Vanilla Sauce or whipped cream and chopped nuts.

4 servings

Neapolitan Cheesecake

Thick, tangy and rich tasting, this cheesecake is actually quite low in calories, because it's made with yogurt instead of cream cheese.

1	Graham Crumb Crust (page 116)	1
6 cups	yogurt	1.5 L
³/₄ cup	honey	180 mL
¹/₄ cup	candied citrus peel, chopped	60 mL
	peel of 1 lemon, grated	
¹/₂ cup	pine nuts	125 mL
1	egg	1
2	egg yolks	2

Make up and chill the crust. Line two bowls with disposable cloth and measure 3 cups (750 mL) yogurt into each. Tie up bags to drip for 1 hour. Discard liquid whey (unless you want to use it to make bread), and empty both bags of drained yogurt into one bowl. Add honey, peel and pine nuts. Beat together egg and egg yolks and add them, beating well. Pour into crumb crust and bake at 300°F (150°C). Cool before serving.

6–8 servings

Raspberry Melba Sauce

Serve with pudding, custard or ice cream.

1 Tbsp.	cornstarch	15 mL
1 cup	raspery juice	250 mL
¹/₂ cup	red currant jelly	125 mL

Mix cornstarch with raspery juice, then mix with jelly in a small pan. Heat slowly, stirring, until the jelly dissolves and the cornstarch thickens.

1¹/₂ cups (375 mL)

Chocolate Fudge Sauce

Excellent on ice cream, this is also very good on cakes.

3 Tbsp.	butter	45 mL
5 Tbsp.	unsweetened cocoa	75 mL
1/2 cup	boiling water	125 mL
1 cup	sugar	250 mL

Heat butter and cocoa in a small pan over low heat. Add water and sugar, bring to a full rolling boil, and cook for 5 to 7 minutes, or to 230°F (110°C) using a candy thermometer. Cool.

1 cup (250 mL)

Vanilla Sauce

Serve with a plain cake or chocolate pudding.

1 cup	milk	250 mL
1/4 cup	honey	60 mL
1 Tbsp.	cornstarch	15 mL
2 tsp.	vanilla extract	10 mL

Heat together milk, honey and cornstarch in a small pan, stirring until mixture thickens. Cool, then add vanilla.

1 cup (250 mL)

Lemon Custard Sauce

This is a thick, lemony sauce, good with plain cake or gingerbread. It will keep well, like an icing, up to three days.

1 cup	water	250 mL
1/2 cup	sugar	125 mL
3 Tbsp.	cornstarch	45 mL
1	lemon peel	1
4 Tbsp.	lemon juice	60 mL
2	egg yolks	2
pinch	salt	pinch

Mix water, sugar, and cornstarch in top of a double boiler over boiling water. Wash and dry lemon before grating peel into the mixture. Squeeze, strain and measure in the juice; if there's not enough, add bottled lemon juice. When the mixture is good and hot, pour a little into beaten egg yolks, then return all to the pot and mix continually for a minute or two. Add salt, stir well, and remove from heat.

1¼ cups (300 mL)

Maple Syrup Sauce

1 cup	water	250 mL
4 cups	brown sugar	1 L
1 cup	dark maple syrup	250 mL

Heat water, sugar and maple syrup. When the sugar dissolves, cool and bottle.

3²/3 cups (825 mL)

MAKING ICE CREAM

Real ice cream tastes much more delicious than commercial products, which seldom contain any fresh flavors such as those of fruits, milk, cream and eggs. Edible oil products, chemical emulsifiers, artificial flavorings and colorings are not things that we would put in our own ice cream, if we had a choice. We still do have choices, and in celebration of them we all deserve a dish of real ice cream, once in a while. There are a full range of churns available, from the Victorian hand-crank machine to the new electric ice cream makers which can be filled, plugged in, stuck in the freezer and left to make dessert automatically; the electric wire flattens to allow the freezer to shut, and freeze the ice cream mixture as the churn slowly turns.

ABOUT CUSTARD

"Custard" in ice cream, is a mixture of hot milk and sweetening thickened slightly with egg yolks. The yolks bind the solids and liquids together, so they don't separate as the ice cream softens on the plate or in the cone.

Until you are familiar with the process, it is best to make custards in top of a double boiler, over (not in) boiling water. Heat milk and sugar or honey first, then add beaten egg yolks or (as is sometimes the case) beaten whole eggs. To insure that the egg yolks don't harden and become granular when suddenly introduced to the hot liquid, pour a little of the hot liquid into them first, mix well, then return this mixture to the pot, mixing steadily during and after the procedure. Cook custard over boiling water for 10 minutes, stirring from time to time. This procedure can be accomplished over low direct heat, taking less time, but needing more stirring.

If you're out of eggs, the mixture can be thickened with a little custard powder, even instant pudding. These are generally pre-sweetened, so you can leave out the sugar.

CHURN-FREEZING

The first stage of ice cream making, the mixing of ingredients, takes place hours or even a day in advance, so that the mixture can be well chilled after cooking.

The second stage is the loading and churning. If you have an old-fashioned hand crank or electric crank machine, here's what you do:

First, fill the churn or inner container with the ice cream mixture. It should never be more than ²/₃ full, as the mixture will expand by a third. Adjust churn, dasher and lid before packing ice and salt in the outer compartment. You will either need 3 bags of ice cubes, for this purpose, or a couple of gallons of frozen water, crushed in a sack with a hammer or baseball bat. Any salt will do. Layer ice about 6 in. (15 cm) deep, then spread a handful of salt; continue to top.

Second, churn the ice cream steadily, not rapidly, for about 20 minutes. This is a long time for one person. Four or five is better. Add more salt and ice as needed.

When the ice cream begins to get thick, churn a little more rapidly. Don't give up until it's impossible.

Third, remove dasher, replace lid, and cover churn with wet towels and ice. Allow to sit and harden for 30 minutes.

Creamy Vanilla Ice Cream

Most ice cream flavors are a variation of vanilla, so this is a really basic recipe. It is, in fact, such a good recipe that I find it is the most frequently asked for flavor among the neighborhood children for each of whom, traditionally, I make a birthday batch. Try it with Chocolate Fudge Sauce (page 121) or Raspberry Melba Sauce (page 120).

2 cups	whole milk	475 mL
4 cups	white sugar *or*	1 L
1 cup	honey	250 mL
4	whole eggs	4
pinch	salt	pinch
1 Tbsp.	pure vanilla extract	15 mL
3 cups	light cream	725 mL
1 cup	whipping cream	250 mL

Mix 2 cups (475 mL) milk and sugar in the top of a double boiler and heat over boiling water. Meanwhile, beat eggs and salt in a mixing bowl. When milk mixture is hot, pour a little of it into the eggs, stirring constantly. Return this mixture to the remaining mixture in the pan, stirring as you do. Cook this about 10 minutes, stirring occasionally, but remove from heat as soon as it thickens. Cool and chill for several hours, or overnight.

When you are ready to make ice cream, add vanilla, remaining milk, and creams.

4 qt. (4 L)

VARIATIONS

CHOCOLATE ICE CREAM

3 Tbsp.	butter	45 mL
½ cup	unsweetened cocoa powder	125 mL
½ cup	white sugar	125 mL

Melt and mix these together in the top of a double boiler. Proceed with Creamy Vanilla Ice Cream pouring milk and sugar directly into the melted chocolate. You need not add vanilla at the end, and in chocolate ice cream you may use evaporated milk rather than cream.

STRAWBERRY OR PEACH ICE CREAM

1 cup	strawberry or peach purée	250 mL
2 Tbsp.	lemon juice	30 mL
1 tsp.	pure vanilla extract	15 mL

Follow directions for Creamy Vanilla Ice Cream but substitute fruit purée for an equal amount of milk in the second part of the recipe, just before churning. Also substitute lemon juice and vanilla for the vanilla in the original recipe.

Orange Sherbet

This sherbet looks and tastes creamy, but contains neither milk nor cream — just fruit juice, gelatin and egg whites. Smooth and delicious, it's the perfect end to a summer day.

1 Tbsp.	gelatin	15 mL
1/4 cup	cold water	60 mL
1 cup	sugar	250 mL
1 1/3 cup	water	330 mL
1	lemon	1
1	orange	1
	lemon and orange juice	
3	egg whites	3

Soak gelatin in the small amount of water. In a small pan, heat sugar and the larger amount of water. Add gelatin mixture, stir, and cool. Wash the lemon and orange thoroughly, then grate their skins into the mixture. Squeeze the juice from the lemon into a measuring cup, and add bottled or fresh lemon juice to make 1/2 cup (125 mL). Add to mixture.

Squeeze the juice from the orange into a measuring cup and add orange juice to make 2 cups (475 mL). Add to mixture. Chill until ready to churn. Just before churning, beat egg whites until stiff but not dry. Pour mixture into churn, and churn-freeze.

2 qt. (2 L)

Strawberry Popsicles

These are just straight strawberries, frozen solid in a popsicle shape. Kids love them. No sugar, no food coloring, no artificial anything!

In strawberry season, wash and pick over fresh strawberries. Freeze in bags or plastic containers. A day or two before serving, remove from freezer and thaw slightly. Place strawberries in a blender and blend at low-speed intervals until they are a solid mush. Fill popsicle containers, insert sticks, and re-freeze for at least 6 hours.

Raspberry Sherbet

8 cups	fresh or frozen raspberries	2 L
2 cups	white sugar	475 mL
3 cups	water	725 mL
1/4 cup	lemon juice	60 mL
3	egg whites	3
1 cup	whipping cream	250 mL

Mix raspberries, sugar and water in a saucepan and bring to the boil. Cook for 5 minutes. Cool and add lemon juice. Chill thoroughly. Just before churning, beat egg whites until stiff but not dry. Add them to mixture. Then beat whipping cream until fully expanded and add it to the mixture in the churn. Churn-freeze.

3 qt. (3 L)

Orange Cream Popsicles

2 cups	yogurt	475 mL
6 Tbsp.	orange juice concentrate	90 mL
1 tsp.	vanilla	5 mL

Mix yogurt, partly thawed orange concentrate and vanilla with a blender or rotary beater. Pour into popsicle molds and freeze for 1 hour. Insert sticks when partly frozen. Complete freezing for 2 hours or more. Remove from molds by dipping in a little hot water. Serve at once.

6–8 popsicles

Country Baking

Some of my earliest memories are of my father or mother making bread. Homemade bread leans more to ritual than recipe. First of all, there's the moment when you realize you're almost out, and plan a day to make the next batch. Then there's the mixing, deciding which goodies will go in this time: Shall we make raisin bread? Is there a little wheat germ around? How about one loaf mixed with thyme and garlic?

Then the kneading. My mother used to put a big enameled baby bathtub with dough in it on the kitchen floor and let us pound and fold it with clean hands as long as we liked. Finally, the whole house was transformed by the smell of baking bread, and anyone in it suddenly found some good excuse to hang around the kitchen, waiting for a "test" slice. The big loaves cooling on clean cloths are a lovely sight, and when a neighbor stops by, you give one loaf away because how can you not? It's such a luxury to have fresh bread — you feel so rich, yet have spent so little.

I have continued to feel this way not only about baking bread, but also the making of cakes and cookies, biscuits and muffins, pies and squares. Country cooks often do their baking all on one day of the week, which is very much more efficient than going at it piecemeal, when you consider cleanup time. It's a nice way to share time with a friend, large or small.

This is a collection of recipes which satisfies a wide variety of purposes. Some are for holidays, birthdays, and special occasions. Others are for the more frequent purpose of providing wholesome snacking food. Everybody has their favorites among them.

MAKING BREAD

STARTING THE YEAST

Unlike baking soda or powder, baker's yeast is a living organism, and care must be taken to handle it properly. Never subject it to too much heat. The right temperature for maximum yeast growth is about 80°-95°F (27°-35°C) so yeast is started in this temperature range. Later, when flour and other ingredients have been added, the yeast dough is raised at the slightly lower temperature range of 75°-85°F (24°-30°C).

Yeast can be bought in small packets, containing 1 Tbsp. (15 mL) each. It is also available in loose form, from health food stores, or in moist block form. There is not a great deal of difference between them, except that the moist form is kept refrigerated until used.

Before you start a bread recipe, always mix up the yeast, a little tepid water, and a little sweetening. Within 5 to 10 minutes, the mixture should begin to bubble and swell, which is a sign that the yeast is dividing and multiplying. If it doesn't do this, you should consider the yeast dead, and not bother to try and make bread with it.

MIXING THE LIQUIDS

For every loaf of bread you need about 1½ cups (375 mL) of liquid. Most breads also include some fat or oil, sweetening, and salt; some include eggs, milk, or other in-gredients for flavor, texture, or nutrition. All this gets mixed into the liquid, along with the yeast mixture, before the flour is added. If the fat is in solid form it may be melted, but be careful not to kill the yeast when pouring it into the mixture.

WHOLE WHEAT BREAD SPONGE

When making whole wheat bread, it is especially important to soften the gluten in the flour enough to make it elastic, so that when the yeast begins to release carbon dioxide, small bubbles like little balloons will form in the dough. The best way to insure this process is to mix up all the wet ingredients with only ⅔ of the whole wheat flour and let it sit and rise, covered, for the first hour in a "sponge" form. As you beat down the sponge, you will notice its gluey quality; the dough follows the spoon in long wet strands.

ADDING FLOUR

As you add flour, bread dough becomes drier and firmer. At first you add flour by cupfuls, then by half cups, and then by small handfuls. After each addition it is important to mix in the flour thoroughly, at first by stirring with a wooden spoon, later by folding and kneading the dough on a floured surface.

KNEADING IN FLOUR

Kneading is a method of mixing dough by hand after it is no longer possible to mix it with a spoon. The best working surface is a wooden board, because flour adheres to it, which helps keep the dough from sticking to the surface.

When the dough is soft and wet, it's incredibly sticky. Care must be taken to keep the working surface and your hands lightly floured at all times. Roll, pat, flatten and fold the dough with a delicate touch. Gradually, as the dough incorporates the flour, it becomes stiffer and less sticky. You can work with a firmer touch, pressing and working the floury dough. The amount of flour which is actually used in any given recipe varies from one batch of bread to the next, because of variations in humidity and the moisture content of the flour. The way you know that you have added enough flour is that instead of sticking to your hands, the dough begins to "clean" your hands.

KNEADING A LITTLE EXTRA

The difference between dry, crumbly bread and smooth, fine textured bread is often the amount of kneading done after the final addition of flour. After you make bread a few times, you will gradually become aware of what a well-kneaded dough feels like: smooth and elastic and a little warm. Until you do, make a practice of kneading the dough for 10 minutes after you stop adding flour. Keep the kneading surface very lightly floured as necessary.

LETTING THE DOUGH RISE

Set the dough to rise in a container which is at least twice the size of the dough, because it will double in size. Keep the dough moderately warm, at 75°-85°F (24°–30°C). One way to do this is to rinse a heavy ceramic bowl in hot water before placing dough in it. Cover the container with a damp, smooth dish towel to keep a crust from forming on top (this is particularly important when making white flour breads).

Bread dough should double in size in one hour, unless it is a sourdough or rye bread, which takes a little longer. Wheat flour dough which doesn't rise at all is usually cold. To get it working again, place it in a warm bowl and reshape the dough every 15 minutes. Also be careful that your warm place is not too warm: the shelf above a wood stove, for example, is too hot.

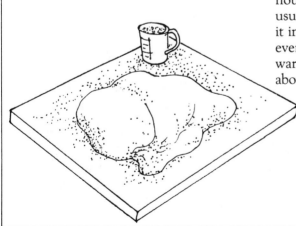

SHAPING LOAVES

It is best to bake no more than three loaves at a time in an ordinary oven. First, grease or oil the pans carefully. Turn all the dough on to a lightly floured surface and knead it a little. Cut, rather than tear off· pieces to be made into loaves. No matter how large or small your bread pans, the dough should fill it no more than three-quarters full. Flatten each piece, fold, and flatten again. Do this about four times per loaf, before you press and pinch the bottom edges together. Pop it in the pan, seam-side down.

RISING BEFORE BAKING

Once you set the loaves to rise, pay attention to the clock and the oven. White flour breads take about 20 minutes to rise, whole wheat flour breads take 30 to 40 minutes, and sourdough or rye breads take longer, depending on the recipe. The oven should be preheated (see below). Loaves should go in the oven *before* they are fully expanded, because they will expand further in the first 10 minutes of baking. Loaves that go in the oven too late come out full of holes and slice poorly.

BAKING

It's a good idea to set the oven 50°F (25°C) above the temperature you're going to bake at, when preheating the oven during the last rising of loaves, because the introduction of the loaves will cool the oven down rapidly when the bread first goes in. As soon as it's in, however, turn it down to the correct temperature, and bake for the required length of time.

Fresh bread smells heavenly, but before you take it out, make sure it's done. Tap the top lightly: it should sound hollow and have a crisp surface. (If baking in a wood stove, tap the bottom, instead of the top, to make sure it's done)

COOLING

As soon as your bread is baked, remove it from the pan to "breathe" or release moisture as it cools. If cooled in the pan, bread will be soggy on the bottom. You may place it on a fine mesh rack or a clean dish towel, on its side. A loaf takes about two hours to cool completely, before you can store it in plastic or in tin.

STORAGE

In a cool, dry place, most bread will keep for about a week. French bread, which has no fat in it, becomes stale in 24 hours, but dark rye, on the other hand, will sometimes keep up to two weeks. Bread with a slight mold on it is not toxic and if you remove the mold it may be used. For long storage, freezing is recommended.

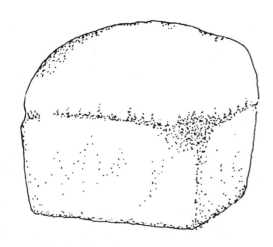

Dissolve yeast in a bowl with ½ cup (125 mL) warm water and 1 Tbsp. (15 mL) molasses until foamy, about 10 minutes. Mix milk, 4 cups (1 L) water, oil, remaining molasses, salt and yeast in a large ceramic bowl. Add 6 cups (1.5 L) whole wheat flour and beat thoroughly with a wooden spoon. Set the bowl in a warm spot, covered, to double its size in about an hour.

Beat down the sponge thoroughly, and add 7 cups (1.75 L) whole wheat flour, one cup at a time, beating well after each addition. At some point in this procedure it becomes impossible to mix the dough any longer with a spoon. Sprinkle flour on a work surface, and scrape the dough out of the bowl. Sprinkle it over with flour, patting and folding until it becomes workable. Knead in the remaining flour very gradually, and knead for 15 to 20 minutes. Cover and let rise for 1 hour, in a warm place. Divide the dough into three equal parts, and grease three loaf pans. Shape loaves and place them in pans seam-side down. Cover and allow to rise for 30 minutes. Meanwhile preheat oven to 400°F (200°C). Put loaves in the oven and reduce heat to 350°F (175°C). Bake for 40 minutes, or until the top sounds hollow when tapped. Remove loaves from their pans and cool 2 hours before storing.

3 loaves

Hovis Whole Wheat Bread

This is very much like the British Hovis Bread, which they started making during the war for nutritional reasons, and continued afterwards because it is so delicious. A firm bread, easily sliced, it's very good toasted or used for sandwiches.

2 Tbsp.	dried baker's yeast	30 mL
4½ cups	warm water	1.125 L
1 Tbsp.	molasses	15 mL
2 cups	milk	475 mL
½ cup	vegetable oil	125 mL
½ cup	molasses	125 mL
1 Tbsp.	salt	15 mL
13 cups	whole wheat flour	3 L
3 cups	unbleached white flour	725 mL

Big Baddeck Brown

For those who like a tender, unsweet rye bread.

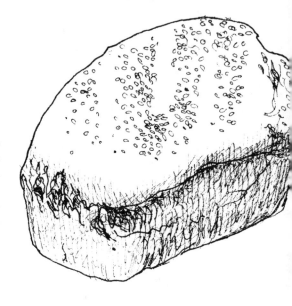

5 cups	warm water	1.2 L
1 Tbsp.	baker's yeast	15 mL
½ cup	blackstrap molasses	125 mL
¼ cup	vegetable oil	60 mL
1 Tbsp.	salt	15 mL
1	egg	1
2 Tbsp.	caraway seeds	30 mL
6 cups	unbleached white flour	1.5 L
7–8 cups	dark rye flour	1.75–2 L

Mix together water, yeast and molasses in a large ceramic bowl. Let sit and dissolve for 10 minutes, or until foamy. Then add and beat in oil, salt, egg and caraway seeds. Add white flour and beat well. Cover and let rise for 1 hour, or until doubled in size, in a warm place. Add rye flour by cupfuls, beating well after each addition. When it is no longer possible to mix the dough with a spoon, turn it out on a lightly floured board and knead in more rye flour gradually, stopping before the dough becomes too stiff to be pliable. Rye dough is a little more sticky, when finished, than white or whole wheat dough. Return to the bowl, cover and let rise for 1 hour or until doubled. Turn out on to floured surface and cut into 4 equal pieces. Grease 4 pans and shape loaves; let rise for 30 minutes. Preheat oven, meanwhile, to 350°F (175°C). Bake 45 minutes or until browned on top and crisp on the bottom.

4 loaves

Anadama Bread

As the story goes, this fellow had a wife named Anna who used to bake his bread. One time she up and left him, so he had to bake his own. "Anna, damn her," he said bitterly, as he threw everything in his dough except the kitchen sink.

2 Tbsp.	baker's yeast	30 mL
3½ cups	warm water	850 mL
1 cup	cornmeal	250 mL
2 tsp.	salt	10 mL
½ cup	vegetable oil	125 mL
⅔ cup	molasses	160 mL
2	eggs	2
½ cup	wheat germ	125 mL
½ cup	instant skim milk powder	125 mL
1 cup	soy flour	250 mL
4–5 cups	whole wheat flour	1–1.25 L

Mix yeast and ½ cup (125 mL) warm water; set aside. Meanwhile, bring remaining 3 cups (725 mL) water to the boil in a small saucepan. Sprinkle in cornmeal and salt, stirring constantly. Cook and stir over medium heat as cornmeal thickens. Remove from heat and add oil and molasses. Pour into a large ceramic bowl. Let mixture cool. When it is lukewarm, add foaming yeast. Stir well, then add eggs, wheat germ, skim milk powder, and soy flour. Add whole wheat flour a cup at a time, beating well after each addition. When you can no longer beat it, turn dough out on a lightly floured surface and knead, adding flour gradually until it is no longer sticky. Put dough in ceramic bowl, cover, put in a warm place and let it rise for 1 hour or until doubled. Turn out, reshape, return to bowl and re-cover; let rise a second time. Punch down, turn out and cut into three pieces. Shape loaves and place in 3 well-greased loaf pans and let rise 1 hour, or until almost (but not quite) doubled. Preheat oven, meanwhile, to 375°F (190°C). Bake 40 to 45 minutes, or until crusty all over.

3 loaves

Herb Bread

This bread has the most incredible aroma when it's baking. It makes a great holiday gift.

| ¼ cup | molasses | 60 mL |
| 1 Tbsp. | dried baker's yeast | 15 mL |

3 cups	warm water	725 mL
2 tsp.	thyme	10 mL
1	egg	1
½ cup	instant skim milk powder	125 mL
1 Tbsp.	salt	15 mL
¼ cup	dark sesame oil	60 mL
½ cup	soy flour	125 mL
6–7 cups	whole wheat flour	1.5–1.75 L
1	onion, chopped	1
2	cloves garlic, crushed	2
2 Tbsp.	fresh parsley, chopped	30 mL
1 Tbsp.	fresh chives, chopped	15 mL

Mix molasses, yeast, and 1 cup of the water; set aside 10 minutes or until foamy. In a large ceramic bowl, beat together yeast, remaining water, thyme, egg, milk powder, salt, 2 Tbsp. (30 mL) oil, soy flour, and 3 cups (725 mL) whole wheat flour.

Add remaining flour by cupfuls, beating well after each addition, until dough cannot be mixed with a spoon. Turn out on a smooth, floured surface and knead in flour until dough isn't sticky anymore. Put it back in the bowl, cover, and set in a warm place to rise. Meanwhile, heat remaining oil in a skillet and sauté onions and garlic until transparent. Cool and add chopped parsley and chives. When dough has doubled, in about an hour, turn it out on floured surface and roll it out about ½ in. (1 cm) thick, and spread it with onions and herbs. Roll up dough like a jelly roll, and then knead it so that the herbs are well mixed in. Shape into 2 loaves, and put in 2 greased bread pans. Preheat oven to 350°F (175°C) as bread rises in pans. Bake 35 to 45 minutes, or until nicely browned.

2 loaves

Porridge Bread

This is a traditional Cape Breton recipe for a light, moist oat-flavored white bread.

1 cup	rolled oats *or* oat flour	250 mL
2 cups	boiling water	475 mL
1 Tbsp.	baker's yeast	15 mL
1/4 cup	warm water	60 mL
1/2 cup	molasses	125 mL
1 tsp.	salt	5 mL
1 Tbsp.	butter	15 mL
5–6 cups	unbleached white flour	1.25– 1.5 L
1	egg	1

Measure rolled oats or oat flour into a large ceramic bowl, pour on boiling water, cover, and let sit 10 minutes. Meanwhile, mix yeast and warm water in a smaller bowl to sit for 10 minutes. Add molasses, salt, butter and 1 cup flour to oats in large bowl; when the mixture has cooled to lukewarm, add foaming yeast. Add the flour by half cupfuls, beating after each addition, until it is no longer possible to stir the dough with a spoon.

Turn out on a floured surface and knead in flour until the dough is smooth and elastic. Return to bowl, cover, and let rise for 1 hour, or until doubled in size. Turn out on to a floured surface and knead 2 to 3 minutes. Cut into four equal pieces, and shape each into a smooth bun. Grease 2 bread pans and fill each with two buns. Break egg into a small bowl and beat it. Brush tops of each bun with beaten egg.

Preheat oven to 400°F (200°C) while you let the loaves rise for 20 minutes. Bake at 400°F (200°C) for 10 minutes, then reduce heat to 350°F (175°C) and bake for 35 minutes.

2 loaves

Holiday Bread

Eggs help provide the light, dry, tender texture of this European holiday bread.

4	eggs	4
	warm water	
1 Tbsp.	dried baker's yeast	15 mL
1 cup	honey	250 mL
1 cup	instant skim milk powder	250 mL
1/2 tsp.	cardamom	2 mL
1/4 cup	vegetable oil	60 mL
2 tsp.	salt	10 mL
2 cups	whole wheat flour	475 mL
2–3 cups	unbleached white flour	475–725 mL

Beat eggs together in a large ceramic bowl, then pour them into a measuring cup. Add warm water to make, in all, 2 cups (475 mL) liquid. Return it to the bowl and add yeast and honey. Beat well. Let sit 10 minutes, or until foamy. Then add milk powder, cardamom, oil, salt and whole wheat flour. Beat well. Add white flour by half cupfuls until you can no longer mix with a spoon. Turn out on to a floured surface and knead the flour in, as needed, to make a smooth, glossy dough. Put it in the ceramic bowl, cover, and place in a warm place for 1 hour or until doubled. Punch down. Allow to rise again 1 hour.

When the dough has risen a second time, shape into 2 loaves. Place in greased pans to rise 30 minutes. Preheat oven 400°F (200°C). Bake at 350°F (175°C) 30 to 40 minutes.

2 loaves

VARIATION

BRAIDED HOLIDAY BREAD

This is a marvelous treat to present to guests on a holiday morning.

Holiday Bread

1 cup	currants *or* raisins	250 mL
1 cup	walnut pieces	250 mL
½ cup	citron pieces (optional)	125 mL

ICING

1 cup	icing sugar	250 mL
4 Tbsp.	water	60 mL
½ tsp.	almond flavoring	2 mL

Follow instructions for Holiday Bread, but after the dough has risen for the second time, knead in currants, walnut pieces and citron.

Divide dough into 3 equal pieces. Knead each into a firm bun and let sit for 5 to 10 minutes on a floured surface. Flatten one piece into an oval the size of your hand. Fold it over and seal firmly. Roll it gently into a tube shape. To roll it out into a strip, place both hands lightly in the middle of the dough and roll back and forth, gradually moving your hands out towards the ends. Work slowly, repeating the process as often as needed (with repairs around raisins), until the strand is about 2 ft. (60 cm) long. Repeat the process with the other two pieces.

Lightly oil a large cookie sheet. Braid the three strands together to make a wreath-shaped loaf. To seal the wreath, tuck and pinch ends together. Cover and let rise for 1 hour, or until doubled in size. Place in a preheated 400°F (200°C) oven and reduce heat at once to 350°F (175°C). Bake for 35 to 45 minutes or until golden brown.

Combine ingredients for icing, and decorate loaf when it has cooled down. You may sprinkle on top: walnut or almond pieces, citron or cherries.

If you prefer not to ice your bread you may glaze it, before baking, with a beaten egg, and sprinkle ground nuts on top. This gives the ring a very nice appearance without the sugary icing.

1 braided loaf

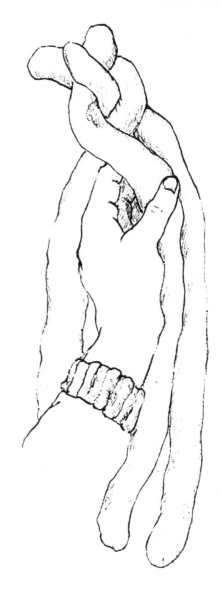

IF YOUR BREAD ISN'T ALL YOU EXPECTED

IF YOUR BREAD IS TOO HEAVY AND DENSE, one possibility is that your yeast didn't work vigorously enough. Always test yeast first by mixing it with warm (never hot) water and sweetening; it should bubble and rise within 10 minutes. Keep dough warm throughout breadmaking so the yeast will continue to work.

Another possible cause of heavy bread is adding flour too fast, without sufficient kneading. The dough should always be pliable, never stiff and unworkable.

Finally, it may be that you like a bread with more white flour in it. Always use unbleached flour, which is not only better for you, but also makes lighter bread.

IF YOUR BREAD SAGS IN THE MIDDLE, you could be letting it rise in the pan too long, or you could be adding too little flour.

IF YOUR BREAD TASTES YEASTY, the oven is at too low a temperature.

IF YOUR BREAD HAS A BIG HOLE IN THE MIDDLE, you let it rise too long before putting it in the oven. It should go in when it's around ⅔ of the way up to where you want it.

IF YOUR BREAD IS TOO DRY AND CRUMBLY, switch to unbleached white flour, or try adding some whole grain flours. Use vegetable oil rather than shortening; honey or molasses rather than sugar. Make sure you knead it enough.

IF BREAD BURNS BEFORE BAKING THROUGH, likely your oven is at fault, not the bread. The temperature should be high when the bread goes in, and then can drop a little for the rest of the baking. The other possibility is that you're adding too many strange ingredients for the amount of yeast and wheat flour.

IF YOUR CRUST ISN'T CRISP ENOUGH, the way to get a thick, crunchy crust is to permeate the crust with water and then bake it out, at a high temperature. Try brushing water on the crust in the last 15 minutes of baking, or you may put a pan of boiling water in the oven before baking the bread.

Shaped

Risen

Baked

ABOUT SOURDOUGH

Sourdough is made with the same yeast we buy, baker's yeast, to make other breads with. The difference is that the yeast remains in the flour and water mixture at the right temperature for a much longer time. It eats up not just some, but all of the sugar in the flour. It creates a great deal of carbon dioxide, and, finally, running out of air and food, it dies — not, however, without leaving some seeds behind, dormant, just in case conditions should ever happen to improve. The reason it is called sourdough is that in eating up every last iota of sweetness, it makes the flour sour-tasting.

Sourdough is, according to most cookbooks, supposed to be kept in a sealed, sterile container, in a cool, dark place, and renewed once a week or so. However, I have heard stories of trappers who came upon deserted cabins and scraped the inside of the old sourdough crock back of the rusty stove and used the scrapings to get bread going.

Sourdough Starter

1½ cups	boiling water	375 mL
½ Tbsp.	dried baker's yeast	8 mL
1 cup	rye flour	250 mL

Pour boiling water into a clean container and allow to cool to room temperature, about 75–85°F (25–30°C). Add yeast and flour. Cover container and set in a warm place where it will rise, or bubble up, and fall back, in about 24 hours. When it stops working, store it in a cool place, labelled with the date.

Sourdough Bread

The night before you make sourdough bread, the culture must be renewed — that is, warmed up and fed something, to wake up the yeast.

1 cup	Sourdough Starter	250 mL
4 cups	warm water	1 L
½ cup	vegetable oil	125 mL
1 Tbsp.	salt	15 mL
4½ cups	rye flour	1.125 L
5 cups	whole wheat flour	1.5 mL

To renew starter, mix in a ceramic bowl the Sourdough Starter, warm water and rye flour. The mixture should only half-fill the bowl. Cover with a damp cloth and leave, in a warm place, to rise overnight.

In the morning, take out a cupful of the batter and refrigerate in a clean container. This is Sourdough Starter for a future batch of bread.

To the remainder of starter in bowl, add the oil and salt and, by half-cupfuls, the flour, beating after each addition. When the dough is too stiff to beat, turn it out onto a well-floured surface and knead, adding flour as necessary. Dough will be damper than usual in bread dough, but stop adding flour before it gets too stiff to work. Shape into 2 loaves and place in 2 greased pans. Allow loaves to rise in a warm place for 2 to 4 hours. It should rise only very slightly above the tops of the pans.

Preheat oven to 400°F (200°C). When you put in bread, turn oven to 375°F (190°C). Bake 1¼ to 1½ hours. For a crisp crust, brush with water in the last 15 minutes of baking.

2 loaves

Black Bread

This recipe, must be started the night before you bake.

1/2 cup	Sourdough Starter	125 mL
2 cups	warm water	475 mL
7 cups	whole wheat flour	1.7 L
1 cup	cooked, cold cornmeal	250 mL
3 Tbsp.	vegetable oil	45 mL
2 tsp.	salt	10 mL
1 Tbsp.	lecithin	15 mL
1	egg, beaten	1
2 Tbsp.	blackstrap molasses	30 mL
2 Tbsp.	unsweetened cocoa	30 mL
2 Tbsp.	caraway seeds (optional)	30 mL
4 cups	dark rye flour	1 L

To renew starter, mix Sourdough Starter, water and 2 cups (475 mL) whole wheat flour in a ceramic bowl. Cover and let stand overnight at room temperature.

Next morning, take out 1/2 cup (125 mL) of mixture, to keep as future starter. To the remainder, add cornmeal, oil, salt, lecithin, the beaten egg, molasses, cocoa, 1 cup (250 mL) whole wheat flour and caraway seeds. Beat well. Cover and let rise in a warm place for 1 hour. Then beat in the remaining 4 cups (1 L) whole wheat flour and the dark rye flour. When it is no longer possible to mix it with a spoon, turn out on a lightly floured surface and knead flour in gradually. The finished dough will be a little more dense and sticky than ordinary bread dough. Return to bowl, cover, and let rise for 2 hours.

Grease 2 bread pans, shape loaves, and let dough rise for about 2 hours, or until doubled. Preheat oven to 325°F (160°C) and bake for 1½ hours.

2 loaves

Summer Bread

The great virtue of this bread is that it can be cooked very quickly in a low oven, ideal for summer baking.

1½ Tbsp.	dried baker's yeast	25 mL
2 cups	warm water	475 mL
2	eggs	2
3 Tbsp.	molasses	45 mL
1 Tbsp.	salt	15 mL
1/4 cup	vegetable oil	60 mL
1/2 cup	instant skim milk powder	125 mL
3 cups	whole wheat flour	725 mL
2–3 cups	unbleached white flour	475–725 mL
1	egg yolk	1
1/2 cup	sesame seeds	125 mL

Mix yeast and 1/2 cup (100 mL) warm water; let stand 10 minutes. Mix in a wide ceramic bowl: yeast, eggs, the rest of the water, molasses, salt, oil, dried milk, and whole wheat flour. Cover and set in a warm place for 1 hour, or until doubled in size. Add white flour by half cups. When the dough becomes too stiff to stir, turn out on a floured surface and knead in flour until dough is no longer sticky but still workable. Grease 2 cookie trays. Cut dough into 6 pieces. Shape each into a bun, then flatten by hand to 1/2 in. (1 cm) thickness. Place on cookie sheet, coat tops thinly with egg yolk, and sprinkle with sesame seeds. Allow to rise 20 minutes while you preheat oven to 325°F (160°C). Bake 30 minutes or until browned.

6 loaves

English Muffins

For years I tried to duplicate commercial English muffins, thinking nothing else would do. Then one summer during a heat wave I was mixing up a batch of bread dough, and I thought, why not? So I rolled it out, cut a few circles, let them rise, and baked them in a skillet on top of the stove — which is, no doubt, how English muffins first got their start in the world.

3	eggs	3
	warm water	
1 Tbsp.	dried baker's yeast	15 mL
1 cup	instant skim milk powder	250 mL
1/3 cup	honey *or* sugar	80 mL
1 1/2 tsp.	salt	7 mL
2 Tbsp.	vegetable oil	30 mL
2 cups	whole wheat flour	475 mL
1–2 cups	unbleached white flour	250–475 mL
1/4 cup	cornmeal	60 mL

Break eggs into a 2 cup (475 mL) measure; fill the rest of the measure with warm water. Pour into a heavy ceramic bowl and add yeast. Beat well and let stand 10 minutes. Then add milk powder, sweetening, salt, oil, and whole wheat flour. Beat well. Cover and let stand in a warm place for 1 hour. Work in white flour by half cups until dough is too stiff to stir. Turn out on a floured surface and knead in flour as needed to make a smooth, elastic dough. Roll out dough 1/2 in. (1 cm) thick and cut with a round cookie cutter or a cutter made by cutting top and bottom from a 3–4 in. (8–10 cm) can. Sprinkle a heavy skillet with cornmeal, and cover with as many muffins as will fit. Allow them to rise until doubled, about 30 minutes. Cover pan; place over very low heat and bake 10 to 15 minutes per side. If using the same pan for successive batches, cool the pan in between, in cold water.

24 muffins

Farmhouse Sticky Rolls

These rolls may be made with Hovis or Porridge Bread, but Holiday Bread is best. You'll need the equivalent of 1 loaf of bread dough, or 1 1/2 lb. (675 g).

1/2 batch	Holiday Bread	1/2 batch
1/2 cup	honey *or* brown sugar	125 mL
1 tsp.	cinnamon	5 mL
1/2 tsp.	allspice	2 mL
1/4 cup	melted butter	60 mL
1/4 cup	currants *or* raisins	60 mL
3 Tbsp.	walnuts *or* pecans, chopped	45 mL

Roll out dough on a floured surface with a rolling pin to 1/2 in. (1 cm) thickness. Mix honey or brown sugar, cinnamon and allspice with melted butter, and spread mixture evenly on the dough. Sprinkle evenly with currants and nuts. Roll up tightly like a jelly roll and cut into 9 pieces. Butter a 7 x 7 in. (18 x 18 cm) pan and place rolls on end. Allow to rise 30 minutes or until doubled. Bake at 400°F (200°C) for 20 minutes. Brush with butter as they come out of the oven.

9 rolls

Bagels

1 Tbsp.	dried baker's yeast	15 mL
1 Tbsp.	white sugar *or* honey	15 mL
1½ cups	warm water	375 mL
1½ tsp.	salt	7 mL
1½ cups	white flour	375 mL
2 cups	whole wheat flour	475 mL
1 gal.	boiling water	4 L

Mix yeast, sugar and warm water in a mixing bowl and let sit for 10 minutes, or until bubbly. Add salt and white flour and mix thoroughly. Add whole wheat flour gradually; turn out on a floured surface when necessary to knead in flour. Add only as much flour as needed to make a smooth, pliable dough. Cover and let rise in a warm place for 1 hour. Bring water to the boil. Meanwhile, turn out the dough and knead it briefly. Flatten and cut it into 25 pieces, each about the size of a small egg. Roll out each one with slightly damp hands into a tube about the thickness of your finger and 5 in. (12 cm) long. Pinch ends together. Dip each for 5 seconds in the boiling water, then place on an oiled cookie sheet to rise for 20 minutes. While they are rising, preheat oven to 400°F (200°C). Bake for 20 minutes or until golden brown. Cool before storing.

25 bagels

Buttermilk Biscuits

These are the light, flakey biscuits that everybody loves. The secret is the combination of buttermilk and soda.

1¾ cups	unbleached white flour	430 mL
½ tsp.	salt	2 mL
1 tsp.	baking soda	5 mL
5 Tbsp.	cold butter	75 mL
¾ cup	cold buttermilk	180 mL

Preheat oven to 450°F (230°C). Sift together flour, salt, and soda. Cut in butter with a fork, then stir in buttermilk. Knead lightly on a floured surface, into a rough ball. Roll out ½ in. (1 cm) thick with a floured rolling pin. Cut into biscuits. Bake at 450°F (230°C) for 10 minutes.

14 biscuits

Singing Hinnies

A Scottish scone, studded with currants. Hot from the oven, who can refuse them? To soften currants, soak overnight in water.

2½ cups	unbleached white flour	600 mL
2 Tbsp.	sugar	30 mL
2 tsp.	baking powder	10 mL
½ tsp.	salt	2 mL
⅓ cup	cold butter	80 mL
1	egg	1
1 cup	buttermilk	250 mL
1 cup	currants, softened	250 mL

Preheat oven to 375°F (190°C). Sift together flour, sugar, baking powder and salt. Cut in butter with a fork. In a separate bowl, beat together egg and buttermilk. Add currants and mix into dry ingredients. Turn out on to a floured surface and knead lightly into an oval. Roll out 1 in. (2 cm) thick. Cut into biscuits. Bake at 425°F (220°C) for 15 minutes, or until golden brown.

20 biscuits

Bannock

This flat, round, slightly sweet cake is known as Shortbread in New England, where it is served with strawberries and cream.

2 cups	unbleached white flour	475 mL
2 cups	whole wheat flour	475 mL
1 tsp.	baking soda	5 mL
1 tsp.	salt	5 mL
½ cup	brown sugar	125 mL
¼ cup	butter	60 mL
¾–1 cup	buttermilk	180–250 mL

Preheat oven to 350°F (175°C). Sift together white and whole wheat flour, baking soda, salt and sugar. Cut in butter with a fork. Add just enough buttermilk to make the batter moist throughout, but not sticky. On a floured surface, work it lightly into a 10 in. (25 cm) cake, using the flat palm of your hand in a kind of rolling motion. Place on a greased cookie sheet and lightly score in 2 in. (5 cm) squares. Bake at 350°F (175°C) for 30 minutes.

5–7 servings

Whole Wheat Honey Scones

Thin and crunchy, these are baked in a cast-iron skillet over very low heat, on a wood stove or the glowing embers of a campfire.

½ cup	water	125 mL
2 Tbsp.	corn oil	30 mL
2 Tbsp.	honey or brown sugar	30 mL
¼ cup	milk powder	60 mL
2 cups	whole wheat flour	475 mL
1 tsp.	baking powder	5 mL
½ tsp.	salt	2 mL

Mix together water, oil, sweetening and milk powder. Add and beat in flour, baking powder and salt. Divide dough into 2 balls. Pat or roll out ½ in. (1 cm) thick; trim off rough edges and cut each into 4 wedges. Prick with fork. Heat a cast-iron skillet, rubbed with a few drops of oil. Bake wedges slowly over low heat, covered, for about 7 minutes; turn, and bake 5 minutes longer, or until browned.

8 scones

Whole Wheat Biscuits

1½ cups	whole wheat flour	350 mL
1½ cups	whole wheat pastry flour *or* unbleached white flour	350 mL
½ tsp.	salt	2 mL
1 tsp.	baking powder	5 mL
½ cup	butter	125 mL
¾ cup	buttermilk	180 mL

Preheat oven to 400°F (200°C). Sift together flours, salt, baking powder. Cut in butter with a fork, until well mixed. Stir buttermilk swiftly into the dough, and knead quickly for a couple minutes on a floured surface. Roll out dough 1 in. (2 cm) thick and cut into biscuits. Bake on an ungreased cookie sheet for 10 minutes.

15 biscuits

Johnny Cake

This corn bread should be baked in a 9 in. (23 cm) square pan or can be used to make a dozen nice muffins.

1 cup	buttermilk	250 mL
3 Tbsp.	vegetable oil	45 mL
2	eggs	2
3 Tbsp.	molasses	45 mL
1 cup	cornmeal	250 mL
1 cup	whole wheat flour	250 mL
1 tsp.	salt	5 mL
2 tsp.	baking powder	10 mL

To make corn bread, preheat oven to 350°F (175°C); for muffins, preheat oven to 400°F (200°C). Beat together buttermilk, oil, eggs and molasses. Add cornmeal, flour, salt and baking powder. Pour into greased pan or muffin tins and bake bread 45 minutes, muffins 20 minutes.

1 loaf or 12 muffins

Oaten Scones

"Baked" on top of the stove, these scones have a delicious nut-like flavor. Thin and crisp, they never last long around our house.

2 cups	oat flour *or* coarsely ground rolled oats	475 mL
½ tsp.	salt	2 mL
2 Tbsp.	butter *or* corn oil	30 mL
2 cups	rolled oats	475 mL
½ cup	hot water	125 mL

Mix oat flour and salt. Cut in butter or oil. Mix in rolled oats, then hot water. Turn out dough on a floured surface and work into 2 balls. Pat or roll out ½ in. (1 cm) thick; cut into 4 wedges, and prick wedges with fork. Heat a cast-iron skillet, rubbed with a few drops of oil. Bake wedges slowly over low heat, covered, for about 5 minutes; turn, and bake 5 minutes longer, or until browned.

8 scones

Blueberry Whole Wheat Muffins

1	egg	1
1¹/₂ cups	milk	375 mL
¹/₄ cup	brown sugar	60 mL
3 Tbsp.	melted butter	45 mL
2 cups	whole wheat flour	475 mL
2 tsp.	baking powder	10 mL
¹/₂ tsp.	salt	2 mL
1 cup	fresh or frozen blueberries	250 mL

Preheat oven to 400°F (200°C). Beat together egg, milk, brown sugar and melted butter in a mixing bowl. Sift in flour, baking powder and salt. Add blueberries and mix briefly. Grease muffin tins and fill each three quarters full. Bake for 20 minutes.

12 muffins

Bran Muffins

1	egg	1
¹/₃ cup	molasses	80 mL
¹/₄ cup	vegetable oil	60 mL
1¹/₂ cups	milk or buttermilk	375 mL
1 cup	whole wheat flour	250 mL
2 tsp.	baking powder	10 mL
¹/₂ tsp.	salt	2 mL
1 cup	bran	250 mL
1 cup	raisins	250 mL

Preheat oven to 375°F (190°C). Beat together egg, molasses, oil, and milk. Beat in flour, baking powder and salt, then add and stir in bran and raisins. Grease muffin tins and fill no more than ²/₃ with batter. Bake 20 minutes. Cool 5 minutes before removing from tin.

14 muffins

Fruit Roly-poly

A very simple cake, almost a shortbread, with fresh berries cooked in a layer inside. Or you can roll it up, as the title suggests.

3 cups	whole wheat pastry flour	725 mL
1 tsp.	baking powder	5 mL
¹/₂ tsp.	salt	2 mL
¹/₄ cup	butter	60 mL
2	eggs	2
¹/₂ cup	buttermilk	125 mL
3 Tbsp.	honey	45 mL

FILLING

3 cups	fresh raspberries or blueberries or apples sprinkled with cinnamon	725 mL
3 Tbsp.	honey	45 mL
3 Tbsp.	butter, cut in small pieces	45 mL

Preheat oven to 400°F (200°C). Sift together flour, baking powder and salt. Cut in butter with fork or pastry cutter, until mixture is crumbly. Make a well in the center and add eggs, buttermilk and honey. Beat the liquid ingredients lightly with a fork, gradually incorporating the dry ingredients to make a stiff dough. Roll out dough into a 10 × 15 in. rectangle (25 × 38 cm). Cover with combined filling ingredients. Fold the dough in half or roll it up like a jelly roll and pinch the edges together well, using water as necessary. Bake until well browned. Serve hot, topped with whipped cream.

Oatmeal Spice Cake

A popular birthday cake, this combines lightness and whole grain ingredients, and is equally good iced and plain. An easy first cake.

2	eggs	2
1/3 cup	vegetable oil	80 mL
2 Tbsp.	molasses	30 mL
1 cup	warm water	250 mL
1 tsp.	baking soda	5 mL
1 cup	whole wheat flour	250 mL
1 cup	unbleached white flour	250 mL
1 cup	brown sugar	250 mL
1 tsp.	cinnamon	5 mL
1/2 tsp.	nutmeg	2 mL
1/2 tsp.	salt	2 mL
1 cup	rolled oats	250 mL

Preheat oven to 350°F (175°C). In a large mixing bowl, beat eggs, then beat in oil and molasses. Mix warm water with soda before adding. Then sift in flours, sugar, cinnamon, nutmeg and salt. Add rolled oats and beat well. Pour into a greased cake pan and bake at 350°F (175°C) for 40 minutes, or until top springs back when lightly pressed. Cool before removing from pan. A good topping is Coconut Butterscotch Topping (page 147).

Aunt Carrie's Carrot Cake

Aunt Carrie gave me this recipe a long time ago, and I have probably changed it a good deal, but it's still a family favorite. More than once I have made it as muffins.

4	eggs	4
3/4 cup	vegetable oil	180 mL
1 cup	brown or white sugar	250 mL
1 cup	whole wheat flour	250 mL
1 cup	unbleached white flour	250 mL
1 tsp.	salt	5 mL
1 tsp.	baking soda	5 mL
2 tsp.	cinnamon	10 mL
1 tsp.	allspice	5 mL
3 cups	carrots, grated	725 mL
1 cup	walnut pieces	250 mL

Preheat oven to 300°F (150°C). In a large mixing bowl, beat eggs, then beat in oil and sugar. Sift in flours, salt, soda and spices together. Then add and mix in carrots and nuts. Grease 2 loaf pans or 1 removable-rim tube pan. Bake for 1½ hours. Cool before removing from pan.

1 cake or 14 muffins

Cottage Cake

This is a simple little cake with a lot of variations. My oldest daughter, Samantha, likes to make it with ¼ cup (60 mL) butter and 3 eggs, which she separates, beating the egg whites and adding them at the end. Good with Lemon Custard Sauce (page 121).

⅓ cup	vegetable oil	80 mL
½ cup	brown sugar	125 mL
1	egg	1
¾ cup	milk	180 mL
1½ cup	whole wheat pastry flour	375 mL
2 tsp.	baking powder	10 mL
½ tsp.	salt	2 mL
½ tsp.	nutmeg	2 mL

Preheat oven to 350°F (175°C). Beat together oil, sugar, egg and milk; then beat in flour, baking powder, salt and nutmeg. Bake in a greased cake pan, 9 in. (23 cm.) square or round. Cool before removing from pan.

VARIATIONS

COFFEE CAKE

⅓ cup	unbleached white flour	80 mL
¼ cup	brown sugar	60 mL
½ tsp.	cinnamon	2 mL
2 Tbsp.	cold butter	30 mL
2 Tbsp.	vegetable oil	30 mL

Mix flour, sugar, and cinnamon, before cutting in butter with a fork. Mix in safflower oil gradually. Sprinkle over cake batter, and bake as above.

UPSIDE-DOWN CAKE

Make Cottage Cake. Grease and flour a 9 in. (23 cm) square or round cake pan, and arrange on it: sliced apples, peaches, or cored pineapple rings. Sprinkle over them:

¼ cup	brown sugar	60 mL
¼ tsp.	cinnamon	1 mL
2 Tbsp.	butter, cut in small pieces	30 mL
½–1 cup	chopped walnuts or pecans (optional)	125–250 mL

Pour cake batter on top and bake.

Banana Coconut Cake

2	eggs	2
¼ cup	vegetable oil	60 mL
½ cup	brown or white sugar	125 mL
1 cup	mashed banana	250 mL
1 tsp.	vanilla	5 mL
1¾ cups	whole wheat flour	430 mL
2 tsp.	baking powder	10 mL
½ tsp.	baking soda	12 mL
½ tsp.	salt	2 mL
½ cup	dried unsweetened coconut	125 mL

Preheat oven to 325°F (160°C). In a mixing bowl, beat together eggs, oil and sugar. Add banana and vanilla, and beat well. Sift in flour, baking powder and soda, salt together. Add coconut and mix well before pouring into a greased loaf pan. Bake for 1 hour. Cool before removing from pan.

The Most Incredible Chocolate Cake

From a nutritional standpoint there is no excuse for this cake. It is sheer sin, and worth every bite. This recipe is for a single layer cake; to fill two pans, double it. You may use either solid unsweetened chocolate or unsweetened cocoa, but the procedure is a little different for each. Solid chocolate is melted over hot water. To use cocoa, mix cold water gradually with the dry powder, then heat them together.

This recipe is dependent on the action of soda and buttermilk, and will not work if you substitute milk or baking powder.

3 oz.	unsweetened chocolate *or*	75 g
7½ Tbsp.	unsweetened cocoa	113 mL
½ cup	water	125 mL
½ cup	warm butter	125 mL
1½ cups	white sugar	350 mL
2	eggs	2
1 tsp.	vanilla	5 mL
1½ cups	unbleached white flour	350 mL
1 tsp.	baking soda	5 mL
½ tsp.	salt	2 mL
¾ cup	buttermilk	180 mL

Preheat oven to 350°F (175°C). Cook chocolate or cocoa and water together in the top of a double boiler over boiling water. Meanwhile, cream together butter and sugar in a mixing bowl. Beat in eggs and vanilla, then add chocolate in a thin stream, beating well with a whisk. Sift in flour, soda and salt together; then add buttermilk and beat well. Pour into a greased cake pan, loaf pan, or tube pan. Bake at 350°F (175°C) for 30 minutes. Cool before removing from pan.

Gingerbread Cake

Rich, spicy, and sweet without sugar, this is a wonderful cake for a cold winter afternoon. Served with applesauce and a dollop of sour cream, it's an experience worth remembering.

1	egg	1
¼ cup	vegetable oil	60 mL
1 cup	molasses	250 mL
1 cup	milk	250 mL
½ cup	instant skim milk powder	125 mL
2½ cups	whole wheat pastry flour	600 mL
1½ tsp.	baking powder	7 mL
1 tsp.	cinnamon	5 mL
½ tsp.	salt	2 mL
1 tsp.	freshly grated ginger	5 mL

Preheat oven to 350°F (175°C). In a mixing bowl, beat together egg, oil, molasses, and milk. Sift in milk powder, flour, baking powder, cinnamon and salt; add ginger and beat well. Pour into a greased tube pan or 2 loaf pans. Bake for 45 minutes, or until top springs back when lightly pressed. Cool before removing from pan.

Wedding Fruitcake

This is one of those cakes which is better after it ages a few weeks.

1 cup	currants	250 mL
1 cup	black raisins	250 mL
1 cup	white raisins	250 mL
1 cup	water or sherry	250 mL
1 cup	lard or butter	250 mL
1 cup	white sugar	250 mL
3	eggs	3
1 cup	molasses	250 mL
3 cups	unbleached white flour	725 mL
1 tsp.	salt	5 mL
1 tsp.	baking soda	5 mL
2 tsp.	cinnamon	10 mL
1 tsp.	cloves	5 mL
1 tsp.	nutmeg	5 mL
1–2 cups	walnuts, chopped	250–475 mL
1 cup	citron (optional)	250 mL
1 cup	glazed cherries (optional)	250 mL

Soak currants and raisins overnight in water or sherry. In a mixing bowl, combine lard and sugar with a fork. Add eggs and molasses; beat thoroughly. Sift together flour, salt, soda and spices; add and beat into mixture. Add raisins, nuts and other fruits. Preheat oven to 300°F (150°C). Grease and flour a removable-rim pan thoroughly. Fill no more than two-thirds full. Bake 1 hour, or until a knife inserted into the middle comes out clean. Cool for at least 2 hours before removing from the pan. Cool and store in a tin up to a month.

Lemon Chiffon Cake

Always wash lemons and oranges carefully before grating the peel.

7	eggs	7
1/2 cup	vegetable oil	125 mL
1	lemon	1
2 1/4 cups	unbleached flour	560 mL
1 cup	white sugar	250 mL
1 Tbsp.	baking powder	15 mL
1 tsp.	salt	5 mL
1/2 tsp.	cream of tartar	5 mL

Preheat oven to 350°F (175°C). Separate eggs into two large bowls. Beat yolks until light and foamy, then add oil, gradually, beating as you pour it in a thin stream. Grate lemon peel into the mixture, then squeeze the juice into a measuring cup. Add water to make 3/4 cup liquid (180 mL). Add liquid to mixture, beating again. Sift flour, sugar, baking powder and salt into the batter, and mix well.

Wash beaters and beat together egg whites and cream of tartar. When the egg whites are stiff, add them to the batter, folding them in with your flattened hand. Pour the batter at once into an ungreased, removable-rim tube pan. Bake at 350°F (175°C) 30 to 40 minutes, or until a knife inserted in the middle comes out clean. Cool for 30 minutes before removing from pan.Serve plain or top with Lemon Custard Sauce (page 121).

VARIATION

ORANGE CHIFFON CAKE Substitute for lemon juice and peel:

3/4 cup	orange juice	180 mL
1	orange peel, grated	1

〜〜〜〜〜〜〜〜〜〜〜〜〜〜〜〜〜〜〜〜〜〜〜〜〜〜〜〜〜〜〜〜〜〜〜〜〜〜

HOW TO TELL
IF A CAKE IS DONE

Press your finger gently on top. Does it bounce right back? Has it browned on top? Has the cake come away from the sides of the pan? If none of these, it's not done yet. Do not stand around with the oven door open, or move the cake. Close the door and come back to check in five or ten minutes.

ICING CAKES

To get around the use of a lot of sugar, you can try using non-instant skim milk powder (available at health food stores) for part of the thickener, instead of cup after cup of icing sugar. For double layer cakes, use cake fillings between layers, and ice only the outsides. Fillings are easy to make and contain much less sugar than icing.

Mocha Chocolate Icing

This dark mocha icing is delicious on an orange, lemon or vanilla-flavored single layer cake.

1/4 cup	butter	60 mL
1 cup	icing sugar	250 mL
2 Tbsp.	unsweetened cocoa	30 mL
3 Tbsp.	double strength coffee	45 mL
1 tsp.	vanilla *or* dark rum	5 mL
3/4 cup	non-instant skim milk powder	180 mL

Soften butter at room temperature for 1 hour before creaming with a fork. Mix in icing sugar, then coffee, cocoa and flavoring, then non-instant skim milk powder. Let icing sit for 1 hour before icing the cake.

Covers 1 layer, top and sides.

Cream Cheese Icing

Excellent on carrot cake or fruitcake

1/2 cup	cream cheese	125 mL
1 tsp.	vanilla	5 mL
2 Tbsp.	cream *or* evaporated milk	30 mL
1 1/2 cups	icing sugar	375 mL
1 1/2 cups	non-instant skim milk powder	375 mL
1	lemon peel, grated	1

Soften cream cheese 1 hour at room temperature, then cream with fork. Add vanilla, cream, and mix well, then add icing sugar and milk powder and mix until smooth. Wash lemon before grating into mixture.

Covers 1 layer, top and sides.

〜〜〜〜〜〜〜〜〜〜〜〜〜〜〜〜〜〜〜〜〜〜〜〜〜〜〜〜〜〜〜〜〜〜〜〜〜〜

Banana Fudge Frosting

1/4 cup	butter	60 mL
1/2 cup	unsweetened cocoa	125 mL
1/4 cup	banana	60 mL
2 Tbsp.	milk	30 mL
1/2 tsp.	vanilla	2 mL
2 cups	icing sugar	475 mL
1 cup	non-instant skim milk powder	250 mL

Soften butter at room temperature for 1 hour before creaming with a fork. Add cocoa and mix well. Mash banana separately; add to icing with milk and vanilla. Then sift and beat in icing sugar and milk powder.

Covers 2 layers, top, middle and sides

Coconut Butterscotch Topping

1/2 cup	butter	125 mL
1 cup	brown sugar	250 mL
1 cup	unsweetened coconut	250 mL
1 cup	walnut pieces	250 mL
3 Tbsp.	milk or evaporated milk	45 mL

Melt butter and brown sugar in the top part of a double boiler over boiling water. Add coconut, nuts, and milk. Cook 5 minutes. Spread on cooled cake at once and cool before serving.

Covers 1 layer cake, top and sides

NUTRITIONAL YEAST

Added in small amounts, 1–2 Tbsp. (15–30 mL) per recipe, Engivita Brewer's Yeast does almost nothing to alter the chemistry of a cake or cookie, but adds quite a lot of B vitamins and raises the protein level by complementing the amino acids in the grain. I add it to my recipes during periods of high stress, such as traveling, hiking, or exams, when a little something extra in a snack is a big help.

French Butter Icing

1/4 cup	butter	60 mL
1 cup	icing sugar	250 mL
3 Tbsp.	cream or evaporated milk	45 mL
1 tsp.	vanilla	5 mL
pinch	cinnamon	pinch
1 cup	non-instant skim milk powder	250 mL

Soften butter at room temperature for 1 hour, then cream with a fork. Mix in icing sugar, then add and mix cream, vanilla and cinnamon until smooth. Add non-instant skim milk powder and beat until smooth.

Covers 1 layer, top and sides

VARIATIONS

PINK BUTTER ICING Substitute for cream:

2 Tbsp.	cranberry juice or syrup from cooked cranberry sauce	30 mL

YELLOW BUTTER ICING Substitute
for cream:

| 1 | large egg yolk, beaten | 1 |

Nutty Cake Filling

1 cup	walnut pieces	250 mL
1	large egg yolk	1
1/4 cup	honey	60 mL
3 Tbsp.	Engivita Brewer's Yeast	45 mL
3 Tbsp.	non-instant skim milk powder	45 mL
1/2 tsp.	nutmeg	2 mL

Grind or pound walnut pieces until they
are small. Beat together egg yolk, honey,
yeast, milk powder and nutmeg until
smooth. Add nuts.

Covers 1 layer cake

Apple Cake Filling

This can also be used as a cake topping, if
you chill it for an hour or so before spreading it.

2	apples	2
3 Tbsp.	butter	45 mL
3 Tbsp.	honey	45 mL
1 tsp.	cornstarch	5 mL
1 tsp.	cinnamon	5 mL
1/2 cup	walnut pieces (optional)	125 mL

Pare, core and chop apples. Melt butter in a
small pan, and sauté apples 3 minutes over
low heat. Add honey, cornstarch, cinnamon and nuts. Simmer for 5 minutes
over very low heat. Cool and spread between layers.

Fills 1 cake

Mincemeat Cake Filling

1 cup	raisins	250 mL
1/2 cup	water or apple juice	125 mL
2 Tbsp.	dark rum	30 mL
3/4 cup	water	180 mL
2 Tbsp.	cornstarch	30 mL
1/4 cup	molasses	60 mL
1	lemon peel, grated	1
1/2 tsp.	cinnamon	2 mL
pinch	salt	pinch
pinch	cloves	pinch

Mix raisins with water or juice and rum,
and allow to stand overnight. Next day,
mix remaining ingredients together in a
small pan. Simmer over low heat about 5
minutes, or until thick. Add raisins. Stir
well. Cool and spread.

Fills 1 cake

Oatmeal Cookies

³/₄ cup	lard *or* shortening	180 mL
1 cup	brown sugar	250 mL
2	eggs	2
¹/₂ cup	yogurt	125 mL
1 cup	whole wheat flour	250 mL
1 cup	unbleached white flour	250 mL
1 Tbsp.	baking powder	15 mL
1 tsp.	salt	5 mL
2 cups	rolled oats	475 mL

Preheat oven to 350°F (175°C). Soften shortening at room temperature for 1 hour, then cream sugar and shortening together with a fork. Add and beat in eggs and yogurt. Sift flours, baking powder, and salt together into batter and mix well; then combine with rolled oats. Drop by spoonfuls, well spaced, on to oiled cookie sheets. Bake at 350°F (175°C) for 20 minutes.

40 cookies

VARIATIONS

MOLASSES OATMEAL COOKIES
Add:

¹/₄ cup	molasses	60 mL
¹/₄ cup	whole wheat flour	60 mL
1 cup	raisins	250 mL

NUT-CHIP OATMEAL COOKIES
Add:

1 cup	chocolate *or* carob chips	250 mL
1 cup	unsweetened coconut	250 mL
1 cup	walnut pieces	250 mL
1 tsp.	vanilla	5 mL

Great Peanut Butter Cookies

1 cup	peanut butter	250 mL
1 cup	brown sugar	250 mL
¹/₄ cup	peanut oil	60 mL
¹/₃ cup	water	80 mL
1	egg	1
1 cup	dried skim milk powder	250 mL
1 cup	whole wheat flour	250 mL
¹/₂ cup	unbleached white flour	125 mL
2 tsp.	baking powder	10 mL
¹/₂ tsp.	salt	2 mL

Preheat oven to 375°F (190°C). Cream together peanut butter, brown sugar and peanut oil in a mixing bowl. In a separate bowl, mix water, egg and milk powder until smooth. Add to batter. Sift flours, baking powder and salt in together and mix thoroughly. Roll into 1 in. (2 cm) balls. Place on a lightly oiled cookie sheet and flatten with a fork. Bake at 375°F (190°C) for 15 to 20 minutes, or until lightly browned.

30–40 cookies

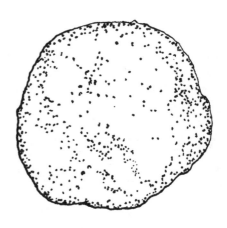

Gingerbread Cookies

When we first came to Cape Breton, we lived on Boulardarie Island, next door to Peggy Ryan. A traditional farmhouse cook, she used to bake mountains of these big, soft gingerbread cookies. They make great cutout cookies if you refrigerate the dough for a couple hours before rolling it out.

³/₄ cup	lard	180 mL
1 cup	brown sugar	250 mL
2	eggs	2
1 cup	molasses	250 mL
¹/₂ cup	strong tea *or* buttermilk	125 mL
1 tsp.	baking soda	5 mL
3 cups	whole wheat flour	725 mL
3 cups	unbleached white flour	725 mL
1 tsp.	salt	5 mL
1 tsp.	cloves	5 mL
1 tsp.	allspice	5 mL
2 tsp.	ginger	10 mL

Cream together lard and brown sugar. Beat in eggs and molasses. Mix tea or buttermilk and soda before adding. Sift flours, salt and spices in together gradually, beating after each addition. Chill 1 hour. Preheat oven to 350°F (175°C) as you roll out dough ¹/₄ in. (.5 cm) thick and cut into shapes. Bake 12 to 15 minutes on lightly oiled cookie sheets or until browned at edges. Cool and remove from sheet.

About 50 cookies

Cape Breton Oatcakes

Light, crisp cookies with a natural oat flavor, these are favorites all around the Maritimes.

2 cups	unbleached white flour	475 mL
1 cup	whole wheat flour	250 mL
1 cup	white sugar	250 mL
1 tsp.	salt	5 mL
1 tsp.	baking soda	5 mL
1 cup	cold lard	250 mL
¹/₂ cup	cold butter	125 mL
3 cups	small flake rolled oats	725 mL
³/₄–1 cup	buttermilk	180–250 mL

Preheat oven to 350°F (175°C). Sift together the flours, sugar, salt and baking soda. Cut in lard and butter with a fork or pastry cutter, until mixture resembles coarse cornmeal. Add and mix in rolled oats. Add buttermilk gradually, mixing as you do, until the mixture will hold together in a rough ball. Turn out on a lightly floured board, pat into a flat shape, and roll out ¹/₄ in. (5 mm) thick. Cut with a pizza cutter into 2 in. (5 cm) squares. Place on ungreased cookie sheets and bake 15 minutes or until lightly browned.

60–70 cookies

Shortbread

1¹/₂ cups	unbleached white flour	375 mL
¹/₂ cup	cornstarch	125 mL
¹/₂ cup	white sugar	125 mL
¹/₄ tsp.	salt	1 mL
1 cup	cold butter	250 mL
¹/₄ cup	cold water	60 mL
	jam or jelly	

Sift together flour, cornstarch, sugar and salt. Chop butter into small pieces and cut in with a fork or pastry cutter. When the mixture is as fine as you can make it, add cold water. Shape lightly into 2 flat patties and refrigerate, covered, for 1 hour or longer.

Preheat oven to 325°F (160°C). Turn out patties on to a lightly floured surfaced. Dust rolling pin very lightly with flour. Roll out dough ¼ in. (.5 cm) thick and cut into small rounds. Make a shallow depression in each and fill with jam or jelly. Bake for 15 minutes, until dry and golden.

50 cookies

VARIATION

PETTICOAT TAILS Roll out each patty to the exact size of your storage tin. Cut into pie-sized wedges. Press around the edges with a fork, and prick in the middle. Bake as above.

Coconut Honey Macaroons

The problem with these delicious macaroons is that once cooked, they stick to anything. My best results have been with brown paper, cut from paper bags, and lightly buttered. Even then, they stick a little bit.

¹/₄ cup	evaporated milk or thick cream	60 mL
1 cup	non-instant skim milk powder	250 mL
¹/₃ cup	honey	80 mL
2 cups	unsweetened coconut	475 mL
¹/₂ cup	unsweetened coconut flakes	125 mL
¹/₃ cup	wheat germ	80 mL
2 tsp.	almond flavoring	10 mL
pinch	salt	pinch
3	egg whites	3

Preheat oven to 350°F (175°C). Mix milk and milk powder into a slightly lumpy paste. Add honey and mix well. Fold in coconut and wheat germ, almond flavoring and salt. Beat egg whites in a separate mixing bowl until stiff but not dry. Fold them lightly into the batter. Cut brown paper to fit 2 cookie tins, and butter them lightly. Transfer batter by tablespoonfuls on to cookie sheets and bake at 350°F (175°C) 15 minutes.

35 cookies

Birdseed Brittle

These thin, crunchy squares of nuts and seeds are great for afternoon snacks at home, at the office, or on the trail. They keep well in a tin.

1 cup	sunflower seeds	250 mL
1/2 cup	sesame seeds	125 mL
1/2 cup	walnuts, chopped	125 mL
1 cup	rolled oats	250 mL
1	egg	1
1 cup	honey	250 mL
3 Tbsp.	vegetable oil	45 mL
1/4 cup	water	60 mL
2 Tbsp.	white flour	30 mL
pinch	salt	pinch
1 cup	currants	250 mL
1/2 cup	dates, finely chopped	125 mL

Preheat oven to 300°F (150°C). Spread seeds, nuts and rolled oats on cookie sheets and roast for 10 to 15 minutes, or until golden brown. In a mixing bowl, beat together the egg, honey, oil, water, flour and salt. Add cooled seeds, nuts and oats, and the currants and dates. Spread mixture on a well-oiled cookie sheet. Bake at 350°F (175°C) for 20 minutes, or until evenly browned. Slice into squares with a pizza cutter or wet knife. Remove with a spatula and cool before storing in a tin.

30 squares

Superballs

Mildly sweet, these treats are flavorful and full of high-energy protein. You can use any kind of peanut butter.

2 Tbsp.	graham cracker crumbs	30 mL
2/3 cup	peanut butter	160 mL
2/3 cup	honey	160 mL
1 1/2 cups	graham cracker crumbs	375 mL
1 cup	non-instant dried milk	250 mL

Put the 2 Tbsp. (30 mL) graham cracker crumbs in a small bowl. Mix all the other ingredients together in a larger bowl. Shape into balls about the size of walnuts, and roll in graham cracker crumbs in the smaller bowl. Store in a tin.

36 balls

Fig or Date Bars

1 cup	dates or figs	250 mL
1/2 cup	boiling water	125 mL
1	lemon	1
1/2 cup	coconut	125 mL
1 cup	whole wheat flour	250 mL
1/2 cup	rolled oats	125 mL
1/2 cup	cold butter	125 mL

Preheat oven to 350°F (175°C). Chop dates or figs into a small saucepan, add boiling water, cover, and simmer 30 minutes. Wash lemon and grate in peel. Meanwhile, mix coconut, flour and oats; cut in butter with a fork. Spread half the dry mixture into a greased 7 × 7 in. (18 cm) square pan. Spread carefully with date mixture and top with dry mixture. Bake for 30 minutes.

9–12 squares

Nutmeg Doughnuts

3	eggs	3
1 cup	white or brown sugar	250 mL
1 cup	milk	250 mL
3 Tbsp.	melted butter	45 mL
3 cups	unbleached white flour	725 mL
1 cup	whole wheat flour	250 mL
1 tsp.	salt	5 mL
1 Tbsp.	baking powder	15 mL
1 tsp.	cinnamon	5 mL
1 tsp.	nutmeg	5 mL
$1/2$ cup	unbleached white flour	125 mL
4 cups	vegetable oil	1 L

Carob Brownies

Carob resembles chocolate, but tastes more like butterscotch. It's good with nuts and currants.

$1/4$ cup	melted butter	60 mL
$1/2$ cup	carob powder	60 mL
2	eggs	2
$1/2$ cup	honey	125 mL
1 cup	unbleached white flour	250 mL
1 tsp.	baking powder	5 mL
$1/2$ tsp.	salt	2 mL
1 tsp.	vanilla extract	5 mL
$1/2$ cup	currants	125 mL
$1/2$ cup	walnuts, chopped	125 mL

Melt butter in a small pan; add carob powder and mix well. Beat eggs in a large mixing bowl. Add honey and beat well. Add melted butter-carob mixture and beat again. Sift in flour, baking powder and salt together. Add vanilla, currants and nuts, and stir together. Pour into a greased and floured 9 in. (23 cm) square cake pan. Bake 20 to 25 minutes at 350°F (175°C). Cool before removing from the pan.

9–12 squares

In a large mixing bowl, beat eggs with a whisk until foamy. Add sugar, milk, and melted butter. Sift in larger amounts of flour, salt, baking powder, and spices. Work in the last $1/2$ cup (125 mL) flour gradually to make a stiff dough. Refrigerate 1 to 2 hours.

Heat oil in a large, heavy pan. Meanwhile, turn out dough on a well floured surface. Roll out to about $1/2$ in. (1 cm) thickness. Cut into narrow strips about the width of your finger and about 5 in. (15 cm) long. Press ends together to make doughnut shapes. Heat fat to 375°F (190°C). At this temperature, a cube of white bread will brown in one minute. Reduce heat to keep the fat from getting any hotter. Fry doughnuts 3 at a time, $2\frac{1}{2}$ minutes on the first side, 1 minute on the second side. Drain on absorbent paper. Cool 1 hour before storing in a tin.

40 doughnuts

Food Storage

Food Storage, a subject near and dear to the heart of many a country cook, is rapidly becoming popular in many an urban and suburban home. The trick is to gather or buy foods when they're available, store them properly, and keep until needed. Thus you have onions in the pantry, carrots in the cellar and a freezer full of delights — ranging from fresh fruits and vegetables to meats, tofu, bread, even whole casseroles.

This chapter is devoted to explaining the methods used to store and retrieve fresh foods at the height of their glory. In many cases, this means a special focus on the freshest, youngest, and tenderest, to get the best taste and texture. It also means that you can serve some things unavailable from the mass markets — things like snow peas, mussels, or fiddleheads. If you're on a tight budget, you can freeze vegetables from the garden, or put away meats on sale. If your problem is a relentless schedule, you can do your baking ahead of time and produce elegant home baked treats at the most hectic moment. Food storage can go in many directions, all of them helpful to the well-rounded kitchen.

Root Cellar Storage

To store roots for any length of time, you must have a damp, cool root cellar. The temperature should be constantly just above freezing, no lower than 32°F (0°C) and never much over 40°F (4°C). The humidity should be from 90 to 95 per cent, or the roots will shrivel after a few months.

There are various ways to make root cellars. The most common is in an unheated part of the cellar of your house, where it will be handy. You should install rodent-proof bins or cans.

Don't try to store anything until cold weather insures that the cellar will be cool enough to keep them. As you bring in each box of vegetables, trim off the tops to within ½–1½ in. (1–4 cm) of the crowns. Gently wipe off excess dirt and check for damage or disease. Store in damp sand or sawdust. Use up damaged roots first. *Potatoes, carrots, beets,* and *turnips* or *rutabagas* will keep all winter. *Parsnips, salsify* and *Jerusalem artichokes* will keep for three to four months, or they can be left in the ground all winter, well mulched, for extra crispness and flavor in the spring.

Cabbage, celery, cauliflower, brussels sprouts, kohlrabi, Chinese cabbage and *head lettuce* may be stored in a cool, slightly damp cellar for several months. The best method is to pull the entire plant and either root it in sand or hang it upside down in the basement.

Fruits and vegetables should not be stored close to one another. Fruits will absorb odors from turnips, cabbages; apples give off a mild gas that makes potatoes and carrots rot. If all you have is one dark hole, store apples in a sealed can of some kind.

Some *apples* will keep all winter. Some won't last three weeks. The best keepers are crisp, dense apples with thick skins. Wrap perfect fruit in newspaper or get a stack of pressed paper fruit racks from your local supermarket. Store at 33°F (1°C), 80 to 90 per cent humidity.

A crate of *oranges, lemons* and *grapefruit* will keep quite well in the root cellar for a couple of months. Optimum temperature: 33°F (1°C), 80 to 90 per cent humidity.

Pick *pears* when full grown but still hard and green. Sometimes they will take months to ripen, but mostly they're all

gone before Christmas. Pack as for apples. Store at 33°F (1°C), 85 to 95 per cent humidity.

Attic Storage

Winter squash, pumpkins, onions, dried beans and peas, and dried vegetables should not be kept in a root cellar, as it is much too damp and they will develop rot. A ventilated attic or room in the house or barn that does not freeze is the best place for them. If you don't have a dry place, surround them with straw or hay to absorb the damp. The temperature should be around 40–50° F (4°–10°C).

Winter Squash and Pumpkins: After the first light frost, cut squash from the vine and leave outside on a bed of straw or hay to cure the shells as they harden in the sun. Handle carefully to avoid bruising. Store them on dry shelves, separated from one another, and check them every week or two for moldy spots. You may stop the mold by wiping it off but, if dark spots develop, use the squash or pumpkin immediately. Mature squashes will keep longer than unripe ones.

Onions: Onions with thick stalks won't keep well. In short growing seasons, you may hasten the decay of the stalks by trampling them at the end of the summer, a few weeks before harvest. At the first good frost, pull the onions and let them sit for a week in a barn or dry shed; turn them over now and then to let all sides dry and paper over. If you wish to braid them, they may be kept in the attic or in any dry, cool room of the house; or you may trim the tops and keep them in a mesh bag. Use those with thick tops first; save the largest and best-formed for longest storage. Onions will keep until the weather gets warm and damp; usually they start to sprout in May. The green tops make very good salad material.

Garlic: Treat as for onions. They may be hung in the kitchen or, for longer storage, in the attic or an upstairs room.

Beans, Peas, and Other Seeds: All such things should be kept in clean, dry glass jars. If you are drying and storing your own seeds, you should first store them in a very warm place and after 12 hours see if any condensation has formed inside the jar; this will warn you that they are not completely dried and will rot in long storage.

Grains: Grains should be kept cool. It doesn't matter if they freeze; the only problem is rodents. One solution is to keep them in galvanized garbage pails; they have nice tight lids and are just the right size for a sack of grain.

Quality Freezing

The most important thing about keeping frozen foods is the maintenance of a constant temperature of 0°-5°F (-15° — 17°C). The second most important thing is the freshness of the food you put in the freezer. Fish, shellfish and vegetables must be absolutely fresh. Fruits are less perishable. The third factor is the packaging. If you are planning to keep the food longer than a few weeks, special freezer wrap is necessary to exclude air and keep in moisture. The food must be wrapped tightly and sealed carefully. Meats and milk products should be double wrapped.

Some fruits and vegetables (or meats) are of a nature that will freeze in a solid brick if the filled bag is placed in a small container. Then the bag can be removed and the container reused.

DEFROSTING FREEZERS

There are several ways of removing ice without damaging the walls of the freezer, but the best one I've heard yet is the vacuum cleaner approach. Plug the hose into the exhaust so that hot air rushes out and defrosts your ice in no time. Be very careful not to dent or scratch the inner surface, which, in some freezers is surprisingly fragile, barely covering the coolant tubes.

Freezing Grains and Nuts

As long as the protective husk or shell of a grain or nut is left intact, there is no need to freeze grains, seeds or nuts. Once you crack the shells or grind them, however, you are faced with a storage problem. After two weeks at room temperature such foods as wheat germ, nuts and shelled seeds lose their flavor. After a month they may begin to go rancid.

Fortunately for those who prefer to buy flour preground and nuts without shells, they may be kept very easily in the freezer for a year or longer.

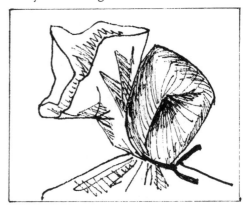

Freezing Fruits

Fruits are very easy to freeze, and keep very well in the freezer. Fruits that have been frozen are very good in all kinds of cooking and baking. To eat them raw, do not allow them to thaw completely; eat frozen or half-frozen. Most freezing instructions will have you using mountains of sugar. If you always add only as much as your taste dictates, you will soon find yourself using much less. Some fruits, such as blueberries or peaches, don't need any at all.

If your fruit comes from commercial growers, it has been sprayed for various diseases, fungi or insects; wash it under cold running water. If you grew it or picked it wild, though, there's no need to wash it unless it's dirty.

DISCOLORATION

As soon as you slice into most fruits, the vitamin C in them begins to oxidize and turn into tannin. There's nothing "bad" about brown fruit, but it does have less vitamin C, and it doesn't look as pretty. The best way to prevent this is to slice it directly into a mixture of:

1 tsp.	ascorbic acid	5 mL
1 cup	cold water	250 mL

Ascorbic acid is just pure vitamin C. As far as I know there's nothing wrong with it, nutritionally speaking, but it you prefer you can use:

1 Tbsp.	lemon juice	15 mL
1 cup	cold water	250 mL

APPLES

1. *Unsweetened Dry Pack* For use in pies, cobblers, other baking. Choose firm, tart apples. Slice around the core, leaving skins on, into acid-water solution. Dry with paper or a towel. Pack in plastic bags.
2. *Syrup Pack* For use in pies, cobblers, other baking, dessert topping. Choose firm, tart apples. Make up a syrup by heating together until well mixed:

4 cups	water	1 L
2 cups	sugar *or*	475 mL
1 cup	honey	250 mL
Cool and add:		
4 tsp.	ascorbic acid *or*	20 mL
	juice of 1 lemon	

Slice apples directly into this mixture, tossing after each apple. When you have enough to fill a plastic container, pack apples in and cover with syrup. To keep apples submerged, wad cellophane or plastic under the lid. Leave 1 in. per qt. (2 cm per L) air space to allow for expansion of liquid when frozen.
3. *Cider* Home-made or unpasteurized unpreserved cider may be frozen as any juice.

BANANAS

Bananas discolor and lose much flavor when frozen, but they can be kept, mashed, for use in banana bread (who cares what color they turn?) Mash and freeze in small containers. If pints are the smallest containers you have, mash and pack in small plastic bags in pint containers. Two bananas are enough for banana bread.

SOFT BERRIES

Blackberries, boysenberries, raspberries and the like, which are seedy when raw, are going to be twice as seedy after freezing. Moreover, the texture of the berry is utterly destroyed when it thaws. Pick over berries before freezing.

1. *For use in syrups, sauce, ice cream and baking* Heat together:

1 cup	water *or* berry juice	250 mL
½ cup	sugar *or*	125 mL
¼ cup	honey	60 mL

Submerge fruit in cooled syrup in pint-sized containers.

2. *For use as separate fruit, as a garnish* Scatter berries on a cookie sheet and freeze. When hard, pack together in plastic bags or plastic containers.

FIRM BERRIES
Blueberries, huckleberries, elderberries, Saskatoon or serviceberries can be bagged just as they are. You don't even have to pick over them if you don't have time. Frozen raw blueberries are a wonderful thing to have on hand.

TART BERRIES
Gooseberries, cranberries, currants. Before freezing, mix:

1 qt.	tart berries	1 L
1 cup	sugar	250 mL

Another method of sweetening tart berries is to mix them with a sweeter fruit. Cranberries, for example, may be mixed with an equal quantity of chopped oranges. This makes an excellent relish for fatty meats such as pork, moose, duck or goose — as well as the traditional turkey.

Never use cardboard containers for packing these berries in wet form, as their extreme acidity sometimes prevents them from freezing completely and the container won't last well.

TART CHERRIES
Before sitting down to the laborious business of pitting them, you may firm them up by soaking for an hour in ice water.

For Pies, Baking Pack raw, dry and pitted, or rolled in:

½ cup	sugar for each	125 mL
2 cups	cherries	475 mL

For Dessert Toppings Mix and heat together:

1 cup	sugar	475 mL
4 cups	water	1 L

Pack cherries in plastic containers. Cover with syrup, leaving ½ in. (1 cm) head room for expansion.

GRAPEFRUITS, ORANGES AND LEMONS
Use half the fruit to make juice. Cut the other half in sections, removing rind but leaving some of the white pith which is an important nutritional part of citrus fruits. Pack fruits in juice, leaving ½ in. space per pint (1 cm per 500 mL) for expansion. Use plastic containers only. To use in fruit cocktails or served raw, these are best if they are eaten half-thawed, with ice crystals still in them.

PEACHES
Peaches are among the fruits that oxidize, or turn brown, most rapidly. There are two separate and distinct methods for dealing with peaches, depending on whether you like peaches yellow or peaches brown. Needless to say, it takes at least twice as long to freeze peaches yellow. I am a personal fan of brown peaches, but I will take them any way I can get them in Nova Scotia.

BROWN PEACHES

If you want to skin them, immerse them in boiling water for 1 minute (using a wire basket for speed and convenience). Peel quickly, slice and pit, and pop into a light syrup or plain water to cover. Freeze packed in liquid in waterproof plastic containers.

YELLOW PEACHES

Heat together, then cool:

4 cups	water	1 L
2 cups	honey	475 mL
	or	
3 cups	sugar	725 mL

Fill a large container with:

2 qt.	ice water	2 L
1 Tbsp.	ascorbic acid *or* juice of ½ lemon	15 mL

Peel peaches under cold running water. Slice or halve each directly into the water-acid bath. Float a plate on top of the bath to keep peaches submerged. When you have enough peaches to fill a container, pack them in, cover with cold syrup, and crumple a piece of plastic wrap on the top to completely submerge them as they freeze. Seal on lid. Defrost until almost thawed. Serve frosty or use in cooking immediately to prevent discoloration.

PEARS

The oxidation which in other fruits is mostly a matter of looks is, in pears, a more vital matter, affecting the delicate flavor and texture as well as the color. Freeze as yellow peaches above.

PLUMS

Soak plums in ice water to firm them before pitting. Pack whole in plastic bags. If you wish to serve them peeled, drop whole frozen plums in ice water and they will peel easily.

For mashed plums, run them through the food mill and mix together:

½ tsp.	ascorbic acid	2 mL
1 qt.	mashed plums	1 L

RHUBARB

The freezing process changes the chemistry of rhubarb so that it requires less sugar to sweeten a pie than one ordinarily needs.
For Pies Pack raw, sliced in short chunks, in bags.
For Desserts Cook and sweeten with sugar or honey as you would for the table. Pack in pint or quart (475 mL or 1 L) containers (plastic only) leaving ½–1 in. (1–2 cm) head room.

STRAWBERRIES

To avoid having them freeze together, spread strawberries thinly on a baking sheet and quick-freeze until solid; then package them together. To serve, do not allow them to thaw completely.

Freezing Meats And Poultry

HANGING AND CHILLING Before freezing, freshly butchered beef is ordinarily hung, to age, refrigerated, for 7 or more days. If you buy your beef ready cut, you may assume that it has been hung and is ready to freeze, after 24 hours of chilling.

Pork, lamb, venison, moose, bear and veal are usually frozen within 1 to 3 days after killing, and need only be chilled for 24 hours before freezing. Rabbit, squirrel and other small game are chilled 24 hours.

Poultry is frozen after 24 hours of chilling; but game birds such as partridge, are hung for 3 days, in a cool place.

PACKAGING MEAT FOR FREEZING

Meat must be carefully packaged for freezing, in two layers of freezer quality plastic or paper, to prevent freezer burn or rancidity. One layer should be moisture-proof and enclose the meat tightly. A freezer quality plastic bag is a good choice: expel the air and twist the neck of the bag, then bend it over double to make a "goose neck" which excludes air. For the second layer of wrap you may choose either another plastic bag or a large piece of freezer paper, folded to exclude moisture and securely taped with broad masking tape. The paper choice is less expensive than another plastic bag, but is only good for evenly shaped pieces of meat.

Ordinary plastic bags, plastic wrap and butcher paper cannot be used for long term frozen meat storage without some sacrifice of the quality of the meat.

HAMBURGERS, STEAKS, CHOPS, and so on may be packaged accordian-style between two layers of freezer wrap so that you can take out just what you need, when you need it.

BONES If you are short of freezer space, bone your roasts and tie them into rounds. Use the bones to make a soup stock, which can be frozen in plastic containers. Be sure to leave 1 in. (2 cm) expansion room in top of the containers.

ODD SHAPED PIECES Ribs and poultry bones must be packaged with extra care to keep the wrap from tearing when moved around by somebody hastily hunting for the ice cream. You can ball up plastic or waxed paper around the sharp bone ends within the package to prevent any problems.

MAXIMUM STORAGE TIMES FOR MEATS, POULTRY, AND FISH: The amount of time you may keep a given piece of meat in your freezer varies.

Here is a list of the maximum storage times for certain cuts of meat. Remember, too, that many states have maximum legal storage times for game meats, and some require licenses for you to keep them frozen.

	MONTHS AT 0°
Beef and Venison:	
Roasts, steaks	14
Stewing size pieces	12
Ground meat, oxtails kidneys	8
Liver, heart, tongue,	4
Brains, tripe	1
Veal:	
Roasts, chops, steaks	12
Thin cutlets, cubes	10
Ground meat	6
Liver, heart	3
Pork (fresh), Moose, Elk:	
Roasts, chops, steaks	12
Cubes	6
Ground	4
Ground and seasoned	2
Liver, heart	2
Pork (cured):	
Ham and shoulder	6
Bacon, small pieces	3
Lamb:	
Roasts, chops	14
Cubes, thin cuts	12
Ground meat	8
Liver, heart	4
Chicken, Turkey, Duck, Goose, Game Birds:	12
Livers	4
Fish, Shellfish:	
Lean whole fish	12
Lean fillets	8
Fat whole fish	8
Fat fillets	6
Cooked shrimp, lobster	3
Shellfish in liquid	10

Thawing Frozen Meat

The more slowly meat defrosts, the more tender and juicy it is. Thus, the best way to defrost it is in the refrigerator, wrapped in its freezer wrappings. The larger and tougher the meat is, the longer it takes to defrost.

Large beef rib or rump roasts, leg of lamb or pork: 7–10 hours per lb., 4–5 hours per kg.

Small roasts, veal, lamb, shoulders: 6–9 hours per lb., 3–4 hours per kg.

Steaks, chops, sliced liver, kidneys: 6–8 hours.

Stewing meat: 10–12 hours.

1 lb. (450 g) ground meat: 10 hours.

Hamburger or sausage patties: 4–6 hours.

If you feel confident about the tenderness of your meat, you may defrost it, in its original wrap, at room temperature and cut the time in half.

Poultry, however, has such a tendency to dry out when thawed at room temperature that I really cannot recommend it. Thaw all poultry in its original wrap, refrigerated.

Whole birds: 6–8 hours per lb. (3–4 hours per kg).

Split broilers: 3 hours per lb. (1½ hours per kg).

Pieces: 2 hours per lb. (1 hour per kg).

COOK IT SOON

All thawed meats, poultry and fish should be cooked within a few hours of becoming thawed; otherwise the meat will spoil rapidly. This is especially true of fish and shellfish, but you should also keep an eye on poultry and ground meat.

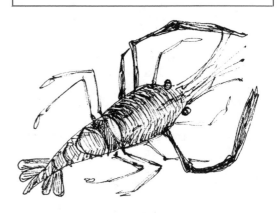

Freezing Fish And Shellfish

First of all, be sure your fish or shellfish is fresh. If you are dealing with a bought fish, make sure it hasn't been frozen already: see if it will float. A thawed one won't.

Behead the fish just above the shoulder bones around the gills, leaving the large bones in to give it structure. Leave the tail on for the same reason.

SMALL FISH

Very small fish, such as smelt or 9 in. (23 cm) trout, are best frozen whole, uncleaned, in liquid — either water or fish broth. Pack them in a suitable plastic container or a bag-lined can. Chill overnight, making sure they are completely covered by liquid, and freeze the next day.

MEDIUM-SIZED FISH

Ordinary sized fish, around 9–15 in. (24–38 cm), may be frozen whole, cleaned, well wrapped in foil or clingy freezer wrap, and again in butcher paper. Be very careful to seal fish packages by folding the edges of the inner wrap together. The outer wrap is important, as it keeps the inner wrap from breaking (frozen fish tails are sharp!). A medium-sized fish may also be filleted.

LARGE FISH

Large fish may be cut into fish steaks and stacked, as you would hamburgers. To save a large fish whole, put fish in the freezer, unwrapped, and freeze it solid for 24 hours in a quick-freeze compartment or against the coldest wall of the freezer. When it is hard through, take it out and dip in cold water. Refreeze until the glaze is hard. Continue to dip and freeze until you have built up a glaze about ¼ in. (.5 cm). No other wrapping is needed, but you should renew the dip every 3 weeks or so.

FRESH FISH WITH VITAMIN C

Fish with a relatively high fat content such as mackerel, lake trout and salmon do not keep as well as the leaner fish like cod, haddock, or sole. To improve storage chances, mix:

| 2 cups | cold water | 475 mL |
| 1 tsp. | ascorbic acid (vitamin C) | 5 mL |

Dip each fish 30 seconds, then drain, wrap twice, and freeze. Pay extra attention sealing tightly. Use fat fish within 2 to 3 months, lean fish within a year.

Thaw fish and shellfish in their wrappers, in a refrigerator. Allow large fish 24 hours to thaw, fillets 4–6 hours, and fish or shellfish in liquid 12 hours.

LOBSTER AND CRAB

These are best cooked whole, chilled 24 hours, wrapped double and frozen.

CLAMS, OYSTERS, MUSSELS

Steam open fresh shellfish, being careful to catch liquid (page 82). Freeze them in a mixture of liquid and steaming water. Keep only 2 to 3 months.

Freezing Vegetables

Freezing vegetables is not quite as simple as freezing meats, fruits and grains, because you don't freeze them raw. They must be blanched first, to destroy enzymes which will otherwise wipe out most of their vitamin content and toughen them slightly. Vegetables frozen raw look the same, and some of them taste the same, but their food value and texture are radically different.

There are two ways to blanch: in boiling water or in steam. Since the vitamin you are most commonly trying to preserve is vitamin C, and since vitamin C is water-soluble, I usually stick to steam.

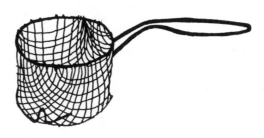

THE STEAM BLANCHING PROCESS

Put at least 3 in. (7 cm) of water in a large pot and bring to the boil, covered. Make sure water is actually boiling before suspending a basket of vegetables over it and covering the pot. Time steaming carefully (see individual vegetables, below). Remove vegetables at once and immerse in ice water. When chilled, remove at once and drain on absorbent paper. Pack vegetables tightly in freezer bags, twist top, bend it back on itself in a gooseneck, and tie tightly. Freeze at once.

Boiling is easier than steaming. If you'd rather boil everything, subtract one minute from the time given below for steaming each type of vegetable.

After blanching, the vegetables must be chilled immediately, to halt the cooking. This is done in very cold water or ice water. They are then quickly dried and packaged.

ASPARAGUS

Freezes well; short, fat tips are the most tender. Chop into 2–4 in. (5–10 cm) lengths; sort tips and stalks for separate steaming. Save woody bases for soup stock. Steam tips 3 minutes. Steam stems 5 minutes. Cool in ice water 3 minutes.

GREEN OR YELLOW SNAP BEANS

Pick only fresh, slightly underripe green or yellow beans and freeze at once. Chop or french-cut large beans. Steam small new beans 3 minutes. Steam chopped beans 3 minutes. Steam frenched beans 2 minutes. Chill in ice water 3 minutes, or until quite cold.

LIMA BEANS

Green lima beans freeze well; white ones are starchy. Steam baby limas 2 minutes. Steam larger limas 3 minutes. Cool in ice water 1 minute.

BROCCOLI

Freezes well. Use dark green parts only. Split large heads, use smaller florets whole. Steam florets 3 minutes. Steam halved heads 5 minutes. Steam peeled, sliced stalks 4 to 5 minutes. Chill in ice water 2 minutes.

CAULIFLOWER

Divide into uniform-sized florets. Inspect carefully for worms, for whom cauliflower is a sort of hotel. Steam florets 5 minutes. Chill 3 or 4 minutes, or until cold.

CELERY

Not, alas, to be used raw, but celery may be frozen for use in stir-fry, soups and stews. String if necessary and cut into 1 in. (2 cm) lengths. Steam 4 minutes. Chill 1 minute in ice water.

CHARD

See Greens.

CORN

Corn really hasn't much in the way of vitamins, so I blanch by boiling it. Pick and husk and plunge corn into boiling water. Fully mature, but not overripe ears are best for freezing. Cook large ears 6 minutes, medium ears 5 minutes. Cool ears 15 minutes in ice water or over ice. Bag no more than 4 together, if freezing whole. To freeze cut corn, use a sharp or serrated knife over a board, cutting off corn on all sides, then measuring into plastic freezer bags.

EGGPLANT
Cut into ½ in. (1 cm) slices, blanch a few at a time. Steam slices 4 minutes. Cool 2 minutes in ice water. Be careful to dry completely. Package in plastic containers with sheets of disposable paper in between.

FIDDLEHEAD
Gather *Ostrich Fern* fiddleheads when tightly curled, keep cool, and freeze within 4 hours of picking. Remove papery brown husks.

1 qt.	water	1 L
2 cups	fiddleheads	475 mL
1 tsp.	salt	5 mL

Bring water to the boil. Add fiddleheads and salt. Boil fiddleheads 1 minute. Remove from water at once and chill in ice water 3 minutes. Bag and freeze at once.

GREENS
Pick only the greenest, freshest, youngest greens, such as spinach, chard, kale, beet greens, lamb's quarters. Boil in a large pot of water 1 or 2 minutes. Chill in ice water 1 minute. Package in bags, expelling all air. Excellent!

HERBS
Certain subtle herb flavors do better in the freezer than dried. They include *basil, parsley, chervil, dill,* and *fresh coriander.* Any fresh herb may be chopped and packaged in small bags, the bags stored in a larger container.

KOHLRABI
Only young kohlrabi freezes well. Trim, slice ½ in. (1 cm) thick, and steam 1 minute. Chill until cold in ice water.

MILKWEED PODS
Gather milkweed pods when they are young and tender. Cut off stems, but leave pods whole. Immerse in boiling water for 1 minute, then drain. Preheat process twice. Chill 2 minutes, in ice water.

MUSHROOMS
My preferred method of freezing mushrooms, both domestic and wild, is to sauté them in a pan with butter for 3 minutes, then cool them over ice before bagging and freezing. For best flavor, domestic and similar types of wild mushrooms (such as meadow mushrooms) should be defrosted rapidly and cooked as briefly as possible.

Chanterelles are a bright orange funnel shaped mushroom abundant in our northern coniferous woods. To freeze them, we sauté in butter, but defrost them by simmering in milk. After that they may be sautéed in butter and oil, or added to a stew or soup.

PEAS
The prince of frozen vegetables, as long as you catch them young. Old peas are pretty disappointing. 2 lb. (1 kg) in the pod equals 2 cups (475 mL). Steam podded peas 1 minute. Chill 1 minute; drain and package.

SNOW PEAS
Edible podded peas freeze well. Slice large pods diagonally, leave small ones whole. Steam 1 cup (250 mL) at a time for 2 minutes. Chill in ice water 3 minutes, dry and pack. I often package these and other vegetables together for a soup or stir-fry. To defrost, steam them, then serve or add to mixture.

SUGAR SNAPS
These edible-podded peas can be eaten when the pods are full, thus eliminating the tiresome chore of shelling. Steam 2 minutes; chill 3 minutes in ice water.

PEPPERS
The best peppers for freezing are the thickest-shelled types. Slice or halve; remove cores. Steam halves 3 minutes, slices 2 minutes. Chill 2 minutes in ice water, dry well, package and freeze.

PUMPKIN
See Squash, Winter.

SPINACH
See Greens.

SQUASH, SUMMER
Frozen after ordinary steaming, summer squash becomes mushy and tasteless. Instead, heat up a little vegetable oil and sauté squash slices about 2 minutes a side. Replenish oil and squash as needed. Drain on absorbent paper, then cool over ice. Package and freeze. To thaw, heat gently in a skillet or saucepan, 10–15 minutes.

SQUASH, WINTER
It is best to freeze pumpkin or winter squash fully cooked. They may be in pieces or mashed. Chill after cooking for 24 hours before placing in freezer.

TOMATOES
Sort tomatoes. Put all the imperfect ones (minus their imperfections) in a juice pot, simmer 1 to 2 hours, and sieve or strain out seeds and skins. Freeze juice as is or use it to pack whole tomatoes in.

To pack whole tomatoes, first skin by steaming or quickly immersing in boiling water; then simmer 5 minutes in water or tomato juice. Cool, then chill in a refrigerator before packing in plastic bag-lined stiff containers. Leave 1 in. (2 cm) space for expansion when freezing.

FREEZING COOKED FOODS
The dishes that make the most sense to freeze are those which take the most time and energy to prepare. Cook or bake them until almost, but not quite done. Cool, chill, wrap and freeze. To revive them, heat in a 400°F (200°C) oven for ½ to 1 hour, covered.

You may freeze casseroles, especially those combining meats and vegetables and sauces such as cream sauce, tomato sauce, gravy, or cornstarch. Meatballs, stuffed vegetables, and meat pastries all freeze well. Whole or mashed cooked beans freeze well. Soup broths of all kinds freeze well and are endlessly useful.

WHAT YOU CAN'T FREEZE

1. Foods that rely on eggs as a basis for texture really don't hold up in the freezer.
2. Cooked grains become watery and tough, even if frozen in a soup or casserole.
3. Raw, baked and boiled potatoes become rubbery and lose their flakey texture — but mashed potatoes are fine.

Freezing Baked Goods

Yeasted and unyeasted breads, quick-breads, pies, cakes and cookies all freeze very well. Freeze baked goods soon after baking them. Wrap tightly to exclude air. Use within 4 months. Defrost at room temperature and use within 24 hours, for best quality.

Many country cooks find it economical to freeze fruit pies in season, purchasing pressed aluminum pie plates to bake pies in and to invert over the top of the pie to keep the top crust safe in the freezer. They may also be frozen unbaked. To bake an un-baked frozen pie, set it unthawed in a 400°F (200°C) oven for 1 hour. To reheat a baked frozen pie, bake at 400°F (200°C) for 30 minutes.

Pies and pastries with custard, or quiches do not freeze well.

Freezing Tofu

Freezing is not only a method of preserving tofu, it is also used to make the tofu drier, more spongey and absorbent. Some darkening also occurs. Before freezing, cut tofu in slabs, or crumble it by wringing in a clean cloth. To defrost, pour boiling water over it and let stand 10 to 15 minutes.

Freezing Eggs and Dairy Foods

Eggs frozen in their shells will expand, cracking the shell; the yolks will also ex-pand and mix with the whites. They are more successfully frozen as follows:

WHOLE EGGS
Mix together:

| 4 | eggs | 4 |
| 1/4 tsp. | salt | 1 mL |

Beat well, and pack in plastic container.

EGG YOLKS
Mix together:

3	egg yolks	3
1/2 tsp.	salt or	2 mL
1 tsp.	sugar	5 mL

EGG WHITES

Mix egg whites gently, being careful not to beat in air, and package in plastic con-tainer. Label all eggs well. They will keep from 1 to 2 years. Defrost in refrigerator and use at once.

MILK AND CREAM
Both should be pasteurized before freez-ing. It is said that cream will whip after freezing but I haven't had much success with it. Milk tastes funny after freezing but it's perfectly good for you.

BUTTER AND LARD
The freezer is a great place for all fats, which freeze easily, keep up to a year, and are unchanged, for all practical purposes, by freezing.

CHEESE
Cheese does not keep its smooth texture, but has very much the same flavor in cook-ing after freezing.

The Pantry

Like the pantry of an old-fashioned farm-house kitchen, this chapter is full of miscellaneous ingredients, without which the cook would be lost. Herbs and spices are a good place to begin. Each has a special essence, a quality which can alter or marry everyday ingredients — like the special smell of sage in the stuffing, of oregano on a pizza. It's very important that herbs be fresh. I used to think this was only necessary in green herbs like basil or savory, but last year a friend brought me some freshly dried black peppercorns from Sri Lanka, and they had a whole bouquet of flavors of which we in the West are unaware, even when we grind our dried peppercorns.

This chapter also contains explanations about certain ingredients, such as baking powder and yeasts; of different types of flour, nuts, oils, eggs, milk; about food additives, and all sorts of tables and charts relating to measure, both standard and metric and in between. I have also included some up-to-date pages of substitution which I've found immensely useful in planning meals: things like 1 lb. (450 g) Cheddar makes 5 cups (1.25 L) of grated cheese, or 1 lb. (450 g) of coffee will make 35 cups of coffee. Some aspects of nutrition are also covered in this chapter — along with a sprinkling of recipes and advice.

Herbs

Herbs and spices add a whole new dimension to cookery. It's fun to try different flavors, and, as you become familiar with them, to experiment. All herbs are better if they are fresh, and dried herbs and spices have a great deal more ambience if they have been picked and dried within the year. Many aren't hard to grow, if you have space; some are available seasonally at ethnic markets.

To dry your own herbs, cut the plants just before they flower, in the early morning of what promises to be a sunny day. Hang herbs to dry upside-down in a warm, dry place, out of the sun. Depending on leaf thickness and the humidity, they will take from three to six days to dry completely. If they are not drying well by the fourth day, take them down and bake them in a slow oven, 120°F (50°C) with the door partly open to allow moisture out.

Crumble the leaves, sorting out stems, and put them in a large covered jar in a warm place for two days. If no moisture appears on the sides of the jar, consider the contents sufficiently dried. Store herbs in covered glass jars in a cool, dry, dark place. I know this rules out all those nice little spice shelves,but herbs deteriorate in sunlight almost as fast as when exposed to heat.

Another way to store herbs is in the freezer. Delicate flavors such as chervil, dill, basil, tarragon and parsley don't carry much of their essence into the dried state, no matter how carefully the process is done. Instead, chop them fine, and pack them by half-cupfuls (125 mL) into little plastic bags. Place the bags in a larger plastic container, label and freeze.

HERBS

Anise Italians like to put anise in their sausage, to contrast with the fiery peppers and heavy meat flavors. You may also try it in meatballs, cabbage rolls, and stuffings. Australians press anise seeds into cookies. Anise-flavored wines and liqueurs are a favorite with Latin lovers, because it is said to sweeten the breath after too much cheese and garlic.

Basil Fresh basil is used in salads, with eggs, cheese, fish, and vegetables, especially tomatoes. If you wish to preserve its pungent aroma, try freezing it. Coat the leaves with a light rubbing of olive oil, crumple them into a plastic bag, and store in a marked plastic container. Or make up a pesto (page 46). Freeze small amounts of pesto in an ice cube tray, then empty the cubes into a marked plastic container. Use as salad dressing or with noodles or rice. It'll definitely knock your dull old January palate right back into the middle of glorious summer.

Bay These are the leaves of the edible bay, useful to mildly sweeten stews, soups, and meats, as well as pickles and baked beans. Bay will not disintegrate either in cooking or in you stomach, so remember to remove it from the pot before you serve.

Borage Borage is a geat big leafy plant with tiny blue flowers all over it, grown mainly to make the garden pretty. The flowers taste a bit like cucumbers, and can be used in salads or cold summer drinks.

Caraway Caraway seeds are strong fla-vored and are used in rye bread, Polish sausage, meatballs, and even, according to Gaelic tradition, on top of cakes and cookies. Caraway's pungent smell is also a marvelous way to mask the smell of cook-ing cabbage or cauliflower: add a pinch to the cooking liquid.

Celery Celery has a fresh, crisp flavor and texture and is used with chicken, fish, and in vegetable salads of all kinds. It's also one of the many flavors in tomato sauce, pick-les, and stir-fries. Use dried seeds or fresh plant.

Chervil This is a delicate-looking cousin of parsley with lacey leaves and a mild anise flavor. Used with eggs, fish, chicken, in salads and sauces, it is also a very nice garnish for rice or potatoes. Chervil, like parsley, is better frozen than dried.

Chives A tiny member of the onion clan, chive tops are used, chopped, as a garnish for egg, fish, and potato dishes. They freeze better than dry, but are not hard to grow in a pot or garden for a perpetual fresh supply.

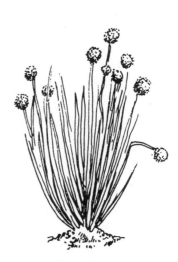

Coriander Leaves and seeds are used in Mexican and Oriental cooking. Coriander leaves are sometimes used in salads or stir-fries, but the chief use is of the ground seeds, which are used to flavor soups, stews, and sauces. In Mexico it is known as *celentro* and used in avocado sauce.

Dill Fresh dill is used in fish cookery and in salads, where its fresh flavor goes well with sour cream or yogurt sauces. It is also commonly used with cucumbers, in dill pickles. Dill is better frozen than dried.

Garlic Garlic is an essential ingredient in cookery the world over, alone or in combination with other flavors. It is chopped fine and fried in oil, like onions, before adding to tomato sauce or vegetable dishes. It may also be crushed with a garlic press for use in salad dressings, pestos, sauces, and fiery Middle Eastern spreads.

GARLIC BREAD CRUMBS

3 Tbsp.	safflower oil	45 mL
3	cloves garlic, crushed	3
2	slices whole wheat bread, crumbled	2

Heat oil in a heavy skillet. Sauté garlic and crumbled bread over moderate heat 3–5 minutes. Add to chopped spinach and fried mushrooms, or use as a casserole topping, to garnish fish or steak, or in meatballs.

Horseradish In Victorian England, no haunch-and-pudding dinner was complete without a dish of freshly grated horseradish with a little vinegar or lemon juice squeezed over it. Horseradish may also be mixed with sour cream, even (if you're adventurous) added to potato salad.

Marjoram Fresh or dried, marjoram is a mild, sweet herb which is good in soups and stews, especially those made with chicken, veal, or mild fish. Fresh, it may be used in salads. It's also a nice herb to stick in a vinegar bottle (See Tarragon Vinegar, page 174).

Mint Mint is known today primarily as a flavor of candy and toothpaste, but it can also be used, fresh or dried, to pick up the flavor of vegetables such as peas or broccoli. Mint sauce is used with lamb. Try a pinch in Hollandaise Alvino (page 42) or with iced tea, for a pleasant change.

MINT SAUCE

bunch	fresh mint leaves	bunch
2 cups	water	475 mL
1 cup	honey	250 mL

Boil leaves in water 15 minutes. Strain liquid, and return to the heat. Add honey and bring to the boil. Bottle. A few spoonfuls of this elixer can be added to Chocolate Pudding (page 120) to make Chocolate Mint Pudding.

Mustard Mustard's yellow seed is sold whole, ground, or mixed with vinegar into a paste. In North America this paste has been developed into an almost tasteless yellow condiment served primarily with hot dogs. Dijon mustard from France has a fine, piquant flavor. Mustard is added to cream sauce, potato salads, ground meats, sausages, and vegetable stir-fries. To make a thick spreadable paste, mix it with oil or other liquid ingredients.

Onions Onions are basic to cookery throughout the world; it is difficult to imagine stews, soups, curries or stir-fries without them. When cooking with them, first chop and sauté in a little hot oil or butter, for best flavor.

There are several varieties of onions. The French swear by shallots, which are more tender than our big yellows. Dry purple Bermuda onions are thin sliced for garnish and salads.

Onions can be difficult to digest, especially for small children or older people. Try using smaller amounts and chopping them finer. Onions are not bad for you – they just take a lot of energy to process.

Parsley Everybody loves parsley. It's easy to grow, has a lovely fresh mild flavor, and does marvelous things for the body. It not only has vitamins A, B, and C, but also E, which restores health and vigor to jaded tissues. Parsley is a biennial, so if you sow it in the same bed two years running, and mulch well during the winter, you might get a permanent parsley patch. Other ways to grow it: in the winter, in flowerpots or a windowbox; in other seasons, beds of parsley look great amongst the petunias or marigolds.

Dried parsley has very little flavor, so if you can't grow it, buy it fresh and keep it refrigerated in a glass of water (change water daily). Use as much as you can to flavor soups, stews, and vegetables. Mountains of chopped parsley can go into sandwiches, stuffings, hamburgers, egg dishes, and salads of all kinds. If you're going to be good to yourself, start with parsley; it's the best.

Chili Peppers Around the Equator, foods spiced with hot peppers are served at every meal, along with gallons of thirst-quenching liquids. They are definitely an acquired taste, but once acquired, it's a nice change to have a meal with a little zip.

You may buy chilies fresh, dried, as dried seeds, or a "mole" or powder. Mole is pounded fresh every day in Mexican and South American kitchens, because it has more flavor when it's fresh.

Chili peppers come in several varieties. The hottest is cayenne. A pinch per pot of food is a good start. Chilies of all kinds are used in stews and meat dishes, with beans, pickled relish, and in tomato sauce.

Peppercorns Unrelated to chilies, peppercorns are also hot, although much less so. Peppercorns lose their fragrance within hours of grinding, which is why many people keep pepper-grinders on the table instead of pepper shakers. The savory aroma of pepper is used in almost all sauces, on meats, eggs, fish, chicken, vegetables of all kinds, including pickles.

Rosemary An aromatic herb with a smell that is faintly coniferous, rosemary should be used with care. It's good in stews, especially lamb or goat, and in marinades, salad dressings, and sauces. But a very little will go a long way.

Sage Sage is that special flavor that we're all familiar with in turkey stuffing. One reason I dislike commercial stuffings is that the sage is always stale, giving it an "off" flavor. Stuffing should be made with sage as fresh as possible.

Summer Savory An exceptionally good dried herb, savory has a spicy flavor which is used in Cape Breton for everything from sausage stuffing to tomato sauce. Soups, stews and casseroles all benefit from a dash of savory.

Tarragon A fragile French herb, tarragon is really only useful fresh, and then only in fast cooking. You would use it on poached fish, but not in stew. It has a very elegant, unmistakable flavor which is almost lost in drying. It may be chopped and frozen for future use.

TARRAGON VINEGAR

4	stalks tarragon	4
2–3	sprigs parsley	2–3
1	bay leaf	1
3 cups	white vinegar	725 mL
4	sprigs tarragon leaves	4
1 cup	dry white wine	250 mL

Cut and hang tarragon stalks in a dark, dry place for 2 days or until well wilted. Place them in a plastic container and add parsley, bay leaf and boiling vinegar. Mark date on the container, cover, and let sit in a cool place for 2 weeks.

Sterilize 2 pint (475 mL) canning jars and lids. Place 1 or 2 fresh sprigs of tarragon in each. Strain the vinegar into an enameled or stainless steel pan and bring to the boil. Divide equally between the two jars; add wine to fill to within ½ in (1 cm) of top. Adjust lids.   **2 pints**

Basil Vinegar Follow directions for Tarragon Vinegar, substituting basil for tarragon, and red for white wine. You may also add a clove or two of fresh garlic, for extra flavor, when steeping the basil for 2 weeks.   **2 pints**

Thyme Thyme is a tiny plant, which looks like it belongs in a dollhouse rock garden, but it can flavor a stew or soup without bitterness.

FINES HERBES

This is a mixture of very finely crumbled herb leaves, to be served as a garnish for an omelet, soup, or in a sauce.
Mix any or all of basil, chervil, celery, chopped chives, marjoram, savory, parsley, sage (not too much), tarragon, thyme.

Spices

Allspice Allspice derives its name from the fact that it smells like a mixture of other spices — cinnamon, nutmeg and cloves. However, it is actually a whole round seed, often used in this form to pickle vegetables or meats. Ground allspice is a wonderful flavoring combined with molasses in cakes, cookies, and pumpkin recipes. It can also be used in fruit dishes. A pinch can be used to brighten the flavor of a sweet-sour sauce, baked beans, or a meat dish.

Almond Flavoring Almond extract is very strong and bitter, so use it with care. It's a very special flavor with an affinity for things like egg whites, nuts, or coconut. You can even use it in oatmeal cookies. Used with care it can also complement chocolate, and it's marvelous in fruit sauce.

Cardamom Cardamom tastes like nutmeg with maybe a little white pepper thrown in. The large seed pods come in three colors: white, green, and black. The white and green pods contain the milder seeds, ground for use in Holiday Bread (page 132) and cookies. The seeds from the smaller black pods are stronger, used to flavor such things as exotic coffee, or barbecue sauce. Pre-ground cardamom has little flavor and is not worth buying.

Cinnamons There are two entirely different "cinnamon" plants. Cinnamon sticks are the rolled bark from the cinnamon tree, which grows in Sri Lanka. Ground cinnamon, which is much stronger and more bitter, is the bark of the cassia tree and comes from Viet Nam.

Cinnamon sticks are used in hot drinks such as apple cider, mulled wine, rum toddy, lemonade, or coffee; they are sometimes cooked in pickle juices.

Ground cinnamon is the most commonly used spice in North America, probably because it does such wonderful things to apple pie. It's also used in a wide variety of baked goods such as molasses cakes and cookies, in fresh and dried fruit dishes, and in puddings.

Cloves Whole or powdered, cloves are very strong. A pinch will often do where a teaspoon (5 mL) of cinnamon or half of a teaspoon (2 mL) of nutmeg would be appropriate. Cloves have a wonderful aroma and can be used for many things besides gingerbread and pumpkin pie. Buy whole cloves and stick two in an onion to marry with the juices of stew or stockpot for a marvelous and not-quite-identifiable flavor. A tiny pinch of ground cloves in a stir-fry or a casserole will have much the same mysterious effect. Whole cloves, along with other spices, are bagged and cooked with pickle juice. Just make sure that nobody sinks their teeth into a whole clove — they'll know what it is at once!

Cumin The strong, nutty flavor of cumin does wonderful things to chicken, meats and vegetables — even eggs or dried beans. In Eastern cooking it's often used in combination with other spices such as turmeric, coriander, mustard, and chilies. The whole seeds are added to marinades and pickles.

Curry Powder Western curry powder is not a spice but a mixture of spices. By "curry," Eastern cooks mean a mixture of spiced foods; they add the spices individually to suit the dish and those who are to eat it. Westerners, however, refer to "curry" as a pre-mixed combination of mustard, coriander, cumin, allspice, turmeric, cardamom and various sorts of hot chilies. Often it is sold as "hot" or "mild" with reference to the chilies. The powder may be used to flavor casseroles, meat or vegetable dishes, or in tiny amounts to pick up the flavor of a cream sauce or gravy.

Ginger Being a root, ginger will keep for months in a humid refrigerator — you do not have to make use of the greatly inferior dried powder. Freshly grated ginger gives a marvelous tang to molasses cookies and cakes, pumpkin or squash, stir-fry dishes and sweet-sour sauces.

Lemon and Orange Peel The peel of either lemons or oranges may be finely grated into cakes, cookies, and other desserts. It can even be used in sauces for meats or vegetables. The drawback is that who-knows-what is sprayed or soaked into the skins these days. I soak fruit for 20 minutes in cold water, then rinse and scrub, and hope for the best. Always use whole fruit to grate; remove peel from grater with a stiff brush.

Nutmeg The kernel of a tall evergreen from the East Indies, nutmeg is famous for its gentle, magical flavor. Keep both fresh and ground nutmeg on hand for use in puddings, cakes, and cookies. Nutmeg was also used traditionally for ground meats

and sausage, stuffing, and pickling mixtures. Whole nutmeg has more flavor, but must be finely grated as you need it. Ground nutmeg, while having less piquancy, is still good in a pinch.

Turmeric Turmeric comes from an Asian root (now cultivated in the West). We buy it as a bright yellow powder. Very popular in southern Asia, it is used in all kinds of meats and vegetable curries, and is also used to color breads and cakes. Because of its mildly unpleasant smell, it is used in combination with strong-smelling spices such as cumin and coriander.

Vanilla In the good old days when vanilla was cheap, thousands of recipes had vanilla added to the ingredients. Lately, it has become too dear to use so freely. I often use almond extract, orange or lemon peel, or spices such as nutmeg and cinnamon instead of vanilla in my cakes and cookies.

Nevertheless, vanilla has a warm, friendly taste, and is especially good in puddings, ice creams, cheesecake, and yogurt popsicles. It's also good in combination with other flavorings, such as chocolate, orange, and lemon.

Also On The Shelf

CHOCOLATE

Chocolate! There's nothing like it. Almost everybody loves it, even though it's not the best thing for you. Chocolate has hardly any nutrition, and many people are unable to eat it without skin problems, weight gain, or a nervous reaction to the high amounts of sugar needed to make it palatable. Chocolate desserts average about 500 calories per serving, and they're empty calories, every one.

The chocolate used in cooking is available in several forms. You may buy it as unsweetened or sweetened cocoa, and as bitter or semi-sweet solid chocolate. Semi-sweet has some sugar, hence less chocolate. The sugar has been cooked at high temperatures with the chocolate to bond them together, a process difficult to duplicate. When cooking with chocolate, it is best to stick to the type recommended in the recipe.

CAROB
Carob is a dark sweet powder made from ground carob beans. It looks like chocolate, but there the resemblance ends; it has a butterscotch-like flavor, and doesn't need the vast quantities of sugar that chocolate requires. Carob goes well with nuts and raisins and vanilla. I have found that while my family enjoys it in cookies, cakes and brownies, they don't like it in uncooked mixtures such as frostings or blender specials.

YEASTS
There are two separate products known as "yeast" in North American cookery, which the novice cook must take care not to confuse: baker's yeast and brewer's yeast. Baker's yeast, used in breadmaking and brewing, is composed of tiny pale balls, or is in a solid cake; brewer's yeast, a nutritional food additive, is a pale powder.

Dried Baker's Yeast Used primarily for baking bread, dried baker's yeast is available in airtight packets, each containing 1 Tbsp. (15 mL), in cans with plastic lids containing larger amounts, or in bulk form from health food stores. There is no difference in these types of yeast. It is important that yeast be kept dry, cool and dark, and used within six months. Some yeasts are sold with expiry dates printed on them.

Cake Baker's Yeast Baker's yeast used to be sold more often in cake form; little squares of cheesey-looking yeast, wrapped in foil, to be kept in the refrigerator and used before the expiry date. The only advantage that I've found to this form of yeast is that it can be spread on toast and used to brew wines, without too much yeasty sediment getting into the fluid.

Beer and Wine Yeasts These are also baker's yeast, but the packages, available at health food stores and delicatessens, contain varieties with a less "yeasty" flavor, for use in brewing wine or beer.

Using Baker's Yeasts Because it is a living organism, you must take some care in the storage and handling of baker's yeast. Yeast is a simple form of plant, purchased in a dormant stage. It remains dormant until exposed to warmth, water and oxygen. The extremes of temperature which it can survive are 70°–105°F (2°–40°C), which means that it grows well in water at about skin temperature, or a little cooler: tepid water. Hot water will kill yeast, so mix water to the right temperature before adding the yeast.

Yeast growth is controlled by temperature. Slower growth makes a finer-textured bread; a higher temperature might cause a bread dough to rise more quickly, with some large air bubbles caused by this rapid growth. If a dough containing yeast is cooled overnight, it can be reactivated by gradual warming over many hours.

Brewer's Yeast A byproduct of the brewing process, brewer's yeast is dead on arrival; it cannot be used to bake bread or brew anything. It has large amounts of B vitamins which can be added to milk or baked goods to increase daily intake of B vitamins. Brewer's yeast comes in various forms: ordinary, debittered, and a debittered form called Engivita. In England, brewer's yeast is sold as Marmite, a brown spread used on bread.

BAKING SODA

Bicarbonate of soda is an alkaline chemical used in baking. It gives off carbon dioxide when combined with an acid ingredient such as buttermilk, yogurt, tea, coffee, molasses, honey, chocolate, or cream of tartar. The carbon dioxide, released into the batter as it solidifies, causes the batter to "rise", or fill with air holes. Baking soda also neutralizes the acidity of the acid ingredient; for this reason, it is sometimes used in combination with baking powder. If there is no acid ingredient in the batter, it will rise a good deal less and give the product an unpleasant flat taste. Thus, if you have a recipe for cookies that calls for buttermilk and soda, and you are out of buttermilk, either sour the fresh milk first with 1 tsp. (5 mL) of vinegar or lemon juice, or substitute baking powder for the soda. Baking powder is not as powerful as soda: 2 tsp. (10 mL) baking powder = ½ tsp. (2 mL) baking soda (plus acid ingredient).

Some people (notably, Adele Davis) object to the use of baking soda because it counteracts vitamin C and the B vitamins. Substitution of baking powder is not a solution, because baking powder contains baking soda. If you feel strongly that you need every vitamin you can get, make your cakes with Baker's Yeast.

BAKING POWDER

Baking powder is a combination of bicarbonate of soda and an acid ingredient. You can make your own baking powder by combining: 2 tsp. (10 mL) cream of tartar and 1 tsp. (5 mL) baking soda. However, this doesn't keep well and must be used up right away. Commercial baking powders mix a little cornstarch in and, rather than cream of tartar, use monocalcium phosphate or sodium acid phosphate.

Double-acting baking powder also uses sodium aluminum sulphate, which is a very successful ingredient in that it doesn't act until heat is applied to the batter. However, many people prefer not to ingest aluminum or alum as part of their diet and therefore stick to baking powders that do not contain this ingredient. The reason is that aluminum is a substance that is foreign to the body.

Vitamins And Minerals In Whole Foods

Vitamins are often thought of as substances which improve health. In fact, they are necessary for life itself. Minute amounts of vitamins A, B, C, D, E, and K are found in almost all foods which have not been refined. For example, there is as much vitamin C in a potato as the average child needs in a day, but it's all concentrated in a waxy layer beneath the skin; there's no vitamin of any kind in a peeled, fried "chip". Grains like whole wheat naturally contain a complex of B vitamins, sifted out when the wheat germ is removed to make "white flour".

People concerned with nutrition have long been aware of this, enough to insist that some vitamins be put back into some refined foods which people eat every day. Thus, we now have "enriched" flour and bread, "vitamin-fortified" fruit drinks and milk. This is a step in the right direction, but a small one, compared to the tremendous amounts of food value lost by refining grains, seeds and fats, cooking eggs, milk and fruits, peeling our roots and boiling our vegetables.

Many people today figure that the situation is bad enough to warrant considerable daily intake of vitamin supplements as pills and powders; that way, no matter what they eat, they're sure of getting adequate nutrition. I'm not so sure. Vitamins, minerals and enzymes in most foods combine in myriad subtle ways, and many are interdependent. You'd really have to be a nutritionist to guess which ones to take, when, and in combination with what foods. Moreover, there are other components of whole, unprocessed, unrefined foods — such as roughage — which are important to the well-balanced diet of a healthy individual. Demand whole foods. Buy them, grow them, cook with them, teach others how to enjoy them. You'll find yourself in good company, with energy to spare, and eating the best-tasting food on earth.

WHOLE GRAINS

Basically, seeds and grains have three parts: the outer shell or bran, the inner germ, and the part in the middle, like the white of an egg, which in wheat is white flour. The bran and the germ are, however, of importance to the human body. Bran provides roughage, which makes it easier to digest the other, richer foods we eat. The germ has all kinds of magical substances, traces of oils needed to keep cells and glands all over the body working, B vitamins needed to be vigorous and healthy. Some of these are returned to flours and cereals. These "enriched" products contain only tiny amounts of some of the vitamins, which is of little use; the reason they are called the "B complex" is that they operate together.

If you lack one, you're low in all. Other than grains, there are very few sources of this B-vitamin complex in the average human diet.

Whole grains we have access to in most supermarkets include whole wheat flour, whole wheat baked goods, and whole grain cereals. From the health food store you can get brown rice, bulgur, millet, kasha, and a variety of whole grain flours such as rye, buckwheat, hard and soft whole wheat.

Hard Wheat Flour The best breads and cereals are made of this flour. It has very high protein for grain, and varies in quality around the world because of climatic and soil differences. Whole grain hard wheat (stone or steel ground) is available in health food stores, or, in bulk, from special distributors.

Hard whole wheat flour has a slightly gritty texture when a pinch of it is rubbed between the fingers. When mixed with liquids, the gluten in the flour softens and dissolves very slowly. Longer rising times and more kneading are needed to make quality whole wheat breads than for making white flour breads.

Soft Wheat Flour A variety of wheat developed more recently for pastry-making, soft wheat has a fat kernel and lower protein. This soft white flour with brown flecks in it is available both from health food stores, where it's sold as whole wheat pastry flour, or from supermarkets, where it's sold as whole wheat flour or graham flour.

Soft wheat flour is excellent for cakes, cookies, and fine for piecrusts, but it does not make high-quality yeasted bread because it has insufficient gluten to rise and set properly.

Durum Wheat Durum wheat is a northern wheat, seeded in the spring. It has the highest level of protein but is a little hard for bread; it makes a rather rubbery loaf. It's used primarily for noodles and pasta.

Unbleached White Flour Like most white flours, this is simply hard whole wheat flour with the bran and the wheat germ sifted out. The only difference is that it hasn't been treated with chemical bleach to whiten and purify it. It looks just the same as white bleached flour, but most cooks agree that it makes better quality products, particularly bread.

SEEDS AND NUTS
Seeds and nuts are similar to grains in their nutritional value, containing B vitamins, essential fatty acids and proteins, but they're more concentrated, richer, and we eat less of them. Unshelled, nuts and seeds will keep for years, in cool storage. With the shells off, however, their high oil content can cause them to become rancid unless you store them in tightly sealed plastic containers or bags in the freezer.

Almonds These are hard nuts, with a special flavor that fades soon after shelling. Almonds are sometimes blanched, by boiling them in water for a few minutes, to remove the skin. They may also be slivered or ground, but are often used whole as delicious decorations on cakes, cookies and breads. Chopped and sautéed in a little butter, they're very good with green beans or on top of a simple broiled fish.

Brazil Nuts Large, soft nuts, Brazils are very good in cookies or as a topping for yeasted rolls and pastry.

Cashew Nuts Cashews are a soft, sweet nut, very good raw in a hiker's mix, or roasted as a snack. Sometimes used on yeast rolls.

Filberts or Hazelnuts Fresh filberts have a wonderful flavor, brought out even more by roasting. Use in breakfast cereals or ground on top of cookies, yeasted breads, iced cakes.

Peanuts Peanuts are a great buy, raw and shelled or unshelled. Roast them for snacks or "pocket food", or eat them raw.

PEANUT BUTTER

2 cups	raw shelled peanuts	475 mL
2–4 Tbsp.	peanut oil	30–60 mL

Spread peanuts on a cookie sheet and bake them in a 150°F (65°C) oven for 1 hour. Grind them in a grain grinder, food processor, or in short bursts of the blender, and add oil for the texture you like. Keep refrigerated and use within 2 weeks.

Pecans Pecans are ridiculously expensive, a wonderful treat. Softer than walnuts, with a gentle flavor, they are good baked on custards, pies or ice cream, and in stuffings.

Pumpkin or Squash Seeds Remove seeds from pumpkin or squash, clean, and toss in a little oil, or oil plus tamari soy sauce. Roast 20 minutes in a hot oven. Pumpkin and squash seeds may also be purchased, shelled, and make a good addition to breakfast cereals or hiker's mixes.

Sesame Seeds Sesame seeds are so flavorful that a few go a long way. Sprinkle them on casseroles, or stick them to the tops of loaves and rolls by first painting the dough with beaten egg. Roasted and coarsely ground with a little salt, they make a wonderful garnish for rice, fish, and other dishes. See Gomasio (page 57).

Sunflower Seeds Very high in protein and unsaturated oils, and very inexpensive compared to other seeds and nuts, shelled sunflower seeds should be kept refrigerated or in a cool storage place. Dry-roasted or sautéed in oil, they make excellent nibbling food. Add them to granola, or roast and add them to familia. Raw or roasted, they may also be added to hiker's mixes, breads, cookies and cakes.

Walnuts Walnuts are best freshly shelled, and are used, whole or ground, on cookies, in nut breads, loaves, and to decorate iced cakes or yeasted breads. Deep-fried walnuts are a treat; fry them for about 2 minutes, cool and drain on absorbent paper, and serve with cold sliced apples.

DRY OVEN ROASTING

Scatter seeds lightly over an ungreased baking sheet. Hulled sunflower seeds: 200°F (90°C) for 20 minutes; Unhulled pumpkin or squash seeds: 400°F (200°C) for 20 minutes; Hulled sesame seeds: 200°F (90°C) for 7 minutes; Peanuts: 150°F (65°C) for 60 to 90 minutes.

TAMARI NUTS AND SEEDS

1 tsp.	tamari soy sauce	5 mL
1 tsp.	safflower oil	5 mL
½ cup	sunflower seeds, peanuts, *or* other nuts and seeds	125 mL

Roast as above.

½ cup (125 mL)

BEER NUTS

2 tsp.	safflower oil	10 mL
1½ cups	raw peanuts	375 mL
2 Tbsp.	honey	30 mL
1 tsp.	tamari soy sauce	5 mL
pinch	salt	pinch

Oil a cookie sheet lightly with half of the oil. Mix honey, soy sauce, remaining oil and salt in a shallow bowl. Beat well, then toss peanuts in the mixture. Roast in a slow oven at 150°F (65°C) for 1 hour. Cool and serve.

1½ cups (375 mL)

Fats

In cooking there are two general kinds of fats: solid (butter and shortening) and liquid (vegetable oils). These types are really quite different, both in the way they work in cooking and in the way they work in your body. Solid fats are saturated with hydrogen, meaning that an extra link of hydrogen is added to stabilize the fat, to make it less likely to oxygenate and become rancid. Solid fats may be used to make certain baked goods (chiefly pies and cookies) light and crisp in texture. However, the extra molecule does not make them easier to digest, and many people find it important to limit the amounts of saturated fats they eat in a day. Liquid fats, mainly pressed from nuts and seeds, are easier to digest, but make a denser cookie or piecrust. They are great for deep fat frying and certain types of baking. They may also be used daily in salad dressing, stir-frying vegetables, braising meats and in yeasted breads. Oils are available both refined and unrefined.

Refined Oils These are the ones in most grocery stores, but health food stores also carry them. They are clear, flavorless, and have no noticeable smell. Refined oils have been extracted and refined by a series of chemical processes involving caustic sodas, bleaches, and extremes of hot and cold. Not only do traces of hydrocarbons remain, but the oils are devoid of values your body really needs — essential fatty acids, lecithins, and vitamins A and B. Another drawback of these oils: because they are tasteless and odorless, there's no way to tell whether they have become rancid (which is likely in a heated grocery store).

Unrefined Vegetable Oils These oils are slightly cloudy with the distinctive flavor of their origin and a fresh, nutty smell. Pressed from living seeds or nuts, they are subject to very little heat in pressing, and thus retain their valuable nutrients.

Over the years, we have tried cold-pressed unrefined oils from many sources: peanuts, corn, soybeans, sunflower, sesame, and safflower. Our preference, for use in cooking, baking, frying and salad dressings has been safflower oil. It has a light, unobstrusive flavor, unlike some of the other cold-pressed oils, and we use about ten gallons a year in various cookery applications. In this cookbook I refer to it, in most places, as "vegetable oil".

Cold pressed oils are somewhat more expensive than chemically refined oils, due to the extra costs of production, storage and shipping. They should be shipped and stored, like all fresh produce, at refrigerator temperatures, and used within a few months.

Olive Oil Olive oil is distinctive in that it is pressed from a fruit, rather than a nut or seed. Widely used in Europe and North America as a salad and cooking oil, olive oil does not have the essential nutrition of oils pressed from seeds or nuts. It is available in both cold pressed and chemically refined forms. The cold pressed variety is cloudy and smells like fresh olives; it should be kept refrigerated.

Butter Butter is made by churning cream, after the cream is separated from the milk. It is a wonderful spread, marvelously light and flavorful to cook and bake with. However, low temperatures must be used when you fry things in butter, or the milk solids will cause it to brown. Butter is often colored with the yellow annatto seed, and is usually lightly salted, which helps make it possible for it to be kept up to two weeks, refrigerated. Unsalted butter will only keep about a week. If you wish to keep it longer, it freezes quite well provided it is carefully wrapped.

Margarine There are dozens of varieties of margarine today. The best ones have long lists of ingredients with very unfamiliar names. Contrary to what margarine companies would like you to believe, they are not better for you than butter. They're based on unsaturated fats, true, but in order to solidify and stabilize them, margarines are saturated, like lard or shortening. They have the same number of calories as butter and none of the flavor. However, they are much less expensive than butter.

Shortenings These are, chiefly, vegetable oils, chemically refined and saturated for stability. They are less expensive than margarines (which are made the same way) because they aren't flavored or colored to resemble butter. Shortening is used in cooking, in the same way as butter or lard, and makes a very nice light texture in pies, cookies, and cakes. It may also be used in deep fat frying.

Lard Lard is a fat rendered out of the fats of a pig. Home-rendered lard is not stable and should be kept frozen or quite cold. Commercial lard is hydrogenated. Lard is excellent in producing flakey piecrust, cookies, and pastries provided it is used and kept cold until it goes into the oven. It can also be used for deep fat frying.

Sugar

Nutritionists often state that there is nothing wrong with sugar as long as you don't eat too much of it, too often, or in place of foods with broader values. The trouble is that people do. Sweet foods are attractive, especially to people on the run. They give you a quick lift and don't require a lot of slow digesting. Sometimes, though, it's more than a lift: it's a rocket launch and crashdown. A snack or short meal made up of sugary foods puts a terrific strain on the pancreas, which is supposed to produce the right amount of insulin, exactly, to balance all the sugar. A blood-sugar high is often followed by a dramatic sense of depression. Children are particularly susceptible. After the birthday ice cream and cake (with candies and icing and pop) it's about half an hour to the first howling casualty.

When you feel the urge for sweets, try to imagine what you'd eat if you were unable to have sugary foods. A piece of fruit? Some freshly cracked nuts? How about some whole grain crackers, cheese, and a cup of hot apple juice? When browsing through dessert recipes, look at the quantity of sugar. Is that what you want to eat? Don't buy cookies or desserts for your kids without tasting them and having a look at the ingredients. I think the answer to the sugar problem isn't whether you use it, but how much, when, and how to go about using less of it.

There are various kinds of sugars available. The most commonly used are:

Molasses Refined or unrefined, this syrup contains a lot of sugar, and, cup for cup, is as sweet as brown, raw, or white sugar. It also has a lot of minerals, some vitamins, and a very distinctive flavor when used in quantity. You cannot really taste the small amounts used in breads, but it is very noticeable in cakes and cookies. They're browner, chewier, and molasses-flavored. It is best to use spices that complement this taste, such as cinnamon, ginger, nutmeg, allspice and cloves.

Blackstrap Molasses This kind of molasses has very little sweetening and a *very* strong taste; some like it and some don't. You will notice the flavor in anything you add it to. You can cook with it, but should not consider it a sweetening but a food additive, like brewer's yeast. It is very high in minerals. You can add a few spoonfuls to bread, cornbread, or grain dishes.

White Sugar This is a purified form of raw sugar. If kept dry, it doesn't become lumpy in long storage. Its only food value is calories, which enter the bloodstream almost at once and are soon used up. White sugar is very light, an easy sweetening to work with, and has no flavor of its own.

Brown Sugar A light brown sugar is popular in Canada; several darker grades are available in the United States. All are made by adding a little molasses to white sugar. Brown sugars don't have much nutrition but have a slightly richer flavor.

Honey Nutritionally speaking, honey is not really much better for you than sugar. It is classified as a glucose (rather than a sucrose), which means that it's slightly easier to digest; to some people, that's important. However, sugar is not very difficult to digest either. Honey is certainly not easier on the teeth or the pancreas, and it's not cheap, either, whether you buy it or produce it yourself. Nevertheless, used in moderation, it has a pleasing taste, and there are many uses for it. Honey can be used in baking, but you must alter the recipe: honey is sweeter than sugar and is, of course, liquid. Best stick to honey recipes, available in honey cookbooks.

Maple Syrup Maple syrup is very expensive and not very flavorful in cooking. It's best used on its own — poured over cake or custard, ice cream, or rice pudding. It has very little nutritive value, other than calories.

About Protein

The most important thing to think about when you plan a meal is protein. Lack of it is what makes you hungry in the first place. Protein provides most of your energy every day, to work and think, to digest food, to grow or heal and mend any part of you that has gotten hurt or sick or worn.

Different people need different amounts of protein at various times, but in general, we can go by this chart:

DAILY PROTEIN NEEDS
(grams per Kg body weight)

Infant: age	0 to 1	2 g
Child: age	1 to 5	30 g
	5 to 10	40 g
	10 to 12	50 g
Boys	12 to 18	50-60 g
Girls	12 to 18	50-55 g
Average woman		55 g
Average man		65 g
Pregnant or nursing woman		75 g

The highest protein foods are animal products such as eggs, milk and milk products, meat, fish and poultry. Protein is also stored in plants in their seeds, so beans, peas, nuts and grains also have varying degrees of protein. In most cases, though, the amount of protein in the vegetable foods is lower than the amount in animal foods. This is partly because the protein in all vegetable sources is lacking in one or more of the nutrients necessary to make all of its protein available to you. But, if you complement vegetable protein foods with other foods that contain the missing nutrients, the level of protein will be greatly increased. For example, a bowl of oatmeal has about 3 g of protein. A glass of milk has about 7. But when you put them together, you will be getting about 12 g of protein, instead of 10, because the milk contains nutrients that oatmeal lacks. Another example: a cup of cooked rice has around 3 g of protein; ⅓ cup cooked kidney beans has 2. Together they provide about as much protein as a commercial hamburger, or a serving of fried chicken

In most cultures there are traditional dishes that incorporate two or three foods that complement each other, to make the level of protein in the whole meal greater than the sum of its parts. Such dishes are legume-grain combinations, such as beans and corn in Mexico, rice and soybeans in the East, noodles and white beans in western Europe, barley and split peas in Scotland, millet and chick-peas in Africa, rice and black beans in South America, bulgur and chick-peas in the Middle East.

Another common combination translated into many cultures is milk products and grains and eggs, which make a good pudding, served hot or cold, sweet or nonsweet. And there are lots of ways to make high protein snacks out of nuts or seeds and grains and dairy products. All these dishes are the result of thousands of generations of cooking by trial and error; we are, by comparison, in a somewhat privileged position, in that we have some idea why such foods combine well to make whole protein out of half proteins. For more on this subject, consult Frances Moore Lappé's book, *Diet for a Small Planet* (New York, Ballantine Books, 1971).

Eggs The egg, the most common ingredient in cooking, is also one of the trickiest. When cooking them, always use low heat. Too hot a pan causes the delicate protein to shrink and toughen rapidly; too hot an oven will deflate a soufflé, or cause a quiche to separate. Eggs should be heated gradually. When adding eggs to hot sauces or soups, first beat the eggs in a bowl, then add a little of the hot mixture to the eggs, mixing as you do. Continue to mix as you pour the egg mixture into the pot, stirring continually. Be careful not to overcook egg-thickened mixtures; remove them from the heat when thick. And, until you're familiar with the process, use a double boiler.

Eggs are wonderfully good for you, containing vitamin A, not available in many other foods, and also lecithin, which helps break down cholesterol.

Home-Grown Eggs Anybody who has ever broken into a home-grown egg can see that there's quite a difference in quality between that and the commercial product. The yolk is dark, not light yellow. The white is thick and gelatinous and doesn't run all over the pan when fried or poached. Part of the difference is that commercial hens, under artificial lighting, lay eggs more often, hence, each egg contains more water. Free-range chickens have a more varied diet, too, which has to account for something. If you feed lobster shells to chickens, the yolks become dark orange.

If you grow your own eggs, you will have noticed these and other differences. Absolutely fresh eggs are wonderful for breakfast, but when making hard-boiled eggs or beating egg whites, choose eggs which are at least three days old. Fresh egg whites stick to the shell, making hardboiled eggs hard to shell. And fresh egg whites absolutely will not expand fully, no matter how long you beat them.

Raw Eggs Many children and some adults are allergic to raw egg whites. There are many recipes for foods with raw eggs, but I hesitate to use them for this and for nutritional reasons. Avidin, a component of raw egg whites, combines with a B vitamin, biotin, and prevents it from reaching your system.

MILK

Fresh Whole Milk When milk first comes from an animal, it's fresh and sweet, and the cream is mixed in with the milk. But, soon, changes occur. The cream rises to the top, and lactic bacteria that are in the milk go to work souring it. Storing milk at optimum low temperatures (34°–40°F, 1°–4°C) will retard bacteria for a few days, but the best way to stop bacterial growth is to kill them by pasteurizing the milk. Pasteurization is also practised to control diseases that could be passed along in milk from an unhealthy cow. However,the process does also kill vitamins and certain beneficial enzymes in the milk. Milk from frequently tested and specially licensed herds may be sold without pasteurization.

Homogenized Milk Most milk today is also homogenized. In this process, the cream is broken down into minute globules so that it won't float to the top of the milk, and so that as the cream ages (in two or three days) it won't clot.

Some people feel that homogenization is not a desirable process. In cooking, it makes the milk (and milk-based custards and sauces) more granular. In the digestive system, the cream globules are so small that they pass through cell walls that would normally keep fats out. People on restricted diets are usually told to drink skim milk only, even if they are allowed some butterfats in their total diet.

Goat's Milk Goat's milk has naturally smaller fat globules than cow's milk (although not so tiny as in homogenized milk). The cream does not rise to the top of the milk readily. Goat's milk also has caprylic acid, which makes the milk taste "goaty" when it gets sour, or is made into cheese or butter. Many people cannot tell the difference between fresh goat's milk and cow's milk.

Dried Skim Milk Dried skim milk has become a common ingredient in cooking and baking. If you buy dried milk for drinking, mix it up at least 1 hour before serving.

There are two kinds of dried skim milk. Instant dried skim milk is widely available in supermarkets; about ⅓ cup (80 mL) to 1 cup (250 mL) of water equals a cup of reconstituted milk. In health food stores, however, there is a dried skim milk which is in the form of a powder, much stronger than instant, which does not so readily combine with water. Only 4 tsp. (20 mL) of non-instant skim milk powder are needed to turn 1 cup (250 mL) of water into milk. To mix powder and water, beat or shake them together in a jar.

CREAM
There are two grades of cream sold in North America. If you allow the cream to rise naturally to the top of fresh whole-milk, in 48 hours it will be in two layers: a light, fluid cream topped by thick, almost solid cream. The top layer is a little too heavy for most cooking purposes: for example it makes a rather buttery whipped cream, unless you add some thinner cream before whipping. A mixture of top cream and lighter cream is what we know as *whipping cream*. *Coffee cream,* on the other hand, is more liquid. It will not whip, but it's great in soups and sauces and in coffee or tea.

To Whip Cream Cream should be whipped just before serving. If it is necessary to hold it for half an hour before serving, keep it chilled. For best and fastest results, chill the bowl, the cream, and the beater before whipping. Don't add any ingredients to the cream, and use only whipping cream (see above) at about 40 per cent butterfat. An electric beater is best for this job, but keep an eye on it! It can turn the cream to butter, if you whip it too long or at too high a temperature. By hand you may use a rotary beater or, if you have an endlessly powerful shoulder and like to do things by hand, it can be done with a whisk. The kind with dozens of wires is best. 1 cup (250 mL) heavy cream = 2½ cups (625 mL) whipped cream.

Evaporated Milk Evaporated milk, which comes in cans, has twice the milk solids of fresh milk. It should be kept in a cool place, and used within six months. It's very useful, because it keeps so well, and has the consistency (if not the flavor, or the calories) of cream. When I don't have cream on the farm, I use it for things like cream sauce, quiches, or puddings. You can also get away with it in chocolate ice cream, but not vanilla. To whip evaporated milk, like cream, chill as for whipped cream and follow directions (opposite page). To use it for drinking, add 1 cup (250 mL) water for every cup of evaporated milk.

Condensed Milk Condensed milk, like evaporated milk, has about twice the milk solids of fresh milk. It also has about half a cup (125 mL) of sugar per can, which makes it only useful for puddings or sweet desserts. However, the sugar helps preserve it; you can keep it up to a year.

About Food Additives

Many people in this day and age are becoming more and more worried about the chemicals used in food production and processing. The more processed a product is, the more likely it is to contain chemical substances that may or may not have been fully tested. By comparing labels, you can avoid jelly with food coloring, bread with preservatives, and soup with monosodium glutamate. But you cannot always be so sure about chemical residues in refined oils, or just exactly what has been used to make the "artificial flavoring" in so many products. Until better laws are passed concerning the need for long-term testing of these minute amounts of chemicals — alone or in combination with other minute amounts of chemicals — it's probably healthiest to stick to foods in as whole a form as possible. Buy nuts, raisins, and fruits instead of cookies and snack foods. Stick to juice, instead of pop; yogurt instead of ice cream.

Wash all fruits and vegetables thoroughly as soon as they are brought into the house. Don't wait until later — you might forget.

In making the washing a part of the buying process, rather than the cooking process, you can also help other members of the household become aware of the fact that unwashed fruits and vegetables are almost certain to have pesticide residues on them. These pesticides are water-soluble, so to get rid of them let them soak for five minutes in a sink full of cold water then rinse and wipe off each piece. Dry thoroughly before storing.

Avoid organ meats such as kidneys and livers from commercial animals. Heavy metals and toxic substances are more likely to be found in these, the "cleaning parts" of the body. Fats are also a storage spot for chemicals, and sometimes there are high concentrations in the neck of an animal, where injections are most often given. Muscle is still the cleanest meat.

Buy from organic producers, whenever possible. Certainly these foods cost a little more. But it's good to support organic growers, because they are the pioneers of the future. The tide is turning against the chemicals in our foods. Organic growers are developing fruits and vegetables that are naturally resistant to bugs and fungi.

Measurement

Europe and Asia are metric, the United States uses standard, and Canada is somewhere in between. This cookbook is in both because it's international. The following charts and tables are helpful in coping with conversion, from standard to metric and vice versa, as it relates to cooking.

SUBSTITUTIONS IN STANDARD MEASURE

Baking Powder, 1 tsp. = 1/2 tsp. baking soda + 1/2 tsp. cream of tartar

Baking Powder, 1 tsp. = 1/4 tsp. baking soda + 1/2 cup buttermilk

Beans, dried, 1 cup = almost 3 cups cooked beans

Butter, 1 cup = 1/2 lb. *or* 225 g butter

Butter, 1 cup = 7/8 cup oil, and decrease liquid in recipe by 1/2 cup

Cheese, 1/4 lb. = 1 1/4 cup grated cheese

Chicken, whole, 3 lb. = 4 cups cooked chopped chicken

Chocolate, unsweetened solid, 1 oz. = 2 Tbsp. unsweetened cocoa plus 1 Tbsp. butter

Coffee, 1 lb. = 35 cups of coffee

Cornmeal, 1 cup uncooked = 4 cups cooked cornmeal

Eggs, 5 large = 1 cup eggs

Herbs, fresh, 1 Tbsp. = 1/2 tsp. dried, *or* 1/4 tsp. powdered

Lemon, 1 whole = 3 Tbsp. lemon juice

Maple Syrup, 1 gallon = 40 gallons maple sap

Noodles, 1 cup uncooked = 2 1/3 cup cooked noodles

Oatmeal, 1 cup uncooked = 2 cups cooked oatmeal

Rice, 1 cup uncooked = 2 cups cooked rice

Sugar, 1 cup = 1 cup molasses, and decrease liquid in recipe by 1/2 cup

Sugar, 1 cup = 1/2 cup honey, and decrease liquid in recipe by 1/4 cup

Sugar, 1 cup = 3/4 cup maple syrup, and decrease liquid in recipe by 1/2 cup

Yeast, 1 pkg. dried = 1 Tbsp. dried yeast *or* 1 cake moist yeast

SUBSTITUTIONS IN METRIC MEASURE

Baking Powder, 5 mL = 2.5 mL baking soda + 2.5 mL cream of tartar

Baking Powder, 5 mL = 2.5 mL baking soda + 125 mL buttermilk

Beans, dried, 250 mL = 750 mL cooked beans

Butter, 250 mL = 225 g butter

Butter, 250 mL = 225 mL vegetable oil and decrease liquid in recipe by 125 mL

Cheese, 125 g = 300 mL grated cheese

Chicken, whole, 1.4 kg = 1 L cooked, chopped chicken

Chocolate, unsweetened solid, 28 g = 45 mL unsweetened cocoa plus 15 mL butter

Coffee, 450 g = 35 cups of coffee

Cornmeal, uncooked, 250 mL = 1 L cooked cornmeal

Eggs, 5 large = 250 mL eggs

Herbs, fresh, 15 mL = 2 mL dried or 1 mL powdered

Lemon, 1 whole = 45 mL lemon juice

Maple Syrup, 1 L = 40 L maple sap

Noodles, uncooked, 250 mL = 580 mL cooked noodles

Oatmeal, uncooked, 250 mL = 500 mL cooked oatmeal

Rice, uncooked, 250 mL = 500 mL cooked rice

Sugar, 250 mL = 250 mL molasses, and decrease liquid in recipe by 125 mL

Sugar, 250 mL = 125 mL honey, and decrease liquid in recipe by 60 mL

Sugar, 250 mL = 200 mL maple syrup, and decrease liquid in recipe by 125 mL

Yeast, 1 pkg. dried = 15 mL dried yeast or 1 cake moist yeast

WHAT'S IN A POUND?

A pint's a pound, the world around — unfortunately only applies to water. Here are some other quantities that weigh a pound:

1 lb. (454 g) butter or lard = 2 cups (475 mL)

1 lb. cooking oil = 2⅛ cups (530 mL) (1 pt. oil = 13 oz.)

1 lb. flour = roughly 4 cups (1 L)

1 lb. sugar = 2 cups (475 g)

1 lb. confectioner's sugar = 3½ cups (825 mL)

1 lb. oatmeal = 2⅔ cups (660 mL) dry, 5⅓ cups (1.33 L) cooked

1 lb. rice = 2½ cups (625 mL) dry, 5 cups (1.25 L) cooked

1 lb. raw potatoes = 2 cups mashed (475 mL)

1 lb. noodles = 4 cups (1 L) dry, 9 cups (2.25 L) cooked

1 lb. cornmeal = 3 cups (750 mL) dry, 12 cups (3 L) cooked

1 lb. dry beans = 2¼ cups (560 mL) dry, 6 cups (1.5 L) cooked

1 lb. kidney beans = 4 cups (1 L) dry, 12 cups (3 L) cooked

1 lb. hamburger = about 2 cups (475 mL)

1 lb. raisins = about 3 cups (750 mL)

1 lb. bananas is 3 or 4 = makes about 2 cups (475 mL) mashed

1 lb. Cheddar cheese = 5 cups (1.25 L) grated

1 lb. Parmesan cheese = 4 cups (1 L) grated

1 lb. mushrooms = 5 cups (1.25 L) sliced raw

AMERICAN STANDARD DRY MEASURE

3 tsp. =	1 Tbsp.
4 Tbsp. =	¼ cup
16 Tbsp. =	1 cup
2 cups =	1 pint
4 cups =	1 qt.
4 qt. =	1 gallon

AMERICAN STANDARD FLUID MEASURE

2 Tbsp. =	1 ounce (oz.)
¼ cup =	2 oz.
1 cup =	8 oz.
1 pint (pt.) =	16 oz., or 1 pound (lb.)
1 qt. =	32 oz., or 2 lb.
1 gallon (gal) =	128 oz., or 8 lb.

METRIC VOLUME MEASURE

In the metric system, there is one volume measure for both dry and liquid: the Litre (L). Anything smaller is measured in a millilitre (mL).

$$1000 \text{ mL} = 1 \text{ L}$$

METRIC-TO-STANDARD DRY MEASURE CONVERSION

A litre is approximately a quart, or 4 cups. A millilitre is approximately ¼ teaspoon. The following conversion is approximate, not absolutely accurate. The metric amounts are a little longer in most instances, than the standard. You can, however, use these equivalencies for making your own conversions.

Millilitre	Approximate Standard Measurement
1	¼ tsp.
2	½ tsp.
5	1 tsp.
10	2 tsp.
15	1 Tbsp.
30	2 Tbsp. *or* ⅛ cup
60	¼ cup
125	½ cup
250	1 cup
475	2 cups *or* 1 pint
1 litre	4 cups *or* 1 quart
4 litres	1 gallon

To find accurate equivalencies, use this:

946 mL or .946 L =   exactly 1 quart

METRIC WEIGHT CONVERSION

The basic unit of weight in metric is the gram, which is a very tiny amount: 28.3 grams = 1 ounce. Larger things are measured in kilograms. 1 kilogram (kg) = 1000 grams (g). To find accurate equivalencies in the standard system, use these figures:

1 lb. =	453.59 g
1 kg. =	2.2046 lb.

METRIC-TO-STANDARD WEIGHT CONVERSION

The following figures are approximate:

¼ oz. =	7 g
1 oz. =	25 g
2 oz. =	50 g
4 oz. =	¼ lb. = 125 g
8 oz. =	½ lb. = 227 g
16 oz. =	1 lb. = 454 g
24 oz. =	1½ lb. = 902 g
35.2 oz. =	2.2 lb. = 1000 g = 1 kg

LENGTH CONVERSION

The standard units of measure are inches, feet and yards.

$$12 \text{ inches (in.)} = 1 \text{ foot (ft.)}$$
$$3 \text{ ft.} = 1 \text{ yard}$$

The standard unit of measure in metric is the metre (m) which is about a yard. Smaller divisions are the centimeter (cm) and the millimeter (mm).

$$1000 \text{ mm} = 100 \text{ cm} = 1 \text{ meter}$$
$$10 \text{ mm} = 1 \text{ cm}$$

To convert centimeters to inches accurately, use this:

$$1 \text{ centimeter} = .3937 \text{ inch}$$

To convert centimeters to inches roughly, use this:

1 cm is slightly less than ½ in.
5 cm is about 2 in.

PRESSURE CONVERSION

Pressure for pressure cookers and canners is measured in kilopascals (kPa) instead of pounds per square inch (PSI)

$$35 \text{ kPa} = \text{approx. 5 PSI}$$
$$70 \text{ kPa} = \text{approx. 10 PSI}$$
$$100 \text{ kPa} = \text{approx. 15 PSI}$$

TEMPERATURE CONVERSION

The Fahrenheit scale of temperature measurement is roughly (but not exactly) twice the size of the Celsius scale. Here are a few familiar temperatures:

	F	C
Deep Freeze	0°	−17°
Just Freezing	32°	0°
Body Temperature	98.6°	37°
Boiling Water	212°	100°
Oven Temperature	350°	177°

To convert Fahrenheit to Celsius, subtract 32, multiply by 5, and divide by 9.
To convert Celsius to Fahrenheit, mutiply by 9, divide by 5, and add 32.
The following is an approximate chart; the figures are rounded off to the nearest whole number.

FAHRENHEIT TO CELSIUS CONVERSION SCALE

F=C	F=C	F=C
0° = –17°	26° = –3°	52° = 11°
2°	27°	53°
3° = –16°	28° = –2°	54° = 12°
4°	29°	55°
5° = –15°	30° = –1°	56° = 13°
6° = –14°	31°	57°
	32° = 0°	58° = 14°
7°		
8° = –13°	33°	59°
	34° = +1°	60° = 15°
9°		
10° = –12°	35°	61° = 16°
	36° = 2°	
11°		62°
12° = –11°	37°	63° = 17°
	38° = 3°	
13°		64°
14° = –10°	39°	65° = 18°
	40° = 4°	
15° = –9°		66°
	41°	67° = 19°
16°	42° = 5°	
17° = –8°		68°
	43° = 6°	69° = 20°
18°		
19° = –7°	44°	
	45° = 7°	70° = 21°
20°		
21° = –6°	46°	71°
	47° = 8°	72° = 22°
22°		
23° = –5°	48°	73°
	49° = 9°	74° = 23°
24° = –4°		
	50°	75°
25°	51° = 10°	76° = 24°

F=C	F=C	F=C
77°	106° = 41°	150° = 65°
78° = 25°		
	107°	155° = 68°
79° = 26°	108° = 42°	
		160° = 71°
80°	109°	
81° = 27°	110° = 43°	165° = 74°
		170° = 77°
82°	111°	
83° = 28°	112° = 44°	180° = 82°
84°	113°	185° = 85°
85° = 29°	114° = 45°	
		190° = 88°
86°	115° = 46°	
87° = 30°		195° = 90°
	116°	
88° = 31°	117° = 47°	200° = 93°
89°	118°	212° = 100°
90° = 32°	119° = 48°	
		225° = 107°
91°	120°	
92° = 33°	121° = 49°	250° = 121°
93°	122°	275° = 135°
94° = 34°	123° = 50°	
		300° = 149°
95°	124°	
96° = 35°	125° = 51°	325° = 163°
97° = 36°	126° = 52°	350° = 177°
98°	127°	375° = 190°
99° = 37°	128° = 53°	
		400° = 204°
100°	129°	
101° = 38°	130° = 54°	425° = 218°
102°	135° = 57°	450° = 232°
103° = 39°		
	140° = 60°	475° = 246°
104°		
105° = 40°	145° = 63°	500° = 260°

Index